Praise for *Hospital, Heal Thyself*

"Our hospitals and health systems are in crisis. Patients are endangered daily. This book is a reminder of the long-simmering underlying causes of that crisis and the fact that no system is safe if it is operated in an unsystematic way. It is also the compelling story of mathematician Eugene Litvak's improbable life and career, from childhood in a multifamily Soviet apartment to managing patient flow in health systems around the world. *Hospital, Health Thyself* lifts the veil on hospital practices in a readable understandable way and offers practical real-world solutions. If you are a healthcare professional or a patient, or plan on ever being one, you need to read this book!"

—**Helen Haskell,** President, Mothers Against Medical Error
and Consumers Advancing Patient Safety, Former Chair,
World Health Organization, Patients for Patient Safety Advisory Group

"*Patients, please read this book.* If surgery, emergency care, pregnancy, or hospitalization could be in your future, read *Hospital, Heal Thyself* to learn why healthcare systems can fail to deliver the best care in emergency departments, operating rooms, and other clinical care areas. Most failures do not stem from malicious intent. But unintentional, less-than-optimal care can still result in unfortunate outcomes, injuries, and death.

"*Nurses, please read this book.* Dr. Litvak's wit, determination, and brilliance inspire me and will inspire you. He understands the priorities of front-line nurses – saving lives, safe patient care, nurse retention, and less overtime. If you want all this and more, read about Dr. Litvak's steadfast journey to a silver bullet solution that incorporates operations management, smoothing patient flow, and minimizing variability. Then advocate for your patients, colleagues, and yourself by convincing hospital executives to implement Dr. Litvak's variability-based methodology. Read about Dr. Eugene Litvak's extraordinary life to understand why he perseveres in his uphill battle to improve healthcare outcomes. Read this book to understand how Dr. Litvak's approach to operations management, smoothing patient flow, and minimizing variability will help broken healthcare systems prevent serious harm to their patients. I read the book and I'm astounded by the emotions it elicited: laughter, tears, sadness, anger, awe, admiration and inspiration."

—Marilyn Rudolph, RN, former Vice President, Quality Improvement, VHA, Faculty Member, Institute for Healthcare Improvement

"More profitability, improved outcomes, greater safety, less stress. If these are a priority for your institution, read this book and courageously act on its lessons. Eugene Litvak has cracked the code of improvement available for all to implement. You can do that. Don't wait; start before you are ready. Everyone mentioned in this book is willing to help."

—James M. Anderson, JD, past President and CEO, now President Emeritus, Cincinnati Children's Hospital Medical Center, Strategic Advisor, Taft Stettinius and Hollister

"A fascinating story of Eugene Litvak, a pioneer in system thinking and work-flow design applied to healthcare delivery. Done well, healthcare systems will be better "prepared" and more "resilient"– two concepts that should be added to the mission of delivery systems."

—Denis Cortese, MD, Professor and Director, Arizona State University Center for Health Care Delivery and Policy, Emeritus Professor and former President and CEO, Mayo Clinic

"This book is a must-read for health system executives and others who want to understand how applying engineering principles to healthcare, and tackling issues such as throughput and operational efficiency, can produce better results all around – for patients, providers, and the nation."

—Susan Dentzer, President and Chief Executive Officer, America's Physician Groups, former Editor-in-Chief, *Health Affairs,* former On-Air Health Correspondent, *PBS NewsHour*

"We all deal with the myriad of problems facing providers of primary care. What we hope they (readers) recognize is that the generosity of experts like

Dr. Litvak in assisting under-resourced institutions is lifesaving. St. Thomas Clinic would likely have gone under without his help. I felt God's grace in Dr. Litvak's kindness."

—**Donald T. Erwin,** MD, Founder and CEO, St. Thomas Community Health Center, New Orleans, Louisiana.

"Eugene Litvak, an extraordinary and visionary mathematician, has developed methods which improve the flow of patients through hospitals and improve safety and efficiency and reduce costs. These changes are critical if society wishes to be able to support adequate healthcare as demand rises. He has partnered with clinicians and hospital managers throughout the world to change the way hospitals schedule their work to smooth flow. His method works everywhere it has been tried, in specialties and whole hospitals, in state and private systems. It is time to stop the need for persuasion; Litvak's methods should be mandatory. Better care for more patients at lower cost."

—**Martin Elliott,** MD, Emeritus Professor of Cardiothoracic Surgery, University College London, former Medical Director, Great Ormond Street Hospital for Children, London, UK, Provost of Gresham College, London

"Mark Taylor's excellent accounting of the history of the Institute of Healthcare Optimization and the genius of its creator and leader, Dr. Eugene Litvak, makes for compelling reading for anyone interested in meaningful healthcare reform, especially as it relates to the US hospital system.

"This book needs to be read by change agents at all levels of healthcare delivery, from the patient level to the C-suite. And more importantly, the principles and practices recounted therein need to be widely adopted by hospitals throughout the country."

—**Ellis "Mac" Knight,** MD, retired Hospital Senior Vice President and Consultant

"When 45% of healthcare costs fail to benefit patients and hospitals sink into debt, something is very wrong in the way they operate. This book presents a foundation for hospital leadership nurtured by the intellect of Eugene Litvak, a savvy driver and leader of healthcare quality who 'thinks' about the inconsistencies of care and provides proven solutions. The Litvak method, based on sensible medical and surgical practices, must be implemented if healthcare is to work for patients and hospitals are to remain viable."

—**Robert G. Lahita,** MD, PhD, Director of St. Joseph's Institute for Autoimmune and Rheumatic Diseases, Professor of Medicine, Hackensack Meridian School of Medicine, Clinical Professor of Medicine, Rutgers, New Jersey Medical School.

"At the Mayo Clinic in Florida, managing variability dramatically improved staff job satisfaction and retention, decreasing nurse turnover by 41%, thereby allowing a stable team of experienced staff to deliver safe care. Anyone looking for a way to better deploy healthcare resources for a safer healthcare system should read this book and explore implementing Dr. Litvak's model."

—**C. Daniel Smith,** MD, Director, Esophageal Institute of Atlanta, former Dean Warren Professor of Surgery, Emory University School of Medicine, former Professor of Surgery and Surgeon-in-Chief, Mayo Clinic in Florida

"Mark Taylor has performed an invaluable service: introducing the work of Dr. Eugene Litvak to a broad range of potential readers who are interested in saving lives and saving money – *at the same time.* He has demonstrated an approach which could benefit the country greatly. Taylor's book should be required reading for hospital leaders, board members, and anyone interested in improving the safety and affordability of America's most important healthcare institutions – and that should be all of us."

—**Mark D. Smith,** MD, former President, California Healthcare Foundation

"This is not just another author with a good idea. Litvak's solutions are straightforward, tried and true. They save lives, improve care and improve staff satisfaction. Hospitals MUST adopt his solutions for the sake of their patients, their staff, their physicians, and their bottom line. Read this book. Take it to your hospital administrator, your chief of surgery, the head of your health department, the Joint Commission, and CMS. Your life may depend on it."

—**Peter Viccellio,** MD, Professor and Vice Chairman, Department of Emergency Medicine/Associate Chief Medical Officer, Stony Brook (NY) University Hospital

HOSPITAL,
HEAL
THYSELF

One Brilliant Mathematician's Proven Plan
for Saving Hospitals, Many Lives,
and Billions of Dollars

HOSPITAL, HEAL THYSELF

MARK TAYLOR

WILEY

Published by John Wiley & Sons, Inc., Hoboken, New Jersey.
Published simultaneously in Canada.

For general information on our other products and services or for technical support, please contact our Customer Care Department within the United States at (800) 762-2974, outside the United States at (317) 572-3993 or fax (317) 572-4002.

Wiley also publishes its books in a variety of electronic formats. Some content that appears in print may not be available in electronic formats. For more information about Wiley products, visit our web site at www.wiley.com.

Library of Congress Cataloging-in-Publication Data:

Names: Taylor, Mark, 1953- author.
Title: Hospital, heal thyself : one brilliant mathematician's proven plan
  for saving American hospitals, many lives, and billions of dollars / Mark
  Taylor.
Description: Hoboken, New Jersey : Wiley, [2025] | Includes bibliographical
  references and index.
Identifiers: LCCN 2024020700 (print) | LCCN 2024020701 (ebook) | ISBN
  9781394283347 (hardback) | ISBN 9781394283361 (adobe pdf) | ISBN
  9781394283354 (epub)
Subjects: MESH: Litvak, Eugene. | Patient Care Management—organization &
  administration | Hospital Administration—economics | Efficiency,
  Organizational—economics | Safety Management | Hospitalization | United
  States
Classification: LCC RA971 (print) | LCC RA971 (ebook) | NLM WX 162 | DDC
  362.11068—dc23/eng/20240603
LC record available at https://lccn.loc.gov/2024020700
LC ebook record available at https://lccn.loc.gov/2024020701

Cover Design: Wiley
Cover Image: © MicroStockHub/Getty Images
Author Photo: © Mark Taylor
SKY10085549_091924

To Marcia, for everything.

Contents

Contents

Preface

If you knew a way to save thousands of lives and billions of dollars, wouldn't you want to share it? Eugene Litvak knows how and for nearly two decades has battled to apply his methods for improving the quality of hospital care and reducing the cost of that care while better protecting patients.

To be clear, Eugene Litvak, PhD, is not a physician. And though he is a well-regarded researcher in the field of hospital operations, Litvak did not study medicine or healthcare at the prestigious colleges he attended in the former Soviet Union. He is that uniquely American creation – the immigrant who built a better mousetrap: in his case, a tested method of improving patient flow and patient care that saves lives, as well as billions of dollars in unnecessary spending.

Litvak laments that between 250,000 and 440,000 people die unnecessarily each year because of hospital admissions issues, according to multiple reputable researchers.[1] That's 10% of US yearly deaths, making it the third leading cause of fatalities after heart disease and cancer (pre-COVID pandemic), according to the US Centers for Disease Control and Prevention (CDC).[2] Litvak is aware that while there is no organized reporting and data collection system tracking medical errors, it is widely acknowledged that hundreds of thousands are reported each year attributable to hospitals; errors that can result in death, costly hospitalizations, and permanent harm. He also knows that as much as one-quarter to one-third of all US healthcare current spending, $4.1 trillion, is considered wasteful or avoidable and that much of that cost, pain, and suffering could be spared.[3] Healthcare costs continue to grow exponentially and are predicted to reach $6 trillion by 2027.[4]

This book details Litvak's story and chronicles his battle to save lives and money and improve care in American hospitals by changing the way they operate. Litvak, born in the Ukrainian city of Kiev in the former USSR, was an applied mathematician there and a rising star in the field of operations management, sometimes referred to as industrial engineering. There, he helped improve the reliability of the telecommunications and computer networks and enhanced the process of efficiently building railroads.

After achieving worldwide recognition for his research in the 1970s in the USSR, Litvak began receiving offers to present his work in other countries. One invitation came from a personal hero, Claude Shannon of the Massachusetts Institute of Technology (MIT), the father of information theory. But Soviet bureaucrats prohibited Litvak from traveling abroad, fearing that, as a Jew, he would not return. So in 1977 he and his wife, Ella, applied to emigrate and requested permission to leave the country. The government also refused that request and Litvak, and his wife immediately lost their jobs and became refuseniks: Soviet citizens, often Jews, who sought to leave the USSR, but whose applications for exit visas were refused and their careers halted.

After years of working menial positions and suffering government persecution and anti-Semitism, including recruitment attempts by the dreaded KGB, the Litvaks and their parents finally received exit visas and joined a Jewish Diaspora fleeing the dying Soviet state. The six émigrés first landed in Vienna before arriving in the United States in 1988, where they initially stayed with relatives and plotted their new lives in Boston.

"The start of our emigration was not very easy," Litvak recalls. "We could take from the USSR no more than $150 each. We had two pairs of old, sick parents, no jobs and little English."[5]

But Litvak has battled bureaucracy his entire life, joking that his time as a refusenik, fighting to emigrate, prepared him for decades of butting heads with America's healthcare bureaucracy. "I truly believe there's a need for a great public uproar and awakening about our healthcare system," he states. "All of us will need advocates to care for us if nothing changes."[6]

Litvak's first encounter with the US healthcare system came when his father, a decorated soldier who had been badly wounded in World War II, was hospitalized at Beth Israel Hospital in Boston the day after the family arrived on US shores. "He was helpless. I couldn't speak English. But I was really impressed with the hospital and the respect and attention of healthcare providers towards my parents and me," Litvak recalls. "I never experienced that in Russia. I knew my father was sick and I had to do something. I felt it was my responsibility to save him, since I brought him to America."[7]

That was 36 years ago. "He received excellent care then," Litvak remembers. "Though today the drugs and equipment are better, the respect, quality of care, and personalized attention are worse than at that time."[8]

For the last two decades as a hospital consultant and co-founder of the not-for-profit Boston-based Institute for Healthcare Optimization, Litvak has combed through hospital finances, quality reporting, and staffing data to track the process of how patients flow through typical American hospitals from admission to discharge. His groundbreaking work in healthcare was driven by a powerful motivator.

"My first incentive to work in this field was hunger," recalls Litvak, who accepted a position as a postdoctoral fellow at the Harvard School of Public Health several years after arriving in the United States. Prior to that, he'd worked as a night manager in a small inn.

"I simultaneously felt like a prince and a pauper," he says. "On one hand, I had recommendations from distinguished scientists. But on the other hand, every company I applied to told me that I was overqualified."[9]

Harvard's School of Public Health wasn't sure how to capitalize on Litvak's skills. He was first assigned to explore testing for the growing HIV/AIDS epidemic and discovered a new screening protocol to detect the virus in donated blood. He and his colleagues developed a method that substantially reduced the cost of screening and significantly improved its accuracy, but faced government health agency intransigence because of the influence of powerful test kit manufacturers.

It was one of Litvak's first battles with American bureaucracies. Later, he worked as an outside consultant at Massachusetts General Hospital in Boston, where managers of its stress lab were seeking more money to grapple with a growing demand. Litvak discovered that the lab was operating with 30% unused capacity, yet still claimed it needed more space to expand.

Working with Mass General researchers, he found similar problems in the hospital's operating rooms and in other departments. He employed complex mathematical theories and algorithms to understand why the Operating Rooms (ORs) and Emergency Rooms (ERs) became overcrowded and how that impacted the cost, quality, and efficiency of care. He learned what creates these predictable weekly overcrowding events there and within most of the nation's 5,000 acute care hospitals.

Emboldened by his findings, Litvak sent letters to every Massachusetts hospital offering to share his research. "Very few even replied, except to say, 'No thanks,'" Litvak recalls. In that era, health maintenance organizations (HMOs), a new health insurance model that achieved savings for its members by cutting healthcare costs and reducing services, began penetrating the Massachusetts market. "Finally, people were talking about healthcare costs," he attests.[10]

Hospital overcrowding, he discovered, isn't just annoying to patients tired of waiting. Well-documented research proves it frequently leads to bad health outcomes and occasionally even death for patients and great stress on the doctors and nurses who care for them. Ambulances are diverted when hospital emergency rooms are backed up and have no space, postponing lifesaving care for patients desperately needing treatment. ER patients lay in hallways and lobbies awaiting space in treatment rooms. Doctors and nurses are stretched thin, working extra shifts caring for ever-growing numbers of patients.

And this was before the COVID pandemic. It has worsened since.

During overcrowding episodes, ER patients requiring hospital admission can wait hours without care or be transferred to open beds, but in inappropriate units. Surgical patients, for example, may be moved to cancer wards because surgical unit beds are unavailable. Sometimes problems occur in the ensuing chaos.

Patients with planned surgeries see their procedures postponed or canceled, causing personal stress and inconvenience and adverse health outcomes. Meanwhile hospitals lose millions in well-reimbursed payments from health insurance plans, revenues that they required more than ever during the pandemic. Declining revenues, often due to canceled surgeries, have contributed to hospital closures around the country.

Litvak has studied these logjams and discovered both the source of the problem and its operational solution. Both relate to patient flow, the journey of a patient through the hospitalization process.

He has widely published the results of his research in prestigious medical journals from the *Journal of the American Medical Association* (*JAMA*) to the *New England Journal of Medicine* (*NEJM*) and *Health Affairs*.

His findings have been endorsed by state hospital associations and the country's leading hospital accreditation agency, the Joint Commission, as well as some of the nation's preeminent healthcare researchers and leaders. These include Donald Berwick, MD, the former administrator of the Centers for Medicare and Medicaid Services (CMS), the federal agency that administers the Medicare program, and Harvey Fineberg, MD, former president of the Institute of Medicine (now known as the Academy of Medicine) and president of the Gordon and Betty Moore Foundation.

In a *JAMA* piece, Stanford University Professor Arnold Milstein, MD, the medical director for the Pacific Business Group on Health, and his co-author, University of California Berkeley Professor Steven Shortell, PhD, estimated that if all US hospitals adopted Litvak's methods for improving patient flow, it could dramatically reduce US spending on hospital care. According to the CDC, in 2019, hospital spending accounted for 37.2% of personal healthcare expenditures. They estimated potential annual savings of 4% to 5% of US annual healthcare spending, between $120 billion and $150 billion ($150 billion to $180 billion in today's dollars), along with reductions in unnecessary patient deaths and medical errors.[11]

Litvak has found a cure for one of the hospital industry's costliest and most vexing issues. His treatment is for a condition previously undiagnosed, but a grave one that hospital administrators prefer to ignore: overcrowding and the resulting peaks and valleys in patient census, which can spark understaffing, chaos, and life-threatening issues.

The cause of his quixotic quest is not as easily identifiable as cancer or heart disease. It's a problem that lurks beneath the surface but is the root of an unnecessary cascade of health complications and steep financial costs.

Litvak's ideas have been tested and validated in the best hospitals in the United States, Canada, England, and Scotland. In one Midwestern medical center, the Cincinnati Children's Hospital, Litvak's methods for improving hospital operations produced over $100 million in annual savings as well as an avoided payment of $100 million on a planned, but unnecessary, new patient tower, along with improved quality of care and patient safety.

Prestigious medical centers such as the Mayo Clinic Health System, the Johns Hopkins Medical Center in Baltimore, and the Boston Medical Center have applied Litvak's methods and saved millions of dollars, as did the New Jersey Hospital Association. His successes have been chronicled by major US news organizations, including *CNN Digital* and *NBC Digital, the Wall Street Journal, Forbes Magazine, Newsweek,* and the *PBS NewsHour.*

As readers will soon learn, Litvak's methods for smoothing patient flow have been tested and proven to work throughout the country and around the world and offer benefits beyond improving hospital efficiency and profit margins. They've been shown to save lives, reduce medical errors, decrease hospital and ER overcrowding, and improve nurse retention and patient satisfaction. But one added value is that improving hospital efficiency can expand access to care, enabling hospitals and other healthcare providers to treat more patients, thereby reducing, albeit indirectly, racial inequities and healthcare disparities.

In 2022 the National Academies of Sciences, Engineering, and Medicine published a report documenting racial and gender-based disparities in the organ transplantation process. That report, "Realizing the Promise of Equity in the Organ Transplantation System," revealed that people of color, poor people, and women receive organ transplants at a disproportionately lower rate and after long waiting times than other patients of similar need. While African Americans are three times as likely to develop kidney failure as White Americans, they are much less likely to receive kidney transplants. And while they suffer higher rates of heart failure, they are also less likely to receive heart transplants than White people.[12]

The report found that more than 20% of kidneys, the most commonly donated organs, are wasted, even as, on average, 17 people die daily awaiting transplants because needed organs are unavailable. The major cause of this waste was a lack of available surgeons to perform those transplants when they were needed for harvest and transplantation.[13]

In an opinion piece for *The Hill* co-authored with Harvey Fineberg, MD, the president of the Gordon and Betty Moore Foundation, and Mark Smith, MD, the former president of the California Health Care Foundation, Litvak said that part of the problem can be addressed with a single management intervention. The authors wrote that hospitals should streamline patient flow by "scheduling admissions, discharges, and visits in a way that alleviates manmade peaks in demand. Such steps can be particularly important in safety net institutions, which are historically under-resourced and were hit hard by COVID."[14] The authors added that "Streamlining patient flow by smoothing surgical schedules can increase access to organ transplants and reduce patient mortality."[15]

They noted that "The COVID pandemic has revealed and exacerbated inequities in health care and produced disproportionate deaths of people of color. It has stretched hospital staffing to the breaking point. In such times of stress, improving health care equity requires more than noble intentions or even money. It requires something more difficult – commitment and practical steps to increase efficiency by overcoming impediments of habit and traditional ways of doing things."[16]

Adopting Litvak's program isn't easy. If it were, many more hospitals and health systems would have employed these methods decades ago. But it is not arduously challenging either. And while the rewards can be great, the alternative – maintaining a status quo that needlessly causes harm and costs patient lives – is far worse.

Litvak conceded that his interventions to reduce variation and smooth patient flow will not cure all of the many problems plaguing hospitals and healthcare organizations. He recognizes that there are other process and quality improvement programs that will also enhance the delivery of healthcare services.

"But unless one can staff to meet the peaks of patient demand – which is not financially feasible for most healthcare organizations – these census peaks inevitably will result in excessive nursing workloads and shortages, medical errors, hospital and ER overcrowding, reduced access to care, and waste," Litvak said.[17]

"Therefore, whatever else is done, whatever other proven interventions are implemented, smoothing those peaks is a pre-requisite to creating a quality healthcare delivery system. In other words, almost everything else a hospital tries to do to improve its system is bound to ultimately fail without addressing the underlying causes."[18]

So why, if those methods have been researched, tested, and proven to work in some of the best US hospitals, haven't all of America's hospitals adopted this lifesaving and cost-effective program?

Litvak blames institutional culture, inertia, and greed for hospital leadership's failure to adopt these proven strategies. He believes a national movement rallying patients, healthcare providers, and policymakers is required to improve patient outcomes by spurring changes in hospital operations.

Sooner or later, most Americans or their loved ones will face hospitalization and may be impacted by the adverse consequences of overcrowding. Litvak and his family were personally impacted when his mother was hospitalized before her death in June 2018.

"I praise the commitment of doctors and nurses to patient care. But I would also inform clinicians that our healthcare system frequently destroys the good work they do," he asserts. "I'd tell families of hospital patients that the system could screw up at any time. Until their loved ones are safely back at home, don't breathe easy."[19]

Litvak's methods are no magic elixir. And adopting them despite their proven success is not painless. It takes time and hard work to fully implement. And they require cultural as well as operational changes.

Hospital association surveys show the average job span for a hospital chief executive officer is 6.6 years. Traditionally, hospital CEOs and their boards of directors have deferred to the wishes of elite specialty physicians who operate within their facilities. These rainmakers – surgeons and other specialists who perform expensive procedures – often have many choices about where they will operate. So hospital CEOs lure and welcome these doctors and the multi-million-dollar revenue streams they channel to their hospitals.

Hospital CEOs are loath to tinker with what they view as a successful model that allows surgeons and cardiologists to set their own operating schedules, usually only a few hours a week and almost always early in the week. Litvak's research proved that this existing model is not only costly and ineffective, but also leads to dangerous swings in patient flow, census overload, and burnout of clinicians, harming patients, and claiming lives.

His solution requires hospital administrators and their medical and nursing staff to change.

Many surgeons resist challenges to their routines, even when those changes have been proven to improve their work schedules and revenues. And most surgeons have the luxury of choice. Facing new and suspected inconvenient administrative or scheduling changes, some doctors warn they'll transfer their surgeries to competing hospitals. Even the threat of that loss of business sends hospital boards of directors searching for new CEOs.

Multiple studies indicate that most hospitals today face over-crowding. Litvak observes, "Adding new Emergency Department beds and building new additions is exactly what hospital CEOs do in this situation and that only increases the overcrowding, because they're increasing traffic to the hospital entrance while blocking the exit flow. And it does nothing to address the underlying issue. Rather, it exacerbates the problem. Litvak cites the noted healthcare researcher Peter Viccellio, MD, vice chairman of the department of emergency medicine for the Health Sciences Center at Stony Brook University in New York, who opined, "One cannot cure constipation by extending the colon."[20]

Litvak notes, "You can only change hospital culture by engaging the CEOs. But most are afraid they will lose their jobs if they attack this problem. They're not looking for a fight. And they wonder: why would I engage in this fight if my rival hospital CEO does not?"[21]

Since the late 1990s Litvak had examined America's healthcare system as an objective observer, a researcher, consultant, and out-sider who had little personal interaction with it. That changed in February 2018, when he was personally impacted by healthcare dys-function when his elderly mother was treated for a brain tumor. The healthcare journey was torturous and frustrating, and if Litvak had not advocated for her, the outcome would have been much worse.

Among the other issues was one that Litvak explained in a *Wall Street Journal* piece. Millions of hospital discharges are driven, not by improved patient health, but because the hospital census reaches its peak on Thursdays and Fridays and hospitals need to free up beds. "On these days it seems patients magically become healthier and are discharged. I knew on Thursday that it could be a problem but thought my mother's serious condition would not allow this practice. I was wrong."[22]

Litvak's mother's painful experience inspires him to complete his mission. "If you want me to summarize what is wrong with our healthcare delivery system, I could do it in two words: almost everything," Litvak states. "The system is broken. It's getting more and more like a combat zone."[23]

Litvak is exhausted by hospital leaders' apathy and inaction. "I am a part of this system, and I can see that people outside of healthcare just don't know what's going on," he bemoans. "Enough is enough. I have studied this problem and know how to fix it. And now I have seen it personally with my own eyes. We are hurting people unnecessarily and that must stop."[24]

Chapter 1

How One Hospital Adopted Litvak's Methods and Saved $100 Million

In 2006 the president and CEO of Cincinnati Children's Hospital, Jim Anderson, realized his hospital faced a daunting crisis. At the time, few outsiders would suspect anything amiss. The prestigious institution, routinely ranked among the best pediatric hospitals in America, seemed healthy. Admissions – from US patients, but also from around the world – were rising and revenue was growing. But several times each week the hospital mysteriously became packed beyond capacity.

Anderson grew concerned when he heard from transplant surgeon Fred Ryckman, MD. During overcrowding episodes, the hospital's care sometimes plummeted to an "inadequate and inefficient" level, Ryckman told him.[1] This was an alarming development from an institution that considered itself world class. The Cincinnati Children's Hospital has been caring for children since 1883.[2] But in 2006 when the 425-bed hospital (700 beds today) contracted with Eugene Litvak and the not-for-profit Institute for Healthcare Optimization (IHO), it was facing routine overcrowding issues, a problem vexing hospitals throughout the United States.

Anderson realized that the hospital could not keep up with the growing patient volume and maintain its high standards. When a surge of new patient arrivals swamped the facility, overstressed clinicians – doctors and nurses – were more likely to make mistakes.

1

Anderson foresaw an escalating cycle of higher costs and more expansion. Plans were already underway to build a 75-bed unit for around $102 million. He knew from years spent in healthcare that the new wing wouldn't permanently fix the problem and overcrowding would return and pressure his staff, potentially leading to deteriorating quality of care.[3] Eventually, something could go disastrously wrong.

"I was tired of seeing children coming in sick and having trouble getting into our operating rooms," surgeon Ryckman said. "If you delay a patient's treatment by more than six hours, their mortality rate goes up. If you delay entry to a hospital room, risk and mortality also go up. There is much data to support that it's a bad idea to make people wait."[4]

Anderson, a business lawyer who worked for manufacturing powerhouse Emerson Electric Company before joining the hospital, wanted to reverse what he feared could become a severe problem. When he hired Litvak, a Harvard professor and the president and co-founder of the Boston-based IHO, he hoped to see a plan for improving patient flow – the journey from hospital admission through discharge. He knew that creating a better, more streamlined patient flow process could reduce overcrowding and decrease the risk of bad outcomes. What Anderson got was much more: a roadmap to improving performance at the medical center, but one that could be deployed across the entire American healthcare system, saving many lives and billions of dollars in unnecessary spending.

Litvak said that the Cincinnati Children's Hospital, like most American hospitals, recorded a daily patient census that, on paper, resembled an electrocardiogram exam, with bed occupancies that could vary as much as 80% from one day to the next, typified by huge peaks and deep valleys. As an applied mathematician who studied queuing, reliability, and graph theories in his native Ukraine during the Soviet era, Litvak knew that variability meant trouble. Canceled surgeries. Crowded hospital emergency rooms. A lack of hospital beds to admit new patients. That variability causes stress on nurses and physicians due to unpredictable schedules and long hours, leading to burnout, early retirements, and nursing shortages. It meant diverting ambulances transporting sick and dying patients to other ERs, putting the patients' lives at risk, and costing the intended hospitals millions in lost revenue. It meant "boarding" ER patients in hallways for hours, sometimes days, aggravating patient conditions, and even costing lives. It meant medical errors, malpractice lawsuits, and sinking reputations.[5]

The United States ranks near the bottom of industrialized nations in average hospital bed occupancy, hovering between 64% and 68%, according to the Organization for Economic Cooperation and Development (OECD), an inter-governmental economic organization comprised of 36 developed nations. Out of 28 nations, the United States ranked 27th, only ahead of Greece. Ireland, Israel, and Canada topped the list in 2017, with occupancy rates that ranged between 95% (Ireland) to 91.6% (Canada).[6]

"Yet we're still overcrowded. Why?" Litvak asked. "Because of the artificial peaks in patient demand. If we could manage patient flow more effectively, our average daily census could be around 80% nationally. The number of Americans who are uninsured is around 10% to 12%. If we could solve this, we could cover hospital care for the uninsured with the savings from hospital spending."[7]

Litvak said Cincinnati Children's Hospital initially hired him for a small assignment – an assessment of its status quo. "In a sense, it was cheating. I don't remember what they paid me, but it was a waste of money for them," he said. "Because I already knew the outcome and could have told them what I'd find."[8] He said IHO performed the assessment – taking an operational temperature of the hospital,

How One Hospital Adopted Litvak's Methods and Saved $100 Million

then meeting with top hospital administrators and physician leaders in Cincinnati. More than 20 attended the morning meeting and listened as Litvak presented his findings.

Litvak said skepticism enveloped the room. "They were suspicious, and I was suspicious, too. Finally, Jim Anderson asked, 'Would you help us walk this road?' I told him no. That was a little shocking to him. He asked, 'Why not?' I said because the very people now smiling at me will create roadblocks later. I knew they would resist any change in their culture. So Jim looked around the room and said, 'If you experience any pushback, call me immediately in my office.' He looked at me again and requested, 'Now, will you do it?' I remember I was smiling when I answered, 'Absolutely.'"[9]

Anderson told the surgeons, "Don't tell me 100 reasons why we can't do this. There are no end-arounds. If this doesn't work, we'll stop and go back to the old system."[10]

Anderson gave a three-to-four-month window to test the program. "But once it was up and running, nobody wanted to go back. We didn't entertain it at all," Ryckman said.[11]

Once the contract was signed, Ryckman flew to Boston on business and Litvak took him to lunch at the Cheesecake Factory. True to his loathing for variability, Litvak is unfailingly predictable in his dining out diet. "I always order the same thing: a salad and chicken."[12]

Litvak said he needed someone within the hospital who was well-respected by the surgical staff to champion the process. The hospital appointed Ryckman. "He took responsibility for his leadership role. I asked him, 'Why did they choose you?' 'Very simple,' Ryckman replied. 'Because I am the most difficult surgeon to deal with.' They knew Fred would deliver. He understands the substance and culture and is very smart, the top surgeon there."[13]

Litvak and his team of IHO analysts gathered hospital data and crunched numbers, applying complex algorithms and mind-numbing mathematical theories to analyze what was happening with the

Hospital, Heal Thyself

hospital's patients. The IHO team's main goal was to understand and document how Cincinnati Children's Hospital handled its patient flow. How do managers schedule surgeries, both elective (planned) and emergency (unscheduled)? What causes all those patient surges, the peaks and valleys? Are they predictable, and how should the hospital respond to ease the burden on its doctors, nurses, and patients?

More than a decade earlier Litvak made the connection between patient demand and hospital capacity using his stealth, but not-so-secret weapon: math. After helping several other hospitals improve their patient outcomes and save millions of dollars, he sought to apply those same tools to Cincinnati Children's Hospital. Only this time, it wouldn't be applied in just one department as other hospital clients did; it would be integrated throughout the entire hospital.

Hospitals are complicated organizations that often employ thousands throughout multiple departments. They are dependent upon costly information technology, use the latest sophisticated and expensive medical equipment – some costing millions of dollars – and require the collaboration and continuity of a symphony orchestra. For decades, individual hospital departments – surgery, oncology, cardiology, to name a few – operated like individual fiefdoms or silos, jealously guarding their territory, revenue streams, and staffing. As long as the hospital prospered, that system worked. But recent changes in hospital reimbursement by insurers, both public (Medicare, Medicaid) and private (Aetna, United Healthcare, for example), are compelling hospitals to deliver higher-quality patient care at lower costs.[14]

These financial pressures have driven medical centers like Cincinnati Children's Hospital to make dramatic changes in how they plan to treat patients. In the past two decades many hospitals have sought out process improvement through programs like General Electric's Six Sigma and Toyota's Lean. These programs are common in the manufacturing world, but somehow escaped adoption

5

by the healthcare industry until recently. Anderson was puzzled by the scarcity of programs to improve patient flow. But IHO's trial run impressed him. He said the results were astonishing.

Litvak remembers telling Anderson and Scott Hamlin, the hospital's chief financial and administrative officer, that the surgeons would meet and vote yes or no on the full project implementation. "I talked individually with each chief of every surgical subspecialty and to each I spoke with, there was a trick," Litvak recalled. "I told them that their unit would benefit more than anyone else. It was not true that one would benefit more than anyone else, but all would benefit. For some people, however, it is important to come out ahead of everyone else."[15]

Ryckman said that back then, few understood the link between poor patient flow and patient safety. He said the greatest risks to hospitals occur when the care they deliver produces bad outcomes and inadequate care to patients.[16] "And in the early days, before we changed, we were offering inadequate and inefficient care. The financial risk is also substantially higher when delivering bad care."

Ryckman pointed out another big risk: headlining the front page of your local newspaper because a patient sat for six hours in the ER and suffered a bad outcome. He felt that one of the most unappreciated and most important resources any hospital can offer is quality nursing care. "Within our hospital Litvak's program has been a driver for nurse retention. Our nurses don't have to routinely work overtime. It doesn't make OT go away but makes it less of a problem. It really changed the way we thought and planned," Ryckman said.[17]

Annual revenue at Cincinnati Children's Hospital rose by more than $100 million during a period when patient volume rose significantly, all without the hospital having to spend $102 million on its planned patient tower, which was no longer needed. Its average daily occupancy increased from 76% to 91%, much higher than the US hospital average. Litvak's methods smoothed the peaks and valleys of the daily census to a more predictable middle level, making it easier for hospital management to staff appropriately and easing the stress on nurses and physicians and, in the process, reducing the likelihood of medical errors.[18]

Hospital officials said that waiting times in the emergency room and the operating rooms reduced significantly, expanding the hospital's capacity to treat more patients while improving quality. "There are fewer mistakes and adverse incidents, and the surgeons are happier because fewer of their scheduled surgeries are canceled," Anderson said, predicting that if Litvak's methods were applied to every hospital in America, "We would see enormous increases in capacity, while saving billions of dollars nationally."[19]

CFO Hamlin said Litvak showed hospital leaders that operating rooms, intensive care units, and emergency departments are all connected and that bottlenecks in one area lead to delays throughout the hospital.[20] In an interview that aired on the Institute for Healthcare Improvement's Wi-Fi internet channel, Hamlin said that in 2004, before the adoption of smoothing, Cincinnati Children's Hospital routinely experienced "operational failures" that caused it to decline referrals or cancel surgeries despite vacant beds.[21]

"You grow up with the idea that you can focus on the patients' needs, or you can focus on the needs of physicians that bring the patients to you. But you fall into the trap of believing those are mutually exclusive things," Hamlin said.[22]

In a May 2016 *Chicago Tribune* story Anderson remembered, "We not only improved patient satisfaction levels, but instead of running around like crazy because of patient overcrowding or sitting doing nothing when few surgeries were planned, our nurses and physicians got home in time for dinner, they made their kids' soccer games, and life got a lot more orderly."[23]

To date, Cincinnati Children's Hospital is the only US hospital that has fully implemented all three phases of Litvak's program to improve patient flow. Other hospitals, including Boston Medical Center and Mayo Clinic in Florida, have adopted portions of the program. The hospital stands as a demonstration of the potential for quality improvement and cost savings by adopting Litvak's program for improving patient flow.

The Cincinnati Children's Hospital success story began with Ryckman, the pediatric surgeon specializing in organ transplantation. He arrived there in 1982 on a surgical fellowship and formally joined the surgical staff in 1984, retiring in 2017. "It was a great way to spend 35 years."[24]

He first heard Litvak lecture at an IHI forum on smoothing surgical schedules in the early 2000s. "I listened to this 90-minute discussion and thought: he's either crazy or knew something no one else did. But it was intriguing to me. The logic behind what he talked about doing seemed clear. He was addressing a very significant problem for us," Ryckman said.[25]

"I thought he hit an important nail on the head. The reason I was passionate to adopt this was that I was tired of patients, children, coming in sick and having trouble getting to the OR [operating room] for needed surgery. This was how we could deliver the best care and prevent kids from getting sicker as they're waiting in the waiting room. The consequence of doing that is we became more efficient taking care of these kids."[26]

He said Cincinnati Children's Hospital was delivering "spectacular surgical care, just not as efficiently as we found that we eventually could. That foundation was in place and allowed us to do the work Eugene taught us."[27]

He admitted that Litvak is not a cookie cutter consultant. "When we first heard his methods for smoothing surgical flow, we were a little skeptical. We had to be convinced that what he was talking about made sense. His methods were very different. The whole concept of mathematical modeling was entirely foreign to how we historically solved medical flow problems in the hospital. We weren't going to listen to a mathematician – instead of a chief of orthopedics – tell us how to run the hospital."[28]

Ryckman said few in the hospital industry discussed patient flow in the early and mid-2000s. "For decades everyone believed that inefficiency was indelibly engrained in the system," he said. "But we learned that it's not about the ED or the OR but understanding how to improve the entire system of care. That's where you'll get the savings and efficiency," Ryckman said.[29]

The hospital saw results within weeks. "We knew what it was like before Eugene [Litvak] came, and it was really clear within the first few weeks that we would radically improve access, especially for children with urgent needs, to get into the OR. Our waiting times decreased. Overtime went down. The data was pretty clear pretty soon," Ryckman said.[30]

Cincinnati Children's Hospital is now, 15 years later, building a new critical care tower. "We needed a better and more modern design that had to include the latest technology. But we were able to put it off for many years. In the first year we improved hospital-wide flow and efficiency by 5% for the entire OR system and it continued to grow for the next few years. That may not seem like much but multiplied across [Cincinnati Children's Hospital's] 20 ORs it's the equivalent of having an additional OR."[31]

Ryckman said Litvak faces an entrenched bureaucracy when he tries to change OR culture. "The people who run ORs still run them the way they did 35 years ago. Surgeons like block time [a scheduled period in an OR 'owned' by a particular surgeon in which no one else can operate, regardless of whether the scheduled surgeon even shows] because they know that they'll be operating on a Tuesday or a Thursday. It requires some adjustments to put Eugene's

How One Hospital Adopted Litvak's Methods and Saved $100 Million

system in place and eliminate surgical block times. Change is hard," he conceded. "The only people who like change are babies with dirty diapers."[32]

Litvak's methods have survived at Cincinnati Children's Hospital. Daniel Von Allmen, MD, the surgeon-chief and senior vice president of surgery there, worked at two other health systems before joining Cincinnati Children's Hospital, logging stints at pediatric hospitals in Philadelphia and Chapel Hill, North Carolina. He said that after arriving five years ago, he helped to orchestrate with Director of Medical Operations Strategy Brooke Mullett how surgeries are planned and continued the surgical smoothing that Litvak and Ryckman introduced.

"Surgeons want patients who need surgery to be able to get it," said Von Allmen, who noted that the hospital is erecting a $600 million critical care tower. "We have maintained those core principles and core approaches. The system has evolved a little bit."[33] He said that today the hospital allocates block times by surgical specialty, not at the whim of individual surgeons.

"We allocate block time based on service, whether that specialty is orthopedics, cardio, or neuro. By having this system and ability to address ED cases, it allows us more flexibility if we're down an OR. We have the ability to run all cases without huge disruptions."[34]

Even 15 years later, Von Allmen said the hospital rarely diverts ambulance patients anymore, a problem plaguing US hospitals that impacts patient safety.[35] "By allocating block times to encourage smoothing out across the week, we reduce the chances of kids coming out of surgery without available hospital beds. In extreme cases, we've kept them in ORs overnight," he noted.[36]

He said Litvak's methods of improving patient flow becomes even more important when a hospital is stressed. "If you have 20 ORs and only 11 are being used, you don't need it. But as pressure goes up on costs and expenses, you cannot have empty ORs waiting for patients to show up. You need to balance supply with demand and that will make it more and more important for people to use this kind of approach."[37]

Mullett said she learned Litvak's theories and methods while working for Ryckman. Mullett, who joined the hospital 11 years ago after working in the pharmaceutical industry, said Ryckman worked to integrate Litvak's program throughout the entire hospital. The Philadelphia native said pediatric hospitals didn't always have to be as mindful about costs. "Now we really need to be."[38]

"We use it across the institution," she added. "There is now a hospital department charged with overseeing capacity and flow. Our chief of staff, similar to a chief medical officer [CMO], manages flow."[39]

■ ■ ■

Ellis "Mac" Knight, MD, chief medical officer and senior vice president of the Atlanta-based The Coker Group, told the *Chicago Tribune* in 2016 that Litvak's time in the USSR fighting the bureaucracy there instilled in him infinite patience. "He has been tilting at windmills for a long, long time," Knight said.[40]

Despite successes like those at the Cincinnati Children's Hospital and others, American hospitals have not rallied en masse to embrace Litvak's methods. Nonetheless, he sounds characteristically optimistic. He said if every US hospital did what the Cincinnati Children's Hospital did to improve patient flow, the savings could pay for US healthcare reform while improving the quality of care in American hospitals.[41]

"Americans can always be counted on to do the right thing," Litvak likes to say, quoting Winston Churchill with a decidedly different accent, "after they have exhausted all other possibilities."[42]

Chapter 2

The Human Toll

Lewis Blackman, a healthy 15-year-old high school student with a bright academic future, arrived on a Thursday November morning in 2000 for a planned surgical procedure at one of America's best children's hospitals, the Medical University of South Carolina (MUSC) Children's Hospital in Charleston.

Lewis was a star student and budding actor born with a concave chest, a congenital deformity known in medical terminology as *pectus excavatum*, a condition in which the sternum and ribs develop abnormally. This "sunken chest," which appears in 1 to 300 to 400 children, often causes embarrassment in locker rooms and on beaches for boys born with it. The condition was long thought to be only a cosmetic defect. However, some researchers have claimed that concave chest patients may later experience chest pain and shortness of breath, and that can sometimes lead to cardiac and respiratory problems, according to Johns Hopkins University research.[1]

Former Johns Hopkins Children's Center pediatric surgeon Fizan Abdullah, MD, now with Lurie Children's Hospital in Chicago, said that sunken chests are sometimes found among children with Marfan syndrome, a genetic disorder with potentially life-threatening complications like arterial aneurysms or aortic ruptures.[2]

"Concave chests can make boys feel self-conscious," said Lewis's mother, Helen Haskell. "This was a cosmetic procedure for Lewis. We thought of it as something like getting braces to straighten his teeth."[3]

Correcting the problem involved a minimally invasive procedure to implant a metal bar to reshape his chest. He'd have a small scar, but a cool one he could later show off. His parents, Helen, an archaeologist, and LaBarre "Bar" Blackman, a high school social studies teacher, waited until after Halloween to schedule the procedure, honoring Lewis's request.[4]

"He didn't want to miss Halloween," Helen Haskell said.[5]

So instead of booking the operation on a Monday, the family moved it to a Thursday. That decision may have played a role in the eventual outcome, because most US hospitals routinely become clogged up later in the week as overcrowding occurs when jammed emergency rooms (ERs) compete with the rush of scheduled surgeries in hospital operating rooms (ORs).[6]

The Columbia, South Carolina, family arrived early on November 2 to MUSC. The surgery took more than twice as long as the predicted 45 minutes and Lewis awakened in pain in the recovery room, Haskell said.[7]

But instead of being transferred to a better equipped hospital surgery ward staffed by nurses trained to monitor and treat Lewis's condition, he was taken to a room within a cancer wing. That transfer was key, Haskell said, because the oncology nurses appeared to be unfamiliar with Lewis's surgery or its pain management and potential complications.

"The hospital never told us that he was not on a surgery floor. We gradually figured it out."[8]

Litvak has proven in multiple research papers that transfers to inappropriate hospital wards or departments are frequently caused by overcrowding and poorly managed patient flow.

This and other hospital decisions, along with many other failures contributed to a horrific outcome. Because his surgery was performed on a Thursday, his family knew he would be hospitalized over the weekend. At most American academic medical centers, medical residents – physicians in training – handle much of the hands-on medical care on weekends. Multiple resident physicians visited Lewis over the next four days, but when the weekend came, no fully trained, credentialed, and board certified doctors examined him between Saturday and Monday morning. Even on Monday, Haskell said, the doctors were busy in the operating room and did not come until Lewis was coded, an announcement of a patient whose heart has stopped. And those resident physicians missed the signs of his rapid decline, a condition marked by a hardening belly and deteriorating vital signs. He was also suffering from severe peritonitis caused by a perforated duodenal ulcer, a postoperative complication Haskell said was due to poorly managed pain management and overdosages of pain medications.

"Any nurse, especially an oncology nurse, should recognize deterioration. What these nurses did not know was what to expect from a surgical patient. This kind of pectus surgery requires near ICU-level care because it has such difficult pain management. Places that do a lot of minimally invasive pectus surgery sometimes have dedicated nurses for this procedure. Some put their pectus patients directly into the ICU. These nurses did not know any of that. I think they saw Lewis as a healthy child having elective surgery, not a sick patient like most of the other children in the cancer ward."[9]

His parents watched helplessly in disbelief as their son lay dying. On Monday he expired after losing 11 pounds and nearly three liters of blood.[10] Hospital physicians were perplexed at the death of an otherwise healthy teenager.

"The whole thing fell through the cracks," Helen Haskell recalled. "What we saw in the hospital there was chaos. There was no rhyme or reason to their care."[11]

Lewis Blackman's death became a national cause célèbre driving patient safety improvement in hospitals. With the proceeds from a wrongful death and medical negligence lawsuit, the Blackmans launched a foundation in his name and created the patient safety organization, Mothers Against Medical Errors.[12]

Today, Haskell is an advisor to the World Health Organization (WHO) Patients for Patient Safety group and works with patient advocacy and safety organizations around the globe.[13]

The Blackmans were instrumental in the passage of the Lewis Blackman Patient Safety Act in South Carolina's legislature and in securing practice changes within MUSC, the hospital where he died.[14]

"I think Lewis's death has been a catalyst," she said.[15]

Haskell met Litvak at a patient safety conference in 2014. They were seated at the same table "when he started talking about my son," she remembered. "He had no idea that I was Lewis's mother. If you have lost children, you want others to remember them, because so often children who die young are forgotten. I was honored that he was so interested in Lewis's story. We've struggled to create a legacy for my son."[16]

Litvak remembers that meeting a little differently.

"When we were introduced she mentioned that she was a patient safety expert. I'd met so many so-called patient safety experts who are unwilling to address the underlying problem in patient safety – recurring excessive patient demand – that I was a little impatient. However, I was trying to be polite. She said she was working to reduce medical errors. I said that should support her nicely until she retires and suggested her time would be spent more wisely studying the Lewis Blackman case. Then she said, 'I am his mother.' I didn't know that. I was almost crawling under the table in humiliation.

Hospital, Heal Thyself

I apologized multiple times for bringing this up. But she couldn't have been kinder."[17]

Before meeting Haskell and inspired by the tragedy of her son's death, Litvak published an opinion piece in the *Wall Street Journal* on December 2, 2013, titled "Don't Get Your Operation on a Thursday."[18]

Since their meeting, Haskell has been supportive of Litvak's work and now understands the hazards of ignoring patient flow.

"America's ER bottleneck is an international disgrace and due to many of the conditions Dr. Litvak described," Haskell said. "What keeps us going is so many people in healthcare like Dr. Litvak are dedicated and committed to change. The zeitgeist has changed. Now the system has to change from the inside. Hospital executives around the country should be galvanized to learn about his ideas and methods of changing hospital care."[19]

Since the late 1990s Litvak had examined America's healthcare system as an objective observer, a researcher, consultant, and outsider who had little personal interaction with it. That changed in February 2018 when an existing benign tumor in his mother's brain grew and caused swelling, intense pain, and fainting. His 94-year-old mother, Anna Litvak, had been transferred in and out of hospital emergency rooms and rehabilitation and long-term care facilities for months and could no longer safely live alone.[20]

She was a patient in a rehabilitation center when the pressure from that meningioma on her brain caused her to go into a coma. The rehab center summoned the Litvak family to say goodbye. Instead, Litvak demanded her transfer to an acute care hospital, where she was treated with life-sustaining medications, including steroids to ease the swelling. Two days later his mother awakened.[21]

"She told me to go home and get some rest. That was the mother in her. I was so happy to be talking with her I was jumping with joy. I said, 'I don't want to leave you, I'm afraid someone will steal you.'

The Human Toll

She said, 'Don't worry, if someone steals me they'll return me to you quickly.' But she was unable to stand or walk."[22]

Litvak's newfound elation was tempered by the news that his mother would be discharged only days after her harrowing admission and seemingly miraculous return to life.

"They needed to free up beds and told me they wanted to bring her back to the rehab facility. I said that was not going to happen and refused. They said they could not hold her, so I had them transfer her to another hospital. To discharge her from the hospital to the rehabilitation facility at that time would have killed her. She would have deteriorated immediately there," he said.[23]

As Litvak once explained in a *Wall Street Journal* piece, millions of hospital discharges are driven not by improved patient health, but because the hospital census reaches its peak on Thursdays and Fridays due to overcrowding and hospitals need to free up beds.[24] "On these days it seems patients magically become healthier and are discharged," he observed.[25] "I knew on that Thursday that it could be a problem, but assumed that my mother's serious condition would forbid the hospital from making this decision. I was wrong."[26]

Litvak said after her transfer to Beth Israel Hospital, the quality of his mother's life improved and she lived another two and a half months, though her condition remained terminal. "Everything was done that could have been done," he said.[27]

"First and foremost, we wanted her to be comfortable and not in pain. The last days of her life were very precious to her and to our family."[28]

That personal connection to hospital overcrowding deepened Litvak's resolve to persuade hospitals to adopt his methods for improving patient flow and patient safety.

Litvak has worked with hospitals and health systems throughout the United States, but also in Australia, Canada, England, and Scotland, including the Ottawa (Ontario) Hospital, a 1,200-bed facility.

Hospital, Heal Thyself

That hospital's chief executive officer, Jack Kitts, MD, said the human costs of hospital and ER overcrowding hit home for him in 2008 even before he became a hospital executive. He was still practicing anesthesiology and had worked for decades in hospital ORs.[29]

Kitts remembered seeing patients in the hospital's same-day surgery OR clinic making sure pre-op surgical patients were ready for their procedures when he was called by a nurse to speak with an elderly female patient and her three grown daughters. OR staff had just told them no bed was available for the woman's scheduled surgery and she'd need to reschedule her procedure. Her surgeon had been overbooked and was stuck in a 10-hour operation.[30]

"She was a distressed older woman lying on a stretcher and scheduled for a major surgery that morning. She looked very pale and fragile and started to cry when she heard the news about the cancellation. She asked when she would have her surgery, and I said I didn't know. Then she asked if she would have to take the onerous three-day bowel preparation again the next time and I said yes, and she began sobbing. Taking those medications had been very hard on her physically. And her daughters had come from as far away as France and western Canada. They'd taken time off work and traveled great distances to be with their mother.

"They didn't know if they would be able to return when the surgery would be rescheduled. I saw a sad, frightened, and distraught family and thought: this should never happen again to anyone," Kitts recalled.[31] That year the Ottawa Hospital would cancel 600 surgeries for lack of available beds.[32]

"I decided then that's no way to run a hospital. I never wanted anybody to go through what this family had to suffer," Kitts said.[33]

A few years later when a physician he knew with the Canadian Ministry of Health told Kitts he'd met a Harvard professor, Eugene Litvak, who could address concerns about OR patient flow, "I almost kicked him out of the room," Kitts remembered. "I was skeptical.

I've studied this like a fine arts student for decades, and this Litvak guy isn't a doctor or hospital administrator, but says he has the answers?"[34]

Nonetheless, Kitts invited Litvak to lecture the hospital's executive committee in May 2011 and the Ottawa Hospital then hired Litvak's company, IHO.

After adopting Litvak's recommendations, Kitts said the hospital added 13 spillover beds for the OR without spending any additional money.[35]

"We haven't had to cancel an elective surgery since [adopting Litvak's system]. We save about $9 million and 40 lives per year because of this," Kitts said.[36]

"Personally, I think the guy's a genius. Here's a man who had no baggage, no experience in an ER. But he didn't need to know how to do surgery. He applied research to a health challenge as he would a challenge in any other business. He applied proven methodologies to solve the patient flow problem and wasn't afraid to try those in the healthcare world. He had the courage of his conviction to do things that have never been done before. He thinks completely outside of the box. I was a 'Doubting Thomas' before, but I came to believe. We need more Eugene Litvaks in healthcare."[37]

Chapter 3

A System in Chaos: US Healthcare at a Crossroad

Unlike the nationalized healthcare systems most industrialized nations adopted long ago – systems that guarantee affordable healthcare services to citizens as a birthright – the US healthcare system is a pastiche of private and public insurance plans funding hospital and physician services in a haphazard, scattershot way that varies widely from state to state.

In 2021, Medicare, the federal program that pays for healthcare services for seniors and disabled Americans (representing 18.4% of the US population), covered 58.5 million beneficiaries. Medicaid, a jointly funded state and federal program, covered 58.7 million poor and disabled Americans (18.9%). Around 11.5 million of those beneficiaries are "dually eligible," meaning they qualify for both Medicare and Medicaid.[1]

Millions of other Americans are insured through specialized government programs, such as the Tri Care Health System for active US military (under 2%), the Veterans Administration (VA) Health System for veterans (1%), and the Children's Health Insurance Program (CHIP) to cover poor children (under 2%).

However, most US citizens are covered by private health plans (66.5%), either by insurance through their employers (54.6%) or through direct purchase or market plans.[2]

Before passage of the landmark Affordable Care Act (ACA) in 2010, more than 47 million Americans lacked health insurance coverage. After the ACA was implemented, the percentage of uninsured fell to 8.3%, around 27.2 million, in 2021.[3]

By early 2022, the uninsured rate had fallen significantly to 8% from the prior low of 9% in 2016, based on new data from the National Health Interview Survey. More than 5 million people have gained insurance coverage since 2020, gains attributable to enhanced marketplace subsidies and Medicaid expansions.[4]

When illness or injury strikes, the uninsured frequently seek care through hospital emergency rooms, the costliest and most inefficient means of accessing treatment. While their emergency conditions are treated, often at taxpayer expense, patients are billed at the highest rates and often sued by hospitals seeking repayment. And once released from ERs or discharged from hospitals, they are often unable to receive the crucial follow up treatment and medication, which means many – up to one-quarter – are readmitted to hospitals or ERs later for the original condition.[5]

According to the US Department of Health and Human Services, more than 21 million Americans were able to access routine physician and hospital care – many for the first time – after the ACA passed, mostly through Medicaid expansions undertaken in some states, and the state insurance exchanges offering subsidies to allow the working poor to purchase care. But ongoing legal attacks and threats to kill the ACA eroded some coverage gains and returned millions to the ranks of the uninsured for several years.[6]

The escalating costs of healthcare, along with growing access problems and periodic reports of quality lapses, have garnered the attention of state and national legislators, healthcare policy experts and hospital and medical leaders. The current cost of the US healthcare system in 2020 was nearly $4.1 trillion, almost 20% of the total US economy, according to the Centers for Medicare and

Medicaid Services (CMS). National health spending is projected to grow at an average annual rate of 5.4% from 2019 to 2028, reaching $6.2 trillion by 2028.[7]

But high healthcare costs and the lack of access to health services aren't the system's only flaws.

A system at the breaking point is bound to leak. In 1999 the Institute of Medicine published a groundbreaking study, "To Err Is Human," that found as many as 98,000 patient deaths occurred due to hospital errors. It was the first time that hospital-related deaths had been quantified, and it shook the industry.[8] As data analysis became more accurate, those early estimates proved low.

A 2010 report by the Inspector General of the US Department of Health and Human Services (HHS) estimated that hospital errors may have contributed to the deaths of 180,000 Medicare patients alone each year.[9] And a 2013 study in the *Journal of Patient Safety* revealed that the annual number of hospital patients dying of preventable causes could be as high as 400,000, which would make it the third-leading US cause of death behind heart disease and cancer.[10]

"How many of those [patients] dying because of avoidable errors were due to uneven patient flow or pressure on the system due to overcrowding? It could be as high as 50 to 75%," estimated Ellis "Mac" Knight, MD, an internal medicine specialist and former chief medical officer for the Palmetto Health system in Columbia, South Carolina.[11]

Knight, whose Palmetto system contracted with the Institute for Healthcare Optimization, said Litvak recognized that hospitals can control the variability of patient flow.

"We can't control how many people get sick or get in car wrecks and come into the ER, but we can control the number of elective surgeries we schedule. Litvak showed that if you can smooth out the number of elective surgeries scheduled throughout the week (instead of allowing surgeons to only operate on particular days at their convenience), you can eliminate the peaks and valleys and dramatically impact the efficiency and safety of hospital operations."[12]

Knight said that in nearly every root cause analysis of hospital deaths he has performed over the decades, the unnecessary deaths were related to overcrowding or understaffing.[13]

"Most were due to providers doing too much with too little in too little time. Thousands – maybe hundreds of thousands of lives – could be saved if every hospital in America adopted Dr. Litvak's methods. And we could make a significant dent in the $4 trillion we spend yearly on healthcare. Even a 5% or 10% reduction could have enormous benefits financially for our healthcare system and our population."[14]

A *New England Journal of Medicine* op-ed suggested those methods could also reduce hospital patient mortality, medical errors, and complications.[15]

"Engineering applications likely represent the single largest group of discrete service innovation opportunities to improve the affordability of US hospital care," said *Journal of the American Medical Association* study co-author Arnold Milstein, MD, aforementioned Stanford University professor and the medical director for the Pacific Business Group on Health.[16] That 2012 study predicted that up to $150 billion per year could be saved if US hospitals adopted Litvak's interventions.[17] "Many hospitals need to understand how they can apply a body of knowledge, such as operations management, engineering, and queueing theory, to get more productivity from their physical and human assets," Milstein said. "The vast majority of that potential is yet to be mined. We still have a fair amount of gold to pull out of the mine."[18]

Milstein said Litvak's approach is "the best near-term play for changing healthcare delivery in a way that would meaningfully reduce spending and improve quality. He is one of these people with the ability to take a form – something working well in one area – and have the vision, insight, and imagination to understand it could bring a lot of value to another area."[19]

He said Litvak was one of the first to practically apply queuing theory – an operations research and industrial engineering concept to predict waiting times – to healthcare settings, and show it could work and bring value to hospital patient throughput. He said some of the most important innovations in human civilization involve the brain of someone who can think metaphorically.[20]

"Litvak's brain allows him to see the applicability of something distant and see that it could work in a hospital environment where the nature of problems you're trying to solve is far different than just manufacturing steel beams. No one imagined you could do that. Most people lack his agility in thinking. He has the mind of a great innovator who can see a cause and effect in one domain and recognize that it could apply to other domains."[21]

Many healthcare policy analysts and cognoscenti believe Litvak possesses a solution that could transform American hospitals, improve the quality of care and save hundreds, perhaps thousands of lives annually. In addition to improving the quality and efficiency of hospital operations and surgical operating rooms, Litvak's methods could reduce ER overcrowding, operating room staff burnout, and employee turnover, ER waits, and may offer great potential for improving outpatient care.[22]

Some of the fundamental underpinnings of Litvak's methods and theories had been employed successfully in other industries but had never been applied to healthcare. His work in understanding patient flow, the process of a patient's journey through a hospital from before admission through treatment and release, has dramatically changed the way his client hospitals operate.

He found that the cause of many problems plaguing US hospitals can be traced to the variability of patient flow. Litvak discovered that in almost every American hospital there are dramatic daily variations

A System in Chaos: US Healthcare at a Crossroad

in bed occupancy (patient census), with the number of patients occupying beds within a hospital rising and falling in peaks and valleys.[23]

That observation is nothing new. Almost every hospital CEO knows that hospital occupancy fluctuates up and down daily. Before Litvak, few questioned the abnormality of those census variations. It was accepted that some days the ER would be swamped, and on those days, patient volume within the ORs for elective surgeries would vary wildly, typified by postponed or canceled surgeries and delayed hospital admissions. Physicians and nurses would work overtime and ambulances would divert patients to other hospitals because of ER overcrowding. ER waits would drag on for hours, even days, and elective surgery patients would seethe in anger and frustration as their scheduled surgeries were canceled. ER patients needing hospitalization could sit on gurneys in hallways because hospital beds in the appropriate wings were unavailable. Hospital overtime costs skyrocket as nurse and physician burnout reach boiling points, jeopardizing patient safety and increasing hospital-acquired infections and hospital readmissions. The day after struggling through 12- to 16-hour shifts, those OR nurses might be sent home early for lack of scheduled surgeries.[24]

Most hospital CEOs throw up their hands, blame it on the gods and unanticipated ER rushes, and beseech their governing boards for millions more dollars for new patient towers or expanded ERs to accommodate the frequent overcrowding. This overcrowding occurs even as the average daily occupancy of American hospitals has hovered around 66%.[25]

"How can you be overcrowded when one-third of your beds are empty most of the time?" Litvak asked.

Few made the connection between the fluctuating daily admissions census and the plethora of hospital problems, from the high cost of care, ER overcrowding, to high OR nurse turnover, wrong bed assignments, ambulance diversions, wasteful capital spending, high readmission rates, and, most importantly, greater risk of medical error and patient mortality. That is, until Litvak pointed it out in his widely published research.

He and his colleague, Michael Long, MD, from the Massachusetts General Hospital, discovered that counterintuitively, the spikes in patient census were not caused by sudden rushes of emergency room patients, but by poor scheduling in hospital operating rooms where elective surgeries are performed.[26]

Litvak said, "That was an aha moment for me."

More on that later.

His reputation spread and some of the most prominent medical centers in America, including the Mayo Clinic and Johns Hopkins University, sought his services.

Knight, the former Palmetto Health executive, said that after hiring Litvak, hospital annual revenue rose by $3 million, primarily by improving "throughput" – the number of patients that can be seen and treated in a day.[27]

Don Berwick, MD, a pediatrician and former president and chief executive officer for the not-for-profit Institute for Healthcare Improvement in Boston, said Litvak's methods hold great promise for improving hospital care. Berwick, who co-authored studies with Litvak, also served as administrator of CMS, the federal agency that administers Medicare.[28]

Berwick said credible research organizations, including the RAND Corporation and the National Academy of Medicine, have estimated that one-third of US healthcare spending is wasted, primarily through duplication, unnecessary tests, and services and medical errors.[29]

"We're spending at least $1 trillion on healthcare of low value or failures due to improper design," Berwick said. "I am not at all surprised that implementing Dr. Litvak's methods could save at least $100 billion annually if they were universally adopted. That figure may even be conservative. If we could bring modern approaches to flow scheduling and managing capacity demand, it is quite possible. It will depend on the skill and courage of hospital leaders."[30]

Berwick said Litvak brought systematic scientific thinking to healthcare operations.

"I think he's brilliant and perceptive. He may be a genius. He has the uncanny ability to see through the underlying dynamics of systems at a high level. And he has sounded the alarm that we're walking past the problems and ignoring the solutions."[31]

Berwick spoke of the hospitals where Litvak has worked. "He's changed their world. People are thinking entirely differently about managing schedules and planning capital spending. He's shown us a totally new way of looking at patient flow and patient safety and shown a strong connection between the two. He's changed people and organizations."[32]

Harvey Fineberg, MD, was the dean of the School of Public Health at Harvard University (now the Harvard Chan School of Public Health) who hired Litvak as a postdoctoral level researcher in the early 1990s. Fineberg, now the president of the Gordon and Betty Moore Foundation, was formerly president of the Institute of Medicine (now the National Academy of Medicine) from 2002 to 2014.

Fineberg said Litvak approaches problems uniquely.

"Some of his answers to questions relative to diagnostic accuracy were intriguing and that's where I started to recognize his talent and brilliance. He's one of those people who speaks so clearly and readily but is not always aware that others have not quite caught up with where his reasoning has taken him," said Fineberg, who also co-authored research and policy papers with Litvak.[33]

Fineberg said Litvak is quick to see through problems to potential solutions.

"It almost seemed as much intuitive as logical, as if he could see the solution and reason how that particular solution was the correct one," Fineberg noted. "He has the ability to envision what the right answers are and the ability to explain them. It's very impressive to witness. He could see six steps ahead while most of us could only see one or two. Eugene possesses a far-sighted brilliance grounded in years of math and logical thinking."[34]

He said improving patient flow through Litvak's methods makes it more likely that ER patients admitted to the hospital will end up on the appropriate hospital floor or wing with nurses who know best how to care for them postoperatively, with cancer patients ending up on oncology floors, not surgery wings.

"He came to understand that patient flow is not only a problem related to ER intake, but occurs throughout the hospital, from intensive care units to cardiac labs and diagnostic suites. And if you applied this notion of flow as an organizing principle for efficiency, as a common pathway for steps to manage patients economically and effectively, it gives you a handle on helping your entire hospital operate with greater efficiency at lower costs."[35]

Chapter 4

The Soviet Years: Maybe I Wasn't Supposed to Be Born

If his grandfather's overcoat hadn't been stitched with such a thick collar when an angry group of drunken Ukrainian soldiers strung him up to hang, Eugene Litvak wouldn't be here to tell this story now.

Litvak's paternal grandfather, Jacob Litvak, was living in a small Jewish village, or shtetl, when the territory of Ukraine sought independence from the Russian empire during the Russian Revolution. He recounted an episode from his family history when soldiers rode into his grandfather's village on horses and demanded money and gold, "because all Jews were rumored to own and hide gold."[1]

They didn't believe Jacob Litvak when he said his family had none. "The soldiers were asking for something that didn't exist," Litvak said.

Symon Petliura, a Ukrainian hero who served as Supreme Commander of its army and president of the Ukrainian National Republic during its brief period of independence (1918 to 1921), had been supportive of Jews and even had Jewish ministers in his cabinet.[2]

However, Petliura's army actively participated in violent, deadly pogroms and attacks against Ukraine's Jewish population. Before the Holocaust of World War II, the largest number of Jews massacred in Europe occurred during the war against Russia for Ukrainian independence, when as many as 50,000 Jews were killed.[3] In one violent attack, drunken members of Petliura's army strung a noose around

Jacob Litvak's neck, hung him from a tree, and left him to die. Luckily, that thick collar prevented the noose from immediately strangling him. Family members and neighbors cut him down and saved his life after the hangmen rode off, also saving the Litvak family line.

"That was a point where my destiny was determined," said Litvak. "My grandfather never discussed it in my presence. When my father asked, my grandfather had one word to describe his attackers: *gonifs* – a Yiddish word meaning thieves, crooks, or monsters."

History spared his ancestors from premature graves on other occasions. Jacob's wife, Faina, had a similarly harrowing episode when Litvak's father, Israel, was just a toddler.[4] In 1919 the White Russian Army launched another pogrom. Faina ran away from the violence, carrying Israel in one arm and pulling his older brother, Emmanuel, with the other, narrowly escaping their attackers.[5] "She told me that she remembered bullets whistling past as she ran away in terror with her sons."

Ukraine, the Russian Empire, and the Soviet Union shared a long, tragic history of anti-Semitism and persecution of Jews. Litvak was born in a country where his career and future were limited by his family's religion, even though few in the family practiced it.

Litvak's maternal great-grandfather was a successful farmer, baker, and windmill owner. His son, Anton, inherited the businesses until just after the Bolshevik Revolution.

"But after the Revolution everything was taken away from them, including their home," Litvak said. "The whole family with small children was thrown out on the street. There was a short 'grace period' after the Revolution when nothing was done to people who were well off. Then they were evicted and lost everything that they couldn't wear or carry. They had to start again from scratch."[6]

Litvak's mother was born Anna Shachnovich in a village in Belarus called Kostjukovichi to Anton and Lisa Shachnovich. As a girl she moved with her parents and brother to the Russian city of Kaluga. There they lived like an average Soviet family.

"But my great-grandfather was labeled a *kulak*, Litvak explained, a pejorative term describing wealthy farmers. The government confiscated everything and only gave them hours to leave. They could take no books, jewelry, or valuables. After that he was poor for the rest of his life."[7]

Litvak remembered his paternal grandfather, Jacob, as a quiet, self-sufficient, and mild-mannered man who kept to himself. "He was a vegetarian, the only person I knew then in the USSR who didn't eat meat. To get from our Kiev house to his workplace he had to walk through a big part of the city, about a six-mile walk one way. Unless it was raining badly, he never used public transportation. He was tall and very thin and ate very little. He really loved me. I was the only grandson carrying on the family name. Sadly, in the late 1950s he fell and broke his hip. He became bed-ridden, then got pressure ulcers and died in his 80s."[8]

Jacob's wife, Litvak's paternal grandmother, Faina, was a few years older than the husband she outlived. "Yet she excluded everything healthy from her diet, never exercised, ate the fat with the meat, and still outlasted my grandfather. She was short and stout, but a survivor."[9]

Litvak said for a Jewish woman of her era, Faina was considered educated and graduated from gymnasium, the Russian equivalent of high school. "She would recite Pushkin's poetry to me by heart," he recalled. "She was strong and demanded respect. I remember my father once punishing me for not being polite enough to her. I did something wrong and she said, 'If you behave like that, you're not my grandson anymore.' I said, 'Okay, that means you're not my grandmother.' She told my father and I was reprimanded. I remember her sitting with her women friends on a park bench near their

The Soviet Years: Maybe I Wasn't Supposed to Be Born

apartment. They would all call each other 'Madame' and relive their memories of life before the Revolution."[10]

Nurse, Lawyer, Mother

Litvak said his mother, Anna, dressed simply around their apartment and wore her hair short. "Never in her life did she have any fancy clothes," he said, also recalling that his mother loved to laugh and appreciated a good joke. "She was dependably optimistic, even if she didn't feel well."[11]

Before World War II Anna was accepted to the Moscow Pedagogical Institute in the department of literature, which inspired her lifelong love of literature. "But the war interrupted that, and she became a nurse, met my wounded father, and nursed him back to health. Her nickname was "Anya," and she shared a fairytale romance with my father. During the war, she married him and came to Kiev to start a new life."[12]

Litvak's mother later graduated from law school at Kiev University but didn't work or practice law until her son was in high school. "She wanted to make sure to be home to greet me and feed me after school," he said. "My mother postponed her career and sacrificed her ambitions for me."

Litvak remembers his mother as a good cook who did the best she could under the circumstances. "At dinner in Kiev I was not allowed to leave the table without my father's permission. They knew I needed protein, so they bought meat, but couldn't afford good cuts. Sometimes I remember chewing and chewing and almost vomiting some of the unknown meat-like substances they served me. I was crying and my tears were dropping into this so-called meat. I didn't want any more, and my father said I couldn't leave until I finished eating. I was a little boy, of five or six, and forcefully told them that in a few more years I would be an adult

Hospital, Heal Thyself

and then nobody could force me to eat this. One cut of meat my mother served me was the chicken navel, a dish called *pup*, but pronounced like 'poop.' Everyone ate that. My son asked me once what I ate as a child and I told him, 'Poop.' You should have seen the expression on his face."[13]

Once Litvak was in high school and his mother began working as a lawyer for a Soviet clothing company, the Litvak family rose to the "People's Paradise" version of middle class. "We bought a television. She started preparing better and more delicious food, baking cakes, and serving cuts of meat like chicken breast instead of feet," he laughed. "That was very tasty."[14]

Litvak said his mother did not influence him as strongly as his father but was his conscience and moral core. "My career here in healthcare didn't matter to her. Whether I was cleaning streets or teaching as a Harvard professor, she could care less. What she did care about is whether I was a mensch (a Yiddish word meaning a person of honor and integrity). She had a strong moral compass."[15]

When they arrived in America, his mother told Litvak, "Finally I can get more of what I wanted all my life: the time to just sit and read." Litvak said, "I inherited my love of reading from my mother." In the last few years of her life she alternated her spare time between reading, watching television news, and completing crossword puzzles, all in Russian.[16] "For my parents to access truthful information in books and newspapers was like finally breathing in fresh air: they could never get enough of it."

"My father was my hero"

Litvak's father, Israel Litvak, was born February 9, 1915, in Bogopol, Ukraine, and lived there until his family moved to the Ukrainian capital, Kiev. Israel Litvak and his older brother, Emmanuel, were Jacob and Faina's only children. Israel became an electrical engineer.[17]

"Recently my wife asked me what I considered my father's main characteristics. I said he was sincere, straightforward, and honest, someone who would not lie even when the truth was unpleasant or could negatively impact his life or career. If you asked his opinion, his response could be brutally honest and direct," he said. "My father was a very strong and active man who was a natural leader. He had black hair and was very good looking. His brother, Emmanuel, was very quiet and subdued and his wife, my aunt, was the master of their house."[18]

Before the Nazis occupied Kiev, Litvak's grandparents evacuated to safer regions south and east of the warfront, again dodging death and escaping the impending Holocaust. Kiev was bombed on the first day of the war and quickly occupied by German invaders. During the occupation, most of Kiev's remaining Jews were slaughtered along with Roma people, Soviet prisoners of war, communists, and Ukrainian nationalists in the ravine outside of the city called Babi Yar, a place immortalized in the eponymous poem by Yevgeny Yevtushenko. "It is estimated that, in total, some 100,000 people, Jews and non-Jews, were murdered at Babyn Yar under the German occupation."[19]

Israel Litvak joined the Red Army and was serving in a tank division when his unit's tanks were attacked near the Ukrainian city of Harkov. An explosion threw him from his tank and the shrapnel nearly split his leg in two from the knee down.

■ ■ ■

"My mother was recruited to train in a hospital in one of the Soviet Asian republics far from the front lines," Litvak said. "The hospital was located in the Kyrgyzstan capital of Frunze, then called Bishkek."[20]

At 18 she became a nurse, where she met Israel Litvak recuperating from his wounds. Doctors were unable to accurately diagnose

Hospital, Heal Thyself

the source of his excruciating pain from causalgia, a burning chronic pain caused by nerve damage. The shrapnel had pinched a nerve between the two shattered bones.

"His suffering was unbearable. He had to keep his hands in rubber gloves with water in them. He remained that way for practically a year, all the while not knowing whether his parents and family were alive," he said. "My mother was assigned to care for him. That's how they met and fell in love. Doctors performed multiple unsuccessful surgeries to repair his leg. The shrapnel had cut his leg vertically, not horizontally. There was little bone left. Finally, on the third surgery, he insisted that doctors operate without anesthesia so he could direct them what to do and what he was feeling. They started the surgery, but he lost consciousness quickly due to the pain."[21]

Fortunately, that operation was finally successful. In 1944 Israel Litvak was discharged. However, the wound never healed properly, and Israel Litvak would limp and walk with a cane for the rest of his life. Fifty years later, after he'd immigrated to the United States, his leg was amputated below the knee after he acquired diabetes. But he learned to walk again with a prosthesis.

Litvak said his father seldom spoke loudly in front of him and only once in anger. "After that he didn't even need to raise his voice. His eyes and facial expressions conveyed what he needed to say. He didn't have to yell. I was always a little afraid of him. It wasn't really a fear of a beating. It was the fear of disappointing him."[22]

Litvak's father set an unachievable gold standard for him. "It was impossible for him to act against his principles, even if that would benefit him personally. For him there was no ethical gray area, only black and white."[23]

As a boy Litvak remembered spilling boiling water on himself. "I sustained second or third degree burns and started crying. My father just shot me a stern look, and I stopped crying immediately. It was impossible to come home and complain that

The Soviet Years: Maybe I Wasn't Supposed to Be Born

somebody beat me or did something to me. He did not believe in complaining."[24]

Litvak said his father was strongly encouraged by bosses to change his first name from the politically unpopular "Israel," and to join the Communist Party, which would entitle him to a higher salary, bigger apartment, and better living conditions. "But that was a nonstarter for him," Litvak said. "He always refused."

Litvak said his father, whose friends called him "Izja," was also a wise man whose wisdom was gleaned from surviving a difficult life. "He was the valedictorian of his class and extremely devoted to his friends. If a friend in another city needed help, he would travel there by train to offer assistance. His friends always came to him for advice. He was that way throughout his life. When he was in college his nickname was 'Rov,' short in Yiddish for Rabbi. He was not a religious man, but he strongly supported Israel."[25]

Litvak remembers asking his father about World War II but said Izja was always reluctant to discuss it. "I never learned anything about the war directly from him, only through my mother. Maybe the memories were too painful. Every morning and evening until his leg was amputated, my mother applied fresh bandages to it. That was real love. I think that this suffering shaped his character and determined his view of what a man should be. He was stoic and never complained."[26]

Israel Litvak died in the United States in 1998 at age 83, a decade after emigrating.

Childhood

Eugene Litvak was born in Kiev in 1949. His first name in Russian is Yevgeny, nicknamed "Zhenya."

"I remember my father taking me to my first day of kindergarten. There was a metal fence around the school, and that first day

I remember watching him through the slats of the fence leave after dropping me off. I started crying. Our school was relatively close to home near Victory Square. My father took me there on the way to his work. We took a trolley. I really came to love it. I remember taking naps and feeling very safe and comfortable there. Here I first learned how to make and keep friends."[27]

The Soviet Union had survived a brutal war on two fronts with Germany and Japan, and the nation, especially its Communist government, took great pride in its burgeoning military might. As the two superpowers engaged in a barely disguised Cold War, Litvak remembers watching many Soviet military parades as a boy, every May 9 (Victory Day) and the commemoration of the 1917 October Revolution.[28]

"It was compulsory then to go out onto the street and celebrate with red banners and flags. You could not escape it. This always reminds me of a joke. A guy came to Red Square in Moscow carrying a blank banner. A policeman stopped him and asked: 'Why is there nothing written on your banner?' The man replied, 'Because everyone already knows what I would like to say.'"[29]

Like most citizens of the USSR, the Litvaks figured out how to exploit the onerous bureaucracy of the Soviet system. There were frequent food shortages and lines for everything, he recalled, but especially for food.

"When I was three or four the amount of food that any person could buy was limited by the government, which issued ration cards. So my mother, like other women, learned that if two of us stood in line for food we could double the portions we were allowed to take home," he recalled. "After that I always accompanied her to the store."[30]

Litvak attended elementary school with boys five or six years older, children whose parents were killed during the war. He said those boys had missed years of classes. He learned that the first

The Soviet Years: Maybe I Wasn't Supposed to Be Born

lesson in life was a child must be able to defend himself. "If you were passive and quiet, you'd constantly get beaten. You had to establish yourself. This helped to shape my character."[31]

Following World War II there were many criminals inhabiting the streets of Kiev seeking easy money, Litvak recalls. Many were displaced by the war, the Soviets' forced evacuations, or the loss of parents and family members. Though the USSR implemented many measures to protect orphans, more than 2.5 million homeless children remained after the war.[32]

"I was surrounded by those guys. They taught us how to pick pockets like Dickens's characters from *Oliver Twist*. I was exposed to them from early childhood. But I never had problems with any of them."[33]

Litvak said as a boy he didn't remember being at home much, except in the evenings. "We didn't have TV. My fun and education came from reading books at bedtime and spending time on the streets during the day. After dinner, my parents would let me go out to play. The older boys were petty criminals who taught us interesting tricks, and I wanted to be like them. What I learned later was that my father watched all this transpire but had never told me. He believed, as an only child, that I needed to learn how to survive. I was old enough to digest the important lessons I learned from these criminals, particularly about human nature. I discovered that some people would rob or steal money and could even be violent. But they were not all bad people. They had difficult lives and few other options."[34]

He counted the local street hoods as friends. "But it was more like a student-teacher relationship. It was probably luck that they never beat me up. Nobody ever touched me. Somehow, they accepted me into their group, though I was not one of them. I think that my sense of humor protected me. When you can make people laugh, they look at you differently. If I was older, they might have forced me to fight."[35]

Hospital, Heal Thyself

He said his hoodlum friends were trying to teach neighborhood boys how to steal money, but mainly how to engage in funny pranks. "We would place an empty wallet on the street with an almost invisible fishing line attached and when someone bent to pick it up, we'd slowly pull on it to frustrate them. It was entertaining for us to see adults try and fail to grab the wallet. And when they moved faster to get it, we pulled the string even faster."[36]

He admits he wasn't talented in sports. "So in order to compensate for that, I was always creating some non-sport competition that I could dominate and win, usually mental challenges or games that would put me on an equal footing with my bigger and stronger friends," he recalls. "This was my saving grace."[37]

Litvak said his family scraped by in the lean years of the 1950s and early 1960s. "I don't remember wearing pants without patches. My family couldn't yet afford new pants, so my mother patched the old ones. But we weren't alone. Everyone struggled in those years. It was hard times in the Soviet Union after the war. We lost more than 20 million people. Many cities, including Kiev, were still in ruins for many years."[38]

The Nazis bombed Kiev in the summer of 1941. Ten to 15 years later, much of that devastation remained, often masked by fresh coats of paint or other superficial remodeling.[39]

"Even when I was a young boy in the mid-1950s much of the city lay in shambles. Many buildings were crumbled and devastated. The government started rebuilding, but just the exterior facades, what you could see from the streets. What was behind those walls you could not see and didn't matter. That part could be fixed later. One of these buildings was around six stories high and was completely gutted and destroyed, but the exterior was left standing. My friends and I loved to go in there to play and explore," he said.[40] "Only now do I understand that we were very lucky we survived playing there. There were no stairs connecting the different building floors and only broken stairs and shattered windows in others. There were unexploded bombs in some buildings around Kiev. But we loved to play among those barren ruins. It was mysterious to us."[41]

Litvak grew up in a Soviet Union that was transforming from a rural, agricultural nation to an industrial and military power. One obvious symbol of that transformation was mechanization and the declining use of farm animals.

"I remember very well when I was five or six, hearing a horse and cart hauling vegetables. It drove right under our balcony. There was something magical about that sound and the feeling it gave me," he said. "But within a few years I no longer heard it, and it disappeared forever, like the neighborhood criminals of my youth."[42]

Litvak said his youthful frailty concerned his father. "On winter mornings before he went to work, my father forced me to stand outside on our balcony and rub snow all over my body. This was supposed to make me stronger and healthier. After he left the apartment, my mother would bring me in. My mother always believed my father was too harsh and tried to defend me. But there was no way I could refuse him. After busy days at work during the winter, he and I would have snowball fights outside or he would help the building superintendent clear snow and ice from the sidewalks."[43]

His father's efforts to transform young Zhenya from a scrawny weakling continued for years. "Back then in the USSR, nobody jogged on the streets for exercise. Even older athletes in their 20s or 30s didn't run on the city streets, but on designated tracks and racing courses. People then would look at you like you were crazy if you tried. But my father ordered me to do this for my health. He would stand on the balcony in the morning and command me to run around a nearby park. I would start out doing that. Then I would sit on a park bench where he couldn't see me and think for a while. After some time, I'd remember I had to come home, so I would run home and breathe heavily when I came in so he would believe his plans were going well. Sadly, my father's efforts were in vain."[44]

Litvak's father also encouraged his son's interest in math, often by challenging him with math puzzles and problems. "When we walked together, he would pose real life math problems of his own creation. My mother, who had a strong aversion to math, did not enjoy these conversations. So he only spoke about math when we were alone to avoid making her feel uncomfortable. He introduced me to some very difficult problems, though he was not very strong in math. He believed it was important to find my talents and discovered that math was my greatest passion."[45]

Litvak's father exposed him to other arts and disciplines, hoping he would excel in one or more. "He believed I should take up painting, so he brought me to somebody giving private painting classes. After a few sessions, this man told my father, 'You are a decent person, and I cannot take your money.' That was the end of it. I was hopeless as a painter."[46]

As a child Litvak felt jealous when he saw other kids playing piano and violin at school. "They put together a school orchestra and one day I received this musical instrument, a baritone horn, which I brought home to our apartment. When I started practicing, the neighbors complained loudly and demanded I stop immediately. That was the end of my musical training. I was 12 and my music career lasted only one week. But math was my greatest love and remained so for many, many years. And that was because of my father."[47]

After 8th grade Litvak graduated to high school. The transition was not pleasant. "I didn't know anybody in the new school. But I was developing some new skills, learning how to make new friends and get along with people," he said.

"I made one friend who was very, very bright and lived in a place in Kiev well known for its criminal activity, Besarabka. Yuli

The Soviet Years: Maybe I Wasn't Supposed to Be Born

[Julius, who was also Jewish] and I competed to be first in class and became very close friends."[48]

Litvak was a voracious reader as a child, devouring Robert Louis Stevenson, James Fenimore Cooper, Jules Verne, and Victor Hugo. "I was also attracted to the Russian writer, Fyodor Dostoyevsky. Dostoyevsky became my obsession and greatest literary influence. As Einstein once said, 'Dostoyevsky gives me more than any scientist.' Who could argue with Einstein?"[49]

Human psychology fascinated him. "Dostoyevsky was my teacher. From my teen years until today I've wondered why people behave the way they do and what motivates their behavior."

Litvak said in high school he desperately wanted to become a physicist. "My father stimulated my interest in math," he said. "But my interest in physics came from a teacher, Grigori Isaacovich, who taught me in 9th and 10th grades [at that time, the equivalents of junior and senior years of high school in the United States]. He was so influential and convinced my best friend, Yuli, and me that we should be physicists. It was like he hypnotized us."[50]

Litvak remembered constantly arguing the laws of physics with Yuli, in and out of class. "Our teacher was always challenging us. We started solving more complex problems outside of class. Yuli became a physicist. He and I were significantly ahead of the rest of our class. Our teacher realized that. So he was constantly increasing the complexity of the problems. Because of him I participated in a physics competition in our city and region and took third place in all of Ukraine," Litvak said. "I was very encouraged. I thought I would become the next Isaac Newton."[51]

Litvak was extremely shy until he left Kiev to attend college in St. Petersburg. "I was serious about achieving my goals. I was not shy in discussing science or in talking with teachers. But in public speaking I was petrified. And around girls, my tongue turned to stone. When my classmates asked me to dance with a girl in high school that was

Hospital, Heal Thyself

as scary as the prospect of sex. I worried that people would make fun of me."[52]

It Was Humbling

Litvak's memories gush freely when he talks about his Kiev home, a small, cramped room within a communal apartment that routinely housed 15 residents. Before the Russian Revolution, the apartment was occupied by a single family. It was the only home he knew for the first quarter-century of his life. In an older neighborhood near the city's center, it was a six-story building with 13 apartments, in an era and environment far removed from his comfortable American home outside of Boston.

Litvak and his parents shared the third-floor apartment with his grandparents and uncle's family; an old Jewish woman and her grandson, who later brought his wife to this apartment; a barber with his wife and two children; and finally an older Ukrainian woman who lived with her daughter there until she married. Residents shared a single toilet, bathroom, and kitchen, as well as common living spaces. "At any given time in the kitchen someone could be cooking or washing their laundry, boiling white clothes in a large steaming pot, while someone on the next burner was making soup or tea."[53]

Litvak's family owned a samovar, a metal device used to boil water for tea, because his grandfather frequently consumed 10 to 12 cups of tea daily, particularly when he read Dostoevsky on the balcony. "Everyone else used small teapots."

Litvak's mother packed him a lunch, though every school staffed a cafeteria. "But when I was little, we didn't have money to buy meals. My mother prepared the same lunch for me every day: a sandwich made with black bread and cheese that sometimes included sausage and butter. When it was warmer, she included fresh fruit if it was available."[54]

Until he reached middle school, the apartment's kitchen did not include a refrigerator. "So during winter, we left our food on the outside windowsills, which kept everything cool. That was our refrigerator. My parents bought a used refrigerator when I was in 5th or 6th grade. Before that, there was no place to safely store perishable food, so we had to shop for groceries every day and wait in the long lines."

Litvak, an only child, lived with his parents in a 140 square foot bedroom that included beds for his parents and him, as well as a wardrobe and a table. "Even if you were slim, you could barely manage to shimmy between these pieces of furniture without crashing into something. Sometimes you felt like you were bumping into yourself."

He said in the kitchen every family had a small table where they could prepare food, as well as a teapot and a cooking pot. Each family was entitled to only one stove burner. "When I was a baby and my mother took care of me, she had to boil water for cooking, cleaning and laundry."

Litvak remembered the lines formed to use the apartment's single toilet. "You had to exercise restraint," he said.

Each tenant family owned separate toilet seats. "People carried their toilet seats around their necks, and their pots in their arms," he laughed. "We went to the public baths in town for bathing. Without hot water, it was not possible to take a bath in our bathroom. We finally got hot water when I was in 9th grade. Everyone knew everyone's business. Sometimes there were conflicts with so many people living so closely together. 'Why did you use my burner?' you could hear someone complain. 'Use your own' 'Why did you leave the light on in the toilet? We have to pay that utility bill.'"[55]

Litvak lived in that apartment from his birth until he married in 1975, except for the time he spent in college in St. Petersburg. Litvak recently located his old home on Google Earth and showed it to his only son, Mark. Today, he said, it is a clean, elegantly painted building housing a bank on the first floor.

On Being Jewish

Litvak said he learned that he was Jewish in the 1st grade. "Then I didn't understand the difference between Ukrainians and Russians and Jews. My mother told me when I asked her in 1st grade why my father was named after this bad country of Israel, as our leaders described it. Then in school I overheard people talking about Jews and learned quickly I was not like everyone else. Maybe, except for anti-Semitism, I would not feel like a Jew now. But the government taught me well. I realized at school that teachers and classmates said bad things about Jews and that my family and I were Jewish. Most of my friends were Russian or Ukrainian and my closest friend was Greek. But my friends' nationality never entered my mind. What was important was whether they were jerks."[56]

Litvak said his parents spoke Yiddish to his grandparents when they didn't want him to understand something. "I never learned the language. It never occurred to me as a child that this country didn't want me. My parents understood this. But I didn't."[57]

Litvak explained that in the former USSR, everyone was issued passports at birth, which showed the holder's first name, father's name, last name, address, and nationality. "In the United States 'nationality' would be called religion for Jewish people. It was famous in the USSR as 'Line 5.' But in the USSR there officially was no religion and no word for it," he explained. "If you had Line 5 listed as 'Jewish,' you could not get into the best colleges or be considered for the top jobs. It was official government policy."[58]

Litvak said despite widespread anti-Semitism, he doesn't believe Russians and Ukrainians are innately anti-Semitic. "Nobody is born a jerk or a bigot. Kids hear this from their parents and neighbors.

Jews were convenient scapegoats. To be Christian then was bad, too. If you were caught praying in a church, you could forget about your career. My grandparents belonged to a synagogue, but my parents did not. In that respect, they were brainwashed products of the USSR. When they grew older, they began to think differently."[59]

Litvak said his parents never discussed anti-Semitism with him. "A kid just wants to belong. Years later, I learned that I had to strive to be much better than others around me because I was a Jew. To get the same treatment as everyone else, I had to work harder and achieve better results. There were some places where, no matter what skills or educational credentials I had, I would not be accepted. I came to understand that reality but didn't want to accept that anyone had that power over me. I knew I wasn't like everybody else, but I would not let them take advantage of me."[60]

School ended in June in Ukraine and students, just as in the United States, enjoyed their summers off. For a few weeks in the summer many parents would take their children to state-subsidized summer camps. Litvak's summer camp was in a suburb of Kiev named Irpin, surrounded by forests.

"We traveled there by train and stayed in dormitories," he remembered. "Parents could visit on special days and bring strawberries and sugary little treats and spend time with the kids. The food wasn't very good. But there were outdoor activities, like swimming and hiking in the forest. We spent time learning about nature. I look back on this time with mixed feelings. Occasionally at bedtime the other kids spoke harshly about Jews. They didn't realize I was Jewish. Then, something happened."[61]

In January 1953 the Soviet Communist Party newspaper, *Pravda*, published a story alleging that a group of nine physicians, mostly Jews, had plotted to poison top Soviet leaders, had killed senior KGB officials, and planned to murder Premier Joseph Stalin. A Russian cardiologist, Lidya Timashuk, blew the whistle on the so-called "Doctors' Plot" and was awarded the "Order of Lenin" for her efforts.[62]

Some of the alleged physician ringleaders were arrested, tortured, and died in custody. News of the "Doctors' Plot" was widely disseminated and the roles of Jews discussed around dinner tables and schoolyards.

After Stalin's death three months later, his successors discovered the "plot" was a conspiracy fantasy created by Stalin to purge his rivals and justify mass deportations of Jews to the Siberian GULAGs (a Russian acronym for the Main Administration of Camps, a government agency that oversaw the Soviet forced labor camps). His death ended that campaign but revealed barely sublimated anti-Semitism.[63]

"The conspiracy was disproven," Litvak said. "But at the time this alleged plot affected the mindset of many people, who still believed that Jews wanted to poison and kill our leaders. Kids heard about this in our summer camp and it started anti-Semitic conversations. I felt very uncomfortable."[64]

Litvak remembered quietly celebrating the Passover seder with his grandparents, parents, and uncle's family. "We dressed in our best clothes, sat around the table, and my grandfather would pray. He read and spoke Hebrew fluently. My parents did not."

He recalled the first time hearing his grandfather praying at a Passover dinner in Hebrew, a language unknown to him. "I was a little boy, and he was speaking in a strange language that made no sense to me. These were funny sounds I'd never heard before. Every time I heard him praying in Hebrew I started laughing. My father shot me an angry look and ordered me to cast my eyes down to the floor. I remember looking down and biting my lips. But I couldn't help myself. The more he spoke in these nonsensical sounds, the more I laughed. Of course, this was a serious and somber occasion, and my behavior was inappropriate. But the more he said the more

The Soviet Years: Maybe I Wasn't Supposed to Be Born

I laughed and the more people looked at me, the angrier they got. How long can a kid sit like that?"[65]

Awakening to the USSR

In high school, after his grandparents died, Litvak said he finally understood what the Soviet government really was. "My father was constantly listening – illegally – to the Voice of America (VOA) and Radio Deutsche Welle from Germany. When they closed the door behind them, I wanted to listen, but knew I shouldn't. However, I couldn't resist when I heard the lovely music to "Yankee Doodle Dandy" that introduced all VOA programs. The VOA signals were often jammed on the orders of the Soviet government, but if I was patient enough and pushed my ear against the door, eventually I could understand. My parents were afraid I'd talk about it outside of our home. I knew not to discuss this with my friends even without my parents' advice."[66]

Litvak said that from listening to the Voice of America, his parents heard the truth behind the sanitized Soviet propaganda, such as Communist Party Leader Leonid Brezhnev's heart attacks, strokes, and news of his declining health that the Soviet state kept secret from its citizens.

"But how can you explain to people that citizens of other countries lived better than we did? We would tell people we won the war and saved the USSR and Europe and the United States. And we would say we just needed some time to catch up. But 'some time' lasted 75 years until the Soviet Union finally collapsed."[67]

■ ■ ■

Albert Einstein, one of Litvak's heroes, famously said, "Intellectual growth should commence at birth and cease only at death."

Hospital, Heal Thyself

But the Father of Relativity also pointed out, "A person who never made a mistake never tried anything new."[68]

Litvak's life is punctuated by astonishing accomplishments and dismal failures. His journey after high school graduation to study telecommunications technology in St. Petersburg, 700 miles from his native Kiev, was driven by two disparate factors: his failure to gain admittance to the prestigious MFTI and the deeply rooted anti-Semitism of the USSR, particularly in Ukraine. Those events were related, Litvak said, because anti-Semitism caused his rejection by the "MIT of the Soviet Union."

A Foregone Conclusion

Litvak dreamed of becoming a physicist and knew the best place to study would be the Moscow Institute, home of several Nobel Prize winners. He had won a third-place medal in a Ukrainian national physics competition and felt certain his grades and talents would qualify him. His father was patient with his aspiration to be a physicist but insisted he formulate a backup plan just in case.

"Fortunately, the physics exam at the Moscow Institute was held earlier than other college entry exams. My father said if I failed there, then I would go where he suggested. And I agreed because I had no doubt that I would be accepted in Moscow."[69]

But for his physics entry exam in Moscow, a professor asked him a single trick question. With everything riding upon it, the professor posed a riddle one could not study for that was designed to weed out Jews and other "official undesirables." The question was: How do you photograph an empty crystal wineglass glittering in the sun to eliminate glare? "I suggested several ideas, including wrapping it with paper. The examiner accepted none of those ideas. Finally, he told me that the glass should be put on ice, which would form dew drops on its surface. Later I learned that this is a trick used by some professional photographers. What it had to do with physics, nobody knows."[70]

Litvak failed to answer the question correctly, as expected. "And that ended my career in physics," he recalled. "They did not accept me. So I went to Leningrad. It felt like I was going into exile to the Leningrad Institute for Telecommunications."

A New Start in St. Petersburg

Fortunately, Litvak said he was itching to leave Ukraine, and St. Petersburg, then named Leningrad, offered the opportunity for escape. "There was anti-Semitism elsewhere in the USSR. But it was deeper and more pervasive in Ukraine. My father was an electrical engineer and wanted me to be an engineer. And through telecommunications he thought I might find the right place for me."[71]

Litvak's parents knew a childless couple, Berta and Alexander, who lived in St. Petersburg and agreed to host their son for a short time. Both families thought the arrangement would offer a soft landing for Zhenya, would save the Litvaks money and postpone moving to a dormitory until he grew acclimated to college life.[72] "That's how my adult life started," he said, gleeful as a child. "I remember these first months in St. Petersburg with real pleasure. I loved it."

"St. Petersburg was an eye opener for me. I didn't know anybody in the city. My head was spinning to be in the hometown of Fyodor Dostoevsky, my hero. I was really overwhelmed," he said. In St. Petersburg he was immersed in the world of art and culture, underground literature and poetry from authors banned by the USSR. It felt both exhilarating and dangerous.

He said that before arriving in St. Petersburg he was extremely bashful. "I was very ambitious to achieve my goals. I was not shy in science or in speaking with school administrators. But in public, around girls, I was ridiculously shy."[73]

After his one-month stay in their home, Berta and Alexander helped Litvak find another living situation for the remainder of the academic year. After his first year at the university Litvak moved into the college's dormitory.

Litvak said in his college days he ate *pirozhki* for breakfast every day at a little shop near the campus. *Pirozhki* are Russian baked yeast buns filled with meat, potatoes, or cabbage, a popular, inexpensive, and common street food. "My lunch was usually soup or cutlets, which might have contained 10% meat, if I was lucky. We only ate dinner when we were hungry. I was extremely thin."[74]

Litvak said he made friends and had a good time as he absorbed the city's fascinating history and culture. Some of his friends' families owned *dachas*, summer homes located in the country, where they traveled on weekends to party and "drink more than we should. Frequently we went to bars, bought cheap beers, and would leave these bars pretty drunk."[75]

Who Knew Attending Classes Was Mandatory?

During his second year, Litvak only attended classes sporadically. "But I found them pretty boring. So I sometimes would read the textbooks in class. One professor, Alexander Yurovsky, taught math and caught me reading the textbook in class. I didn't notice when he approached me.[76] 'Are you checking what I'm teaching, Mr. Litvak?' he asked. 'No,' I replied. 'Because you're teaching the book verbatim.'"

Returning for his third year of studies in St. Petersburg, Litvak grew increasingly aware that his social life was impacting his academics and class attendance. He was staying out late, sleeping in, and missing classes. By the year's end, his bad habits were endangering his academic future. His parents received letters from the university that their son was frequently skipping classes. "I believed if I had good grades, I was fulfilling my college requirements," he said.

One day his father paid an unannounced visit to his son's dorm room. "There were girls and guys in our room drinking, and the tables were topped with bottles of vodka. My father walked in, looked around and left. I ran out after him, apologizing nonstop. Then he stopped and slapped my face but said nothing. Later he told me I shouldn't become a monk."[77]

Litvak said his father was most upset by the letter from the university. "Now when I think about that, I am horrified putting myself in his shoes," he said.

By the end of his third year, the university's frustration with Litvak's behavior had come to a head. Though he seldom attended classes, his grades remained well above average.

Litvak was called to the office of Dean Avakov, a man whom he liked and admired, who told him he would be expelled. "I told him I scored As and rarely Bs on my tests, which he acknowledged. But he said that by not attending classes, I was providing a bad example. He said, 'Others follow you and then fail their exams. We do not want that here. I cannot let you continue this way.' I apologized and attended classes for a few days and then went off track again. He called me in a few weeks later and said it was too late. He suggested completing my degree with distance learning through correspondence classes," Litvak recalled. "He was fair to me. Even as he described my wrongdoing, he felt obligated to explain why he was doing it, that he did this reluctantly. It was my own fault. I was having too good of a time. My father warned me to change, and I promised I would, but I did not deliver."[78]

Forced to return to Kiev, Litvak felt low. "Coming home felt like a biblical catastrophe had struck, something unimaginably crazy and horrible. I had no friends in Kiev anymore and felt isolated and depressed."[79]

Back Home in Kiev

He remembered walking the streets of his hometown the summer after he'd returned in disgrace, scanning the license plates of cars on the streets, trying to spot one from St. Petersburg. "When I found one, I wanted to see if I knew the owner. It was pathetic, but I was absolutely obsessed."[80]

His parents were unhappy with his self-inflicted wounds and treated him accordingly. "My father was the angriest I saw him in all my life," he said. "My mother still blamed me but was more forgiving. They believed I was ruining my future."[81]

There was another reason that Litvak had to leave St. Petersburg and complete his studies through distance learning. "It meant that I could be drafted at any time by the military as a soldier."

Now he would be required to serve in the Soviet Army, not as an officer, but a grunt soldier. "However, when they tested my vision, they pronounced me unable to serve because my eyesight was below the accepted level."[82]

While getting rejected by the military seemed like a victory, he faced another challenge. "I had to continue to take classes through distance learning and take the exams, but I also had to work some-place. In the USSR, if you were not studying full time at a university, you had to work or be declared a social parasite. And Kiev was much more anti-Semitic than St. Petersburg or Moscow then. So finding a good job as a Jew that would employ my skills, intelligence, and ambition was next to impossible."[83]

His luck was about to change. Through his father's cousin in Moscow he learned of a position within the reliability lab of a research center. "I got the lowest possible position within the Kiev Branch of the Soviet Central Institute of Telecommunications in its reliability laboratory. It was 100% pure luck."[84]

He returned to Kiev "absolutely depressed." His Kiev friends had all left to study elsewhere. This offered him a chance for a new life. Almost everyone at the job was older than him.

While it was a failure that brought him home in disgrace, it motivated him to excel. Litvak needed an outlet for his growing ambition. "And that became science. I had a goal in mind: to be the best in reliability theory. I read many books and years later I found a mistake in the Russian translation of an influential American book on reliability theory. That started a snowball."[85]

Finally, Growing Up

Litvak said that at the age of 20, he finally began maturing into a man. "I got angry and vowed that I must become a success. I was determined to show the world how good I was and how wrong they were. That was my motivation."

Litvak learned hard lessons about himself. "In St. Petersburg I had this sense of newly found freedom, combined with classes that did not challenge me and left me bored. There was this vacuum in my life and I filled it with friends, girls, and alcohol. I knew I could always pass the tests and I was right. I learned by reading books, not by listening to lectures."[86]

But back in Kiev he spent most weekends and weeknights after work in the library. "It was a 180 degree turn for me. I had no friends or girlfriends. I became very ambitious and wanted to show everyone that I was worth something. That's what drove me. It was an overnight change. My parents thought I'd moved from one extreme to another. I published my first article even before I graduated. I was on my way."[87]

Litvak eventually graduated from the Leningrad Institute in 1971 with a master's degree in the science of telecommunication.

"I've always identified with the mythological character, Sisyphus," Litvak opined. "We have a lot in common."[88]

Starting in the autumn of 1969 after returning from the more glamorous St. Petersburg, Litvak spent most of his 20s working in the reliability lab. That eight-year era of professional success ended abruptly in 1977 when he applied to leave the Soviet Union. In between those significant bookmarks in his life, Litvak married his wife, Ella; began earning a worldwide reputation for his research; earned a doctorate; and rebuffed a KGB attempt to recruit him to spy on his fellow scientists.

He remembers this era of his life with a mixture of fondness and fear. He said his office seemed typical of Soviet workplaces in the 1970s. The staff didn't socialize much outside of work, but there was a sense of camaraderie. "Except for our lab director, I had excellent relations with everybody in the lab," he said.

There were pervasive inequalities between genders during that era. "I'm embarrassed that at that time there was a common notion that women were pretty, nice, and weak, and men were strong and smart. Men were thought to have an intellectual advantage over women. It took me a few years of living and working here in the United States to surrender these antiquated and stupid ideas and view women as equal or even better. It was never an official stated policy or formally declared notion that men were superior, but it was endemic in the culture."[89]

Litvak's area of interest was the reliability of computer and telecommunications networks, including the survivability of those networks during potential attacks. He spent weekends and weeknights in the library of the University of Kiev for several years after returning from St. Petersburg.

"Any complex systems have failures," he explained. "We were looking at how to ensure that despite failures, every node in a network would still talk to other nodes."

Heading the reliability lab was Vladimir Ilych Pampuro, PhD, whom Litvak described as "socially, a complete idiot. He behaved as if he were the reincarnation of Isaac Newton and that the work he did should be considered a treasure of civilization. Each time he discovered something we had to scream, 'The Emperor's New Clothes.' One reviewer of a manuscript Pampuro submitted wrote, 'This paper cannot be accepted. Moreover, there is nothing that could make it acceptable in the future.'"[90]

If a researcher wants to publish a scientific paper in the United States, he or she submits it directly to the journal or publisher. But in the USSR then, Litvak said, "You needed written permission from your bosses to allow you to send a paper to be published. You could not send it yourself. There was no public access to copy machines. And Pampuro never gave me permission to publish. He wanted to share the credit for something he did not do or take credit solely for himself. I thought it was better not to publish at all than to publish with him. But I needed to publish, to show the world how great I was."[91]

Pampuro's office was in a tiny room separated from the rest of the reliability lab. He sat alone at a small desk and an extra chair. "There was not even room to stand. But that was his personal fiefdom."

Berta Vtorov, a former co-worker of Litvak's who now lives in Livingston, New Jersey, recalled Pampuro as "a pompous little dictator who always put himself first. He wanted credit for everyone else's work." Vtorov emigrated to the United States in 1994 after working 30 years for the institute.[92]

Litvak devised a work-around that would allow him to publish. He waited until Pampuro left on a business trip or vacation to request permission from the Deputy Director Zhuk, who would sign the permission for Zhenya. "Pampuro knew Zhenya was a genius and was jealous," Vtorov said.[93]

Around this time Litvak was invited by the internationally renowned American mathematician and World War II cryptographer,

Claude Shannon to present his research at the Massachusetts Institute of Technology (MIT). Shannon, the "father of information theory" and one of the theoretical contributors of the Arpanet, a predecessor of the internet, was interested in Litvak's research in telecommunications theory.[94]

But Pampuro would not allow Litvak to travel abroad to present his ideas, nor move to another department or claim credit for his own research, because he was Jewish. By 1975 the situation had reached a boiling point. Litvak felt like an indentured servant with no options. When he began publishing his research, Pampuro demanded credit.

"It felt like a kind of intellectual rape that I could not tolerate. As a boy growing up around criminals, I learned that the rule is if someone pushes you, you push back even harder," Litvak explained. "There were more and more conflicts, and they were starting to become public. It was difficult and stressful to work there, but there was no way for me to get another job. Pampuro went to the director of our institute, who was a real anti-Semite, to complain about my behavior and try to get rid of me. This would have meant that as a Jew, I could go nowhere else. My colleagues in the lab banded together and threatened to go to the local (Communist) Party district office if I was fired and informed the director about their plans. Because of that, the director did not fire me, but called Pampuro and asked him to leave instead."[95]

Vtorov said that by the mid-1970s a stultifying bureaucracy was strangling the former USSR. "When we completed a project, we needed to prepare five copies for approvals from different departments," she recalled. "But to make even one copy, sometimes I spent a half day to get the signed permission of a director. Everything was done secretly. Just getting a photocopy required permission from half the institute. Those photocopy machines were closely watched. To change jobs then was almost impossible if you had no connections. It's not like here in the United States where you can just apply, interview, and get hired. There was no job 'market.' It limited your chances."[96]

On Meeting His Idols, "The Gods of Math"

Litvak was part of a proud Soviet educational tradition known as "The Math Movement" that began in the 1930s and mushroomed after World War II. While this Soviet policy to develop a cadre of world-leading mathematicians was not as well known outside the USSR as the nation's fascination with chess was, math events attracted wide interest in the cultural life of the country. Many local, regional, and national competitions were held and drew broad press attention to math problems and contest winners. It "attracted the best and the brightest," wrote Soviet émigré and University of Minnesota physics Professor Mikhail Shifman, in his book, *You Have Failed Your Math Exam, Comrade Einstein.*[97]

Shifman said "mathematical circles" – informal math clubs formed in schools and universities – sprouted up throughout the country with math professors and teachers, students, and mathematicians discussing math problems and theories.

While Shifman believes that the discriminatory policies taken against Jews in math and physics were official government positions, "As far as I know, there have been no official documents found. Some archives are still closed. It was a practice that was well-known to all involved but was never officially discussed or publicized in the Soviet media."[98]

He pointed out that Jews were discriminated against in other areas. "The only employer was the government," he pointed out. "There were no private universities, labs, or companies. Therefore, you could not escape whatever policies and practices that the government was implementing."[99]

He said Jewish culture and religion were rooted out in the USSR after the 1917 Russian Revolution, starting in the 1920s and 1930s. By the late 1940s there were no more Jewish newspapers, theaters, or cultural centers.[100]

"The very word 'Jew' became a pejorative. People were afraid. After Stalin died, there were many fewer people sent to the GULAGs, but this discrimination remained. They spoke about it at home, among close friends and family. You couldn't file a complaint that you were treated improperly. Even now, 30 years after the USSR collapsed, not a single university president has stepped up even to acknowledge this, let alone apologize for it. It has never been officially recognized."[101]

■ ■ ■

Later, on a separate math road trip to Moscow, Litvak traveled to tell the well-regarded operations management researcher Professor Igor Ushakov that he'd made a mistake in his translation of an American book on reliability by Richard Barlow and Frank Proschan into Russian. Rather than be offended, Ushakov, Litvak's senior by 14 years and a member of the editorial board of the Academy of Sciences journal *Engineering Cybernetics*, spent hours with the precocious 22-year-old discussing reliability.[102]

"Here I was, an ordinary engineer, and he was offering to be my advisor on my PhD thesis at the Moscow Institute of Physics and Technology (MFTI), the very institute that rejected me as a student in 1966. I went back to Kiev with my head in the clouds, and we started working together. Because we published together through his institute, we didn't need permission from my institute. He was well known in reliability and had published several books."[103]

He described Ushakov as a gifted and talented renaissance man, a poet, and painter in addition to being a famed operations researcher. He was the author of *Man's First Steps: Tales and Legends of Mathematical Insights* and many textbooks about reliability. He served until 1989 as the head of the Department of Operations Research at the Computer Center of the USSR Academy of Science. Litvak also met the top Soviet mathematician in graph theory, Professor Alexander Zykov, at a conference on that topic in Odessa.[104]

"Once I returned home, I spent every weekend studying graph theory and vowed to succeed. After a year or two, I'd read and digested so much I became pretty good in the field and published several papers in the most prestigious journals. And with Ushakov as my advisor and Zykov as an assigned reviewer, I prepared to defend my PhD."[105]

Based on his published research and scientific activity, Litvak was promoted to senior scientist at his institute, the highest non-administrative rank he could achieve. It was time to take the next step and defend his doctoral thesis.

Defending His PhD in a Rigged System

1977 proved to be a pivotal year in Litvak's life, marked by great accomplishment, discouraging defeat, a close brush with terror and a momentous decision from which there was no turning back.

Litvak said in the former Soviet Union a doctoral degree approved by the government could net its earner an extra month's paid annual vacation and nearly double the current salary, as well as the opportunity to head a department.[106] He defended his PhD at the MFTI before a committee of 13, in the specialty "Mathematical cybernetics. Everyone presents their comments, only then do they vote. For me it was unanimous, 13–0. Everyone was complimentary."[107]

Hospital, Heal Thyself

So "Zhenya" was now "Dr. Litvak." But there remained another hurdle to clear. To receive the financial benefits of that degree, a government committee would need to approve Litvak's dissertation, a process called confirmation. "Once you defended your dissertation, all of the materials go to the government's Supreme Attestation Committee (VAK)."[108]

The person serving as his "black opponent," a kind of devil's advocate, on that committee was an internationally regarded mathematician and member of Soviet Academy of Science, Oleg Lupanov.[109]

According to numerous personal reports from Soviet Jews who emigrated from the USSR, Lupanov, a recognized expert in Litvak's field of mathematical cybernetics, was appointed by the government to prevent Jews from entering that field. "I was invited to VAK. That was already a bad sign.[110]

He defended his dissertation in Moscow in 1977. The chair of the MFTI committee that would confirm his PhD was a member of the Academy of Science, Nikita Moiseev. He came to VAK to defend Litvak's work and speak on his behalf. After the committee interviewed Litvak, they asked him to wait outside of the room.

"Moiseev went in to speak with them, then left, red-faced. He slammed the door and hurried away without saying a word. He was absolutely mad, and his footsteps were loud. He didn't even look in my direction," Litvak said. "For him it was a total humiliation. He was a well-known figure and they practically told him that he and his committee were wrong and didn't know what they were doing."

But during this era the government was not recognizing PhDs for Jews in the field of mathematical cybernetics, Litvak said. "Neither Moiseev nor Ushakov, my advisor, were Jews. They knew that Jews were not welcome, but they were surprised that the government would decide to go against such a prestigious committee."[111]

"Zhenya is absolutely a talented person," his colleague Vtorov said of Litvak. "He was rejected by MFTI. But while we worked together,

The Soviet Years: Maybe I Wasn't Supposed to Be Born

he went to this same university for his PhD for personal and professional satisfaction, to show them he deserved to be there in the first place. I think he was shocked when he was refused."[112]

Former Litvak colleague Iryna Stoianova, PhD, lived in Kiev since 1944, just after the Nazis were defeated. Stoianova, who now assists the European Union on special projects through Ukraine's Institute of Energy Sciences, worked with Litvak for five years in the reliability lab. She said no one from the reliability lab knew Litvak was traveling to Moscow to defend his PhD. Stoianova, who sat in front of Litvak at the institute, observed his growing depression. She died of COVID in 2021.[113]

"One day he showed me a card from the attestation committee that said his dissertation did not meet the requirements and the government would not confirm his PhD. I knew Dr. Vladimir Karmanov, who headed the department of VAK. I called him to ask why Zhenya was rejected, and he called back and said Lupanov was ordered to reject Zhenya's dissertation and write a bad review. It was because Litvak was Jewish."[114]

Vtorov said there was a phrase in the USSR commonly used to describe Jews. "Zhenya was someone with a Fifth Article Problem," referring to the Soviet Union passport which listed "Jewish" as a nationality, targeting them for discrimination.[115]

"Jews, Tatars, and others suffered if their passports said they were not Russian. It was marked on Line 5 on your passport," Vtorov said. "After the Soviet Union collapsed, they removed this line. Unfortunately, that was the atmosphere in the USSR then. It was officially sanctioned anti-Semitism. When Zhenya showed me the card saying his dissertation was rejected, I thought then he might pack his suitcases and leave this country."[116]

Because the government attestation committee rejected his PhD dissertation, Litvak was not entitled to claim the privileges of one confirmed. "No extra money, no extra vacation, and no right to head

Hospital, Heal Thyself

a department. There was nothing for me after that. I wanted to leave my footprint in science, but I wouldn't have that chance, not in the USSR."[117]

Litvak felt his destiny was predetermined in the USSR. "Neither I nor my friends thought about whether we were Russian, Ukrainian, or Jewish. Russians and Ukrainians could reach the top levels of government, academics, and industry. But I couldn't. That was denied me. The government made me a Jew. They did everything they could to make me feel like a Jew. They succeeded."[118]

In his book, Shifman (who was born in 1949, the same year as Litvak, but in Riga, Latvia) chronicled the government's official anti-Semitism and witnessed it in his own life, how "high school mathematics was used as a weapon of racism in the USSR."[119]

But few outside the USSR knew of the insidious efforts of the Soviet state to "blackball" Jewish undergraduate and graduate students from the elite mathematical and physics institutes to prevent them from passing admission exams or earning PhDs or appointments to top jobs and academic posts.[120]

In a 2005 letter, Stanislav Lipovetsky, a Soviet émigré and physicist, also working in Minnesota, wrote that Shifman's book *Comrade Einstein* preserves "the memory of all the young would-be scientists who suffered and perished from Soviet anti-Semitism. What happened was, indeed, an intellectual, mental, and psychological genocide, which was imposed on many, in addition to imprisonments and the very probable murder of selected individuals."[121]

The Swiss journalist George Szpiro wrote in *Notices of the American Mathematical Society* that Jews or applicants with Jewish-sounding names "were singled out at the entrance exams for special treatment."[122] Szpiro wrote that written tests usually posed no problem for talented students. "The hurdles were raised in the oral exam. Unwanted candidates were given "killer questions" that required long computations or reasoning. Some questions were impossible to solve, were stated in an ambiguous way, or had no correct answer," Szpiro wrote. "They were not designed to test a candidate's skill but meant to weed out undesirables. Even if a candidate's answers were correct, reasons could always be found to fail him."[123]

Comrade Einstein author Shifman said he doesn't know how many refuseniks left the USSR or how many of them were Jewish. "I know that when I was growing up there were around three million Jews in the Soviet Union, and today there are around 200,000, mostly in Moscow." He estimated that between 5,000 and 10,000 Jewish math and physics students and professionals were refuseniks who left the USSR. "There was no competition and no choice. All salaries were fixed from Moscow for every job everywhere in the country. Whether you were a genius and worked like God or a humble street cleaner, it didn't matter. That's how extreme socialism works," Shifman said.[124]

Quitting the KGB Before He Started

In the summer of 1976, 27-year-old Eugene Litvak was working for the Institute of Telecommunications Research in Kiev when he received a chilling telephone call from the dreaded "First Department."[125]

Every sizable employer in the former Soviet Union staffed a First Department, a euphemism for "Big Brother," the department within every factory, research institute, or government office that watched over employees to ensure their loyalty to the Soviet Communist Party, prevent security leaks, and report on antigovernment activity. It was almost always occupied by former KGB agents, a cushy retirement job awarded for services performed. "Its members keep track of workers' loyalty, compiling dossiers that detail the political views of all workers and the trips abroad (including the conduct thereupon) of the select few. It also grants or denies permits for employment in secret work," according to the *The Encyclopedia of Soviet Life*.[126]

This had never happened to Litvak before. "It is an invitation that could give you sleepless nights," he remembered, his voice rising, as if triggering a 40-year-old shudder. "But because it came while I was at work, I didn't have time to think about it. I didn't know what the problem was. And that made it even more terrifying."[127]

He sat at his desk and pondered his choices, perplexed and petrified. "So-called First Departments exist in all institutes, regardless of whether their research is classified or accessible to the public. The entire staff of these First Departments consists of secret police agents. Occasionally high-ranking KGB agents are among them."[128] Called the *pervy odtel* in Russian, it was known variously as the First Section, Special Department, or General Department, depending on whether the organization housing it was military, police, research institute, or factory.[129]

On the long, slow walk to the First Department, Litvak felt stressed, anguishing over who might have reported on him and which jokes might have been overheard. Litvak is an inveterate joke teller and party bureaucrats were often the butts of his humor. Telling jokes about government bureaucrats was not uncommon in the former USSR. In fact, it was a time-honored practice to share this humor, but not publicly or indiscreetly. Who had informed on him?

Litvak was ushered into a small, private office by the First Department head, a man in his sixties with a forgettable face who left almost immediately after introducing Litvak to a much younger man with dark blond hair and a casual suit, a man only a few years older than the mathematician nervously seated before him. Litvak was sweating. While he understood that the KGB of 1976 was not the murderous secret police of Felix Dzerzhinsky's Cheka after the Russian Revolution or Lavrenty Beria's brutal NKVD of the 1940s, everyone knew the agency still could ruin careers and lives.[130] "They might not kill or torture me," he recalled. "But they could fire me,

The Soviet Years: Maybe I Wasn't Supposed to Be Born

making me officially a 'parasite of the state,' a crime punishable by arrest and imprisonment."[131]

The KGB agent, who held the rank of captain, presented his badge and quickly reassured Litvak that he was not there because of his jokes, though he was aware of them. "He smiled at me and said, 'Don't even try to think about what you did wrong'."[132]

Litvak felt like the KGB officer was reading his mind. "It was scary because at that moment that was exactly what I was thinking. He said, 'I'm not much older than you. We're of the same generation.' He appealed to my sense of patriotism and understood who I was. He made it seem like we could be friends."[133]

Litvak couldn't recall how long the interview took. "I would not be surprised if you told me it was one hour or one day. They wanted me to collaborate with them," he said, still anxious recollecting the experience decades later. "They had enormous power."[134]

The KGB official asked Litvak, "'How about you help us and we help you? For example, you received an invitation to travel outside the USSR to Germany. So far you have not been allowed to go, but maybe now you could.' He said, 'We decide who goes to the conference. You just tell us what's going on. And no anti-government jokes.'"[135]

Litvak was told the KGB would like to use his skills for the homeland. "You should help us," the captain told the researcher. "He said I would not be required to inform on my colleagues. Rather, I would work with foreigners. That was a very clever move. You don't want to denounce your friends or colleagues. When they tell you this, it seems normal. But after you leave and think about it, it's very scary."[136]

Litvak said the KGB captain did not ask him to sign any document or make any commitment. "He told me to just think about it and that we should continue to be friends. I was not concerned they would take me to jail after that."

Litvak didn't refuse the KGB captain's offer. But he didn't agree either. And he didn't sign anything. He tried to buy himself some time, to figure out how to get rid of this "offer." He knew the KGB would return. The KGB doesn't forget. But he needed to stall. However, Litvak pointed out, losing a job then was not only financially painful, but could end any career aspirations. "To lose a job because of a KGB action meant you'd never be employed again. Period. You become what is called a parasite of society. And if you don't work, you could go to prison. They make you a parasite and then arrest you for being a parasite."[137]

Litvak said the KGB officer told him that he could never tell anyone, including his wife, that he worked for the spy agency. "This was really stressing me out. I stopped coming to work for a while. I got permission from a doctor to stay home. In the USSR, it was very easy then. I just gave the visiting doctor a bottle of vodka and stayed home."[138]

But the KGB hadn't forgotten its offer. "The KGB captain called and said he was sorry to hear that I was sick. He recommended I eat more garlic and chicken soup. 'Take care of yourself,' he advised me, like he's my brother. He said, 'You shouldn't rush back to work. We will talk when you return to work.' It was the KGB as Mother Russia, sympathetic and caring." But Litvak knew that he could not delay the KGB forever.[139] "I understood that eventually, I would have to see him."

Despite warnings, Litvak sought advice from his parents and in-laws about how to deal with the KGB. "The KGB captain told me the first time we spoke that our conversation was private and I would be punished if I ever told anyone else," Litvak recalled.[140]

So here's what he did. "I told him that I talk very loudly in my sleep and my wife is a very outspoken woman. I said that despite my best efforts, my secret would not remain a secret for very long. He perfectly understood what I was doing and completely changed

The Soviet Years: Maybe I Wasn't Supposed to Be Born

his tone. He spoke in a quiet, still voice and said, 'We know you do not want to help us. Let me give you one warning though: if you tell anybody about this, you will be severely punished.' He hinted that there would be terrible consequences if I shared our conversation. That was the end of it. Soon after, we applied for an exit visa."[141]

Litvak said cooperating with the KGB was not an option. He said his father would lose respect for him and even break off relations if he collaborated with the KGB. "I would lose him as a father. But that's not the only thing that stopped me. I wouldn't have been able to do it anyway. So I came up with this strategy."[142]

Around that time, a friend of Litvak's who had applied for the exit visa finally received permission to leave the USSR. "I told him that I was hesitating. He said, 'If you don't know whether you should leave the USSR, just apply for the exit visa anyway. By the time they let you go, you'll understand that you did the right thing.'"

Litvak admitted that he never was a dissident who wanted to change the USSR. "I wanted to get out and let them enjoy their lives and let me enjoy mine. My only goal was to leave. I wasn't fighting for human rights or to overthrow the government. I was not a threat and I don't think they viewed me as one until I applied for an exit visa."[143]

Breaking Up with the USSR

Litvak said his close call with the KGB changed his plans and career path. "That was a big weight on me." Litvak and his wife, Ella, discussed emigration many times. But they concluded that because the issue kept arising, the right decision was to go.

The KGB experience showed Litvak that even as a senior scientist, his career and position meant nothing. "The KGB could call me in at any time. That's no life. I wanted to communicate with

Hospital, Heal Thyself

Western researchers, travel there, and meet with them. But in the USSR, I would never have that chance. That pushed the thumb on the other side of the scale."[144]

Many of Litvak's research manuscripts had been published around the world, and he was able to glean a tiny glimpse into the privileged world of the Soviet elites. "I was receiving a special kind of payment for my articles, checks that could be cashed only in Soviet stores exclusively for foreigners. Normal Russians without such checks couldn't buy anything there and were prohibited even from entering. The exchange rate for my foreign checks was pretty bad. If I earned $100 in US currency, they [the government] would only pay me the equivalent of $10. But for that $10 I could buy comparatively more than I could in a general Russian store. Ella bought a nice pair of shoes there. This was probably the only time my wife benefited from my research," he laughed.[145]

After his dissertation was rejected, Litvak told his co-worker Stoianova that his life was broken. "He felt devastated for a long time. I think Zhenya's life is a very good illustration of what the Soviet regime did to its people. Some people lived normally without ever having problems. But for people like Zhenya, the regime shattered their lives."[146]

Vtorov continued to work for the telecommunications institute until the day before she left the USSR. "I only returned once to Ukraine to visit my mother's cemetery in 2007. I was so happy I moved to America. I thought it would be hard. But every day after departing the Soviet Union, I was pleased that I left."[147]

Litvak said when Soviet communism tried to convince citizens that they had it good, "They had to point out that other countries had it even worse. It's too bad Lenin didn't study Pavlov's research. Otherwise Soviet communist ideas could have been tried out on dogs instead of Soviet citizens. I felt like one of his human experiments, one of those dogs."[148]

Litvak's wife, Ella Tsenter, was born and raised in Kiev. While her parents' occupations would have been considered middle to upper class in the United States, her mother (a pediatrician) and father (a civil engineer) were paid little in the Soviet Union of her youth post–World War II.

"I grew up in a very charming area of Kiev populated by many poor people," she said of her neighborhood, St. Andrew's Descent, which features the famous St. Andrew's Church. Years ago, the Russian writer and playwright and author of *The Master and Margarita*, Mikhail Bulgakov, lived a few doors away.[149]

She recalled her mother working extra shifts for more money. "My mother was able to send me to a school attended by the children of Communist party leaders. I was dressed worse than anyone else, and I was self-conscious about this. We were poor. My mother went to medical school during the era of the famous Stalin Doctors' Plot (the conspiracy that Stalin concocted to eliminate Jewish cabinet members). It was a very bad time to be Jewish in the Soviet Union when I was growing up."[150]

The couple met in their 20s when they worked on separate floors at the Institute for Telecommunications in Kiev and after a few years were formally introduced. "I was studying part-time and working full-time and was very busy," she remembered. "Zhenya scared me to death. He offered me some *samizdat* [illegal underground publications of authors prohibited by the government] and stories from Alexander Solzhenitsyn. 'No thank you,' I told him."[151]

But she relented, and after dating for a few months, the couple married in 1975. Ella didn't have a wedding dress, so she wore a new skirt.

Ella Litvak is a bright, engaging, and energetic woman who, after a successful career in biostatistics, published novels, leads tours of art museums, and remains fiercely loyal to her husband of 49 years.

"Ella is an introvert and I am an extrovert," Litvak said, as if that explained everything.[152]

As a teenager, Litvak's father told him the time would come when he would need to act responsibly. "I think that happened when I met my wife," he said. "When she suggests something, later I quietly accept it."[153]

After months of haggling and debate, Litvak and his wife finally decided to apply for exit visas to leave their homeland. "We applied near the end of 1978 and that very day both of us were fired from our jobs, which didn't bother me very much because we thought we'd get permission to leave soon. We didn't think it would take 10 years. Our plan was we'd sell everything, and we did," he said.[154]

Vtorov said when Litvak was fired, it happened in secret. "The next day he was not at work. Nobody explained anything. He was fired and that was the end of it. We came to visit him after he was fired. It was very hard to see him like that. He was absolutely lost and he could not find a job. For him, reputation was everything. I think it's difficult for Americans who grew up in this country to understand. It's like explaining life on Mars," she recalled.[155]

After they were fired, Litvak delivered telegrams. Ella washed factory floors. Then in December 1979 the Soviet Union invaded Afghanistan, according to the state press, at the Afghanis' request. "Relations between the United States and the USSR got worse. And like thousands of other applicants, our exit visas were declined."[156]

The Litvaks were called to the Department of Visas (OVIR), a branch of government connected to the KGB, where hundreds of others in Kiev were waiting for their destiny. "When they called my name, I was invited to the room where the military major shook my hand and said, 'Congratulations! You are not allowed to go to the stagnating West. Our government took good care of you and prevented this from happening,'" Litvak said.[157]

The Soviet Years: Maybe I Wasn't Supposed to Be Born

For nearly a decade the Litvaks were persecuted by the KGB and secret police, their telephones tapped, their meetings with fellow "refuseniks" disrupted and monitored. Every year they were summoned by the passport authorities and told their exit visas were again denied. And still they persisted.[158]

Shifman said that the only reasons the Soviet government would release Jews applying to emigrate were trade deals or public shaming by world bodies. "It was an ideological thing. The Soviet doctrine said it is the best country in the world for everyday people. But if this country would not let its people leave, everyone would see that's not the case. Only in difficult times would they let the Jews go, such as when a US president pushed strongly, or after a bad harvest the country didn't have enough potatoes or grain to feed its people. Then the Soviet government would make agreements behind closed doors to let refuseniks go in exchange for the US providing grain."[159]

Sometimes, such as when the USSR hosted the Olympics and feared worldwide condemnation, the country also let Jews depart. "By the mid-1990s almost every Soviet Jew known in the scientific world had left the USSR," Shifman said.[160]

In 1988 Ella and Eugene Litvak and their parents were finally granted exit visas to leave their homeland, a decision no one in the family regretted.

Chapter 5

The Litvak Method: A Massachusetts Hospital Became His Test Lab

If there is an origin story to Eugene Litvak's lifelong work – his mission for the past 25 years of improving hospital care – it began at Massachusetts General Hospital, locally known as Mass General, in Boston.

Mass General is the third-oldest hospital in the United States, tracing its beginnings to 1811. It's a 900-bed behemoth, an academic medical center and teaching hospital that is routinely ranked as one of the nation's top 10 and remains the first and biggest hospital affiliated with the Harvard Medical School.[1]

Mass General is also a major research center with a research budget that exceeded $2 billion in 2022 and is one of two original members of the state's largest health system, Partners HealthCare.[2] Litvak met its former president, Peter Slavin, MD, when Slavin (then a senior vice president and chief medical officer) presented a lecture on how hospitals needed to improve cost control efforts to deal with a new player in the local insurance market, health maintenance organizations (HMOs), a model that was taking root in New England.

HMOs offer a health insurance product that covers its member beneficiaries by managing the cost and controlling the care its network physicians and hospitals provide. In theory, managed care companies like HMOs provide better care to their covered members by choosing the highest quality providers who deliver the best care at the lowest costs. In practice, HMOs choose doctors and hospitals that accept their lower fee payments in exchange for a guaranteed number of patients. Those providers get paid less to treat a higher volume of patients, in a sense caring for patient populations and receiving a flat per-patient, per-month payment. "What happened is that HMOs started penetrating the Massachusetts market and all of a sudden hospitals started talking about healthcare costs," Litvak said.[3]

Litvak said in the mid to late 90s, his father, a wounded and decorated Soviet Army veteran and electrical engineer, Israel Litvak, was frequently hospitalized at Boston's Beth Israel Hospital, which was located near the Harvard School of Public Health. He visited his father in the mornings before work and after leaving his office at day's end.

"I found many things that could be improved at the hospital in terms of operations management. And I was listening to conversations," he said. The seeds were taking root.

After that lecture, Litvak introduced himself to Slavin, who invited him to visit Mass General. On that visit Litvak explained how to reduce costs and improve care by implementing operations management tools. He must have been persuasive, because Slavin offered him work.

"While I was there Peter received a phone call from the hospital's stress lab, which claimed to need more resources. 'Would you be interested in working with them and looking into that?' Slavin asked. That's when I started formally working as a consultant with Mass General."[4]

Litvak's two-year contract to perform research with his Harvard benefactor, John Taplin, who had subsidized his work after earlier grants ended, was nearly expired. Litvak was wondering how he would support his family when Slavin hired him as a consultant to

Hospital, Heal Thyself

work with Mass General. "That happened all of my professional life, even up until now," Litvak chuckled. "I could never hold a steady job."[5]

Slavin told Litvak that the stress lab was seeking more money to expand capacity because of frequent overcrowding. Slavin was concerned that Mass General patients were waiting too long – sometimes days – to schedule stress tests, spending unnecessary time in the hospital and driving up the cost of care, while preventing other patients from gaining admission.

A hospital stress lab is a unit where a variety of diagnostic testing is conducted, often for cardiac patients. Those tests may include treadmill stress tests to measure heart performance, as well as other sophisticated diagnostic exams.

When Litvak visited the hospital's stress lab staff, the department leaders told him they were often overcrowded and would need additional resources to meet patient demand. Litvak discovered that the lab scheduled fewer tests on Fridays and asked why. He was told, "Because it's Friday." He found two other problems: no-shows and canceled appointments.

"I drilled deeper into why and found that one reason patients were canceling was due to unexpected illness. They were sometimes not well enough to come in for tests. I found that when a patient has an appointment for an ordered test and that patient doesn't show, the hospital disposes of the chemical agents that would have been used for the test, wasting a lot of money. We're talking thousands of dollars wasted annually in this one tiny cost center."[6]

To grapple with no-show appointments – patients who didn't bother to come – he developed a formula for overbooking patient appointments to combat the wasted costs, frustration, and underused resources.

He explained that staff should understand the potential risks of scheduled overbooking. His formula calculated the risks of scheduling one, two, or three additional tests if the lab overbooked and how it would impact staffing if it overbooked.

He said that if every overbooked patient arrives, staff may have to stay longer to accommodate the extra patients. "But the chance of that happening was small. In my research I found that rather than needing more money to expand, the lab was actually 30% underutilized."[7]

Slavin was impressed and credits Litvak with introducing operations management research to Mass General in a real way and introducing people to the potential power of those analysis tools. "As a result of his work, we improved operations within the stress lab," he said.[8]

Slavin, who earned his undergraduate degree, medical degree, and master's in business from Harvard, is also a professor of healthcare policy at that university. He has a long history with Mass General. He trained in his specialty, internal medicine, at the hospital in the mid-1980s. After hiring Litvak as a consultant in 1995, Slavin was recruited two years later to serve as president of Barnes-Jewish Hospital in St. Louis, a large teaching hospital.

He returned in 1999 to head the Massachusetts General Physicians Organization, a 1,700 independent physicians' organization (IPO). Four years later he was named president of Mass General, Boston's largest employer.[9]

■ ■ ■

Hearing hospital executives in the 1990s discussing HMOs in their markets was akin to terrified European townsfolk fearful of attacks from the barbarians, Huns or marauding Ottomans.

Slavin said the atmosphere in the hospital industry was tense in the mid-1990s as HMOs began penetrating local markets. He described HMOs as "a new creature toughly negotiating to keep

Hospital, Heal Thyself

hospital payment rates as low as possible and trying to keep people out of hospitals as much as possible."[10]

He explained that HMOs were pushing a new form of reimbursement called capitation, now called global payment. Under those payment arrangements, hospitals are paid a lump sum each month for caring for an individual member for one year, regardless of how much care those patients need or use. In one sense the hospital negotiating an insurance contract with an HMO is taking a risk that it can provide enough care to keep the HMO members healthy while not exceeding the per member, per month payment from the HMO. If the hospital is able to treat the patient for less than the agreed upon payment, it makes money. If the cost of care surpasses that payment, the hospital loses money. HMOs incentivized hospitals to reduce the amount and cost of care provided and to become more efficient. "It changed the incentives, making efficiency more important than ever," Slavin said.[11]

The hospital's response was to create Partners HealthCare, merging with rival Brigham and Women's Hospital to get bigger and improve its negotiating clout. That healthcare system now includes 12 hospitals, a health plan, a huge physicians' network and other programs, making it the state's largest private employer and biggest healthcare provider.[12]

"We became a larger organization in a better position to respond to those forces," Slavin said. "We undertook a number of programs to become more efficient."[13]

What Slavin meant was that by growing into the huge provider it became, Partners improved its ability to negotiate favorable payment rates from health plans, particularly the newly ascendant HMOs. Because Partners became such a large market presence, it would be difficult for health plans to exclude it from preferred hospital and physician networks.

When he earned his Harvard MBA in 1990, Slavin said he learned about operations management and how it could improve efficiency within hospitals. "That's what intrigued me when I met Eugene," he said. "I thought that operations management research and patient flow might identify some opportunities to improve efficiency and reduce waiting times."[14]

About six months after Massachusetts General hired Litvak, Slavin told him about an even bigger and more important hospital cost center that was causing problems. Slavin challenged Litvak to investigate the growing disorder and inefficiency in Mass General's operating rooms (ORs). He said elective surgeries were being canceled, costing the hospital millions of dollars. The daily census was at the over-crowding level one day, while the next day the halls might be empty.

History is replete with famous duos whose talents complement one another, making the sum greater than the individuals: Laurel and Hardy. Batman and Robin. Simon and Garfunkel. Sam and Dave. In healthcare there were the Mayo Brothers. And, beginning in 1996 and for years to come, there was Litvak and Long, the Dynamic Duo of Mass General and improving patient flow.

Mass General's deputy OR director was an anesthesiologist and former Army surgeon who had served tours in Vietnam, Mike Long, MD. When Slavin introduced Litvak to Long, it was, in the words of Rick Blaine in *Casablanca*, "the beginning of a beautiful friendship."[15]

Long had been an outspoken department leader in the hospital's OR. He said meeting Litvak was like discovering his long-lost twin. He described that meeting as "a fortuitous occurrence. The synergy just happened. We became friends very quickly. There was no bullshit or posturing. Everything was open and honest, the way I've worked with people all my life. In that respect we're the same kind of person," he said. "We both knew what we knew and what we didn't know. And there was enough overlap of what we did know so we could talk with each other."[16]

It was at Mass General that Litvak and Long researched and collaborated on his theories about patient flow. "Long's mindset is that he wants to get to the bottom of everything. He is a researcher by nature," Litvak said of his partner.[17] "What happened was each of us had something that the other one needed and wanted. I clearly had little idea of how healthcare was delivered, particularly surgery, while Mike had no idea about how operations management worked. In the beginning we called each other not only on weekdays, but on weekends."[18]

Long said he'd been at Mass General for decades and "knew where bodies were buried and where all the skeletons and problems were. But we had never put anything together before to tackle these problems."[19]

Long had been so vocal about how the hospital's OR was inefficient and dysfunctional that leadership urged him to join an improvement project intending to correct it. "If you think you can fix it, have at it," he recalled being told. "They provided some support and brought in a consulting company to work with us," defining a consulting group as "someone who borrows your watch to tell you the time, then steals it." He called the consulting group useless with one exception. "For the first time we had systematic data gathering about the numbers and types of cases we did."[20]

Long said the then-OR manager was a semi-retired surgeon only interested in making sure that everyone on the surgical staff got what they needed. "He was interested in basic care, but not in any kind of efficiency. And since we had little or no information about the OR, it was part of my job to develop an information system to give us some data to work with."[21]

Long said that he spent five years and Mass General spent $2 million to create an information system to capture and illustrate what he and Litvak were doing. The hospital appointed Long to spearhead the program.

The Litvak Method: A Massachusetts Hospital Became His Test Lab

"We were struggling," he said. "We had a bunch of committees doing what all committees do: complaining. We weren't going anywhere. The only reason the hospital did this was the leaders were scared silly. Managed care was coming fast, and everybody feared it would slash hospital revenue. They believed they needed to clean their own house before someone like Medicare or private payers looked over their shoulders and did it for them."[22]

Long said Litvak quickly understood how healthcare was delivered at Mass General. "He became more and more surprised about how inefficient and wasteful our healthcare system is. Almost immediately he began to see widespread dysfunctional patterns. That's where the variability came in. We developed a theory that there are two types of variability in healthcare: natural and artificial – and they were not confined to operating rooms, but present throughout the hospitals. That variability occurred basically everywhere and posed problems for achieving efficiency. If you don't care about efficiency, there is no reason to think about this stuff. Any other industry would have applied the brakes to the kind of runaway money spending you see in our business. But not in healthcare."[23]

Long suggested Litvak begin attending the weekly 6 a.m. Thursday meetings held before surgeries were scheduled. For six months Litvak showed up for those early morning gatherings and listened. "I learned that the surgeons prefer to operate the first thing in the mornings early in the week because they want to be fresh. But there was another reason. If you do all your surgery on Mondays and Tuesdays, then the rest of the week is yours," Litvak said. "It's personal convenience."[24]

He said that if surgeons operate on a Thursday or Friday, their patients are likely to remain hospitalized over the weekend. "That means surgeons have to come to the hospital to make rounds over the weekend to check on their patients' progress. And that's taboo," Litvak said. "In addition, some hospital services, like physical therapy

Hospital, Heal Thyself

and certain diagnostic testing, are unavailable on weekends in most hospitals."[25]

This practice practically makes hospitals a Monday to Friday business, even though many customers – patients – remain hospitalized, requiring care even on weekends. If a surgery is performed on Monday, he said, most patients are discharged by Thursday or Friday.

"This practice has nothing to do with patient well-being," Litvak said. "Both surgeons and hospitals do everything possible to make sure their patients aren't there on weekends. That's how we use our valuable, expensive real estate."[26]

Long served as Litvak's anthropological guide into the strange, unknown culture of surgeons. The mathematician found surgeons frequently battling with each other for the best morning block times at the beginning of the week for surgery and access to the OR. Surgical block times are periods of time within a half-day or a day when a surgeon operates. When a surgeon is assigned a block time, he or she essentially owns the operating room during that period and can schedule successive surgical procedures.

Or not.

Litvak was beginning to see that there are many problems with this time-honored practice. If too many elective, or planned operations are scheduled, they may conflict with unscheduled patients coming into the emergency room requiring immediate surgery from automobile or industrial accidents or gun violence, which take precedence over planned surgeries. The planned surgeries then get canceled or postponed, often leading to 12- to 18-hour days, huge patient inconvenience, overcrowding and nurse and physician stress and burnout. Also, sometimes surgeons don't completely fill their assigned block times, leaving surgical nurses and staff present without work to do, costing hospitals a great deal of money.

"I didn't understand how important those morning block times were. There were real passionate arguments. I asked Mike to explain, saying these surgeons fight for block time like men fight for their spouses. Mike replied, 'You don't understand. They would rather give up their spouses than their morning block times.' Later I understood."[27]

Long explained Mass General institutional practices, cultural norms, and peculiar routines as well as the pecking order and relative status of physician specialties, providing Litvak a Who's Who and what's what primer of the hospital. And Litvak spoke daily to physicians, nurses, and staff.

"I had no high rank or status, so people talked frankly to me about their routines and work and what their lives were like and the problems they faced. I asked them what they would like to change."[28] Diving into the trenches was a practice he began in the USSR when he helped a Soviet state-owned construction company build rail lines more efficiently. He knew he needed to get up close to understand the challenges. "Nurses were being stressed during peak patient demand periods."[29]

■ ■ ■

One day Slavin, who returned to Mass General in 1999 as hospital president, showed Litvak the bed occupancy charts that revealed the daily patient census. "The charts showed me that the average daily census was rising, while the peaks and valleys remained the same."[30]

When the patient census was low, the peaks did not hit the ceiling. But when that census was high, those peaks taxed the hospital's capacity to staff appropriately and deliver the best quality care, he said. Litvak compares patient flow to a traffic pattern.

Imagine driving to the beach. "If you leave at noon on a hot summer day the traffic would be different than if you leave at 2 a.m.

Hospital, Heal Thyself

on a cold February day. If you see a car accident ahead with police cars and ambulances on this hypothetical three-lane highway in February, it's not likely to slow you up very much. But if that same accident occurred at noon on a hot August afternoon on the same road, the density of traffic would be much higher and your driving time much longer."[31]

So Litvak and Long began researching the problem, starting with the hospital's emergency department (ED). "I was not a healthcare researcher. My background was in computers and telecommunications. Everything in those worlds was logical. Logically, if you have peaks in demand, you must have more patients. So why was there this variable line? And who brings this variability? What causes it? To me it was absolutely clear who was responsible. Every normal person would think it was the emergency department – more people coming into the ER."[32]

Litvak said hospitals don't pay as much attention to the census "valleys" as they do the peaks in demand. "That's because we don't feel the valleys. The valleys manifest themselves as waste in healthcare. Too many people caring for too few patients. Except for paying for unneeded staffing, it doesn't have a direct effect on quality of care or patient safety," he said. "But we feel the peaks immediately."[33]

Typically, hospitals experience the peaks at the beginning of the week when high volumes of elective surgeries are planned, but they also may vary at differing times in the same day. That variability is problematic on weekdays. The biggest and longest valley of the week occurs on weekends, he said. But despite offering fewer services and less staffing, the hospital still has fixed costs: the employees that work in the ER, utilities, meals, housekeeping, and other services. "It's like having a really beautiful and expensive rental property, but only leasing it out for two-thirds of the week," he said.[34]

So, the "Double L Twins" attempted to retrieve data from the ED to validate their hypothesis. Litvak said in hospitals, however,

85

departments are not always eager to share data and don't welcome strangers looking over their shoulders. "We were given many excuses. They didn't have the data then, but might have it in the next century. But the bottom line was we could not get any ED data."[35]

So Long retrieved that OR surgical data instead and compared it under a transparency sheet to the hospital census showing the daily patient peaks and valleys. The data included all the scheduled surgeries from the OR and the hospital bed occupancy. The figures overlapped, matching almost perfectly to hospital census and OR case volumes.

"For me this was an 'aha moment.' I was shocked. It meant that OR scheduling determines the hospital bed occupancy and causes those census peaks," he said. "It was very counterintuitive. The vast majority were elective [scheduled OR] cases."[36]

Litvak and Long called their discovery moment unforgettable. The two were able to access and use data from the hospital's operating rooms (ORs) because Long headed the hospital's OR committee, its information technology (IT) project, and served as the deputy director of the OR.

They discovered the cause of the peaks and the valleys, and their research began to quantify the human and monetary costs. So the solution became apparent. It emanated from existing hospital practices and was not attributable to nature's whim. The solution was something doable. Or so they thought. Little did they realize the rocky path awaiting them.

■ ■ ■

In the mid-1990s most Boston-area hospitals were creating cost-reduction task forces to prepare for the bloodbath they anticipated would come from these new creatures, HMO contracts. Litvak likened talking to Mass General's task force about operations management to parachuting into distant, isolated primeval forests to discuss physics with illiterate natives.

"I was told that I am a mathematician who knows nothing about health or surgery. I'm here on an isolated island. I thought when I met Mike that this well-respected accomplished doctor could bring me from my island to the mainland. After working together for a year, I discovered there were now two of us on this isolated island."[37] It was going to be a tough slog breaking through the surgeons' resistance. Litvak calls Mike Long "a scientist who believes all ideas can be divided into right and wrong. And if they are right – evidence-backed and demonstrated to work – people should accept that and adopt them. When he feels resistance, he gets angry."[38] Long said there was little understanding of operations management theory in medicine at that time.

"Those principles have been around since WWII and adopted by many other industries, including telecommunications. Healthcare was this black box thought to be immune to the discipline of operations improvement," Long said. "It took the pair of us to begin to change awareness of that."[39]

Long said it became obvious that the US healthcare system would benefit vastly if American hospitals operated 7 days a week, 24 hours a day, like factories, hotels, and airports. "That delivers the biggest benefits and greatest efficiencies. Today most hospitals effectively close at 5 p.m. on weekdays and further restrict services on weekends, though they have patients around the clock. Some heart centers claim to deliver good, around-the-clock care. But try to get a catheterization, physical therapy appointment, or find specialty doctor coverage over a weekend."[40]

Long said physicians and hospital leaders hold their breath and pray that nothing bad happens overnight and on weekends. "Hospitals try to cram seven days of work into three, especially with surgery departments. And that creates an intense, overloaded environment with people constantly putting out fires, stressing out their staffs and doing the best with the resources they have under difficult circumstances."[41]

And Long said much of it is unnecessary, self-inflicted wounds. He said the duo faced the same problems and the same resistance wherever they went. "Every hospital says it's different with different patient populations and different cultures, resources, and responsibilities," Long said. "And that is true. But when it comes to patient flow, they're all the same."[42]

When Long served in the US Army during the Vietnam War, he had planned to become a surgeon in medical school, even attending the University of Colorado for a surgical residency. "I looked around and found every single surgeon I met was divorced. I was working 120 hours a week and decided that lifestyle would not be conducive to living a long and happy life with my wife," he said.[43] So he pursued Plan B in anesthesia. He said Litvak's methods are an easy sell for anesthesiologists.

"Once you talk with them and they realize you've been there and done everything and faced these same problems, the anesthesiologists come onboard right away. But I was only a surgical intern and never practiced surgery after Vietnam. Even though I've been observing surgeries for over 25 years, I was not a surgeon in the eyes of surgeons."[44]

He said most surgeons are reluctant to change their practices, even when confronted with evidence that they could improve patient safety and outcomes. "When you already have what you want, whatever you want at whatever the cost, why would you welcome any change? Surgeons were, and will continue to be, a hard sell when they've been in total control. They can command hospital leaders to jump and then tell them how high to jump."[45]

After sharing their findings with Slavin, the question became: What happens next? "We learned what the problem was and then we found the solution."[46]

From 1997 to 1999 while Slavin was leading Barnes Jewish in St. Louis, the late James Mongan, MD, served as Mass General president. Mongan, who went on to head Partners HealthCare in 1999, was also supportive of Litvak's work. Litvak said when he first explained operations management research to Mongan, the executive was interested to learn more, and he gave him a copy of the book, *Principles of Operations Research,* by Harvey Wagner.

After reading it, Mongan told Litvak, "We're already doing 80% of this. Why are you being so critical?" Recalls Litvak, "I told him the book was published in 1969, nearly 30 years earlier. A lot's changed since then."[47] Litvak complained of the strong resistance Long and he faced, and Mongan told him, "You're just ahead of your time."[48]

Years later when Mongan was president of Partners, Litvak phoned him. "I really liked the guy. I told him that Mike Long had gone and I left, too. I said I respected him. He told me, 'Many people say that you and Mike were right. But you should understand it's difficult for them to publicly acknowledge. I don't think I would have had the guts to do this.' I always appreciated Jim's honesty, but it was a forecast of things to come.'"[49]

Litvak said that before he and Long published their 2000 paper on variability in ORs, hospitals blamed the ED for overcrowding.[50] "There were too many people coming into the emergency rooms or too many people who shouldn't be coming to EDs to get primary care they should have gotten from their family practitioners. It was a problem of access to health insurance and the absence of primary care physicians."[51]

But he and Long discovered it was the way hospitals scheduled their elective surgeries that caused big disruptions and chaos, leading to a lack of empty beds a few days every week.

"We introduced that idea," he said.

And they began to prove that those longtime practices had consequences, leading to overcrowding in the hospital and the ED,

The Litvak Method: A Massachusetts Hospital Became His Test Lab

medical errors, nurse and physician stress, and burnout and higher risk of dying unnecessarily in the hospital. They published their first piece together, "Cost and Quality under Managed Care: Irreconcilable Differences?" in *the American Journal of Managed Care.* In it they explored how managed care companies, such as HMOs, could control costs without compromising quality of care. The authors espoused the theory that employing operations management tools to improve patient flow and reduce artificial variability could improve the quality of care while reducing costs.[52] "The application of variability-based methodology is in its infancy but has the potential to distinguish effective cost-control interventions in healthcare from those that would only waste money or even damage the healthcare system," Litvak and Long concluded. "More importantly, variability analyses can be used to determine the threshold at which further attempts at cost reduction will compromise quality of care."[53]

Litvak said when they published their first piece, they were attempting to reduce healthcare costs in America. "The first inclination of hospitals in response to the growth of managed care was to lower the costs of the materials they purchased. Then they hired consultants."[54] They published two other papers in well-regarded journals in 2000 and 2001 and shared co-authorship four more times over the decade.[55]

Slavin said he wasn't surprised to learn that Mass General's OR was creating more non-random variability than the emergency department. "But we wanted to quantify it," he said.[56]

Still, Litvak and Long grew frustrated that despite all their research and data, Mass General never adopted their solutions to the OR dysfunction. They faced too much resistance from surgeons. "We hit a dead end in the OR," Slavin agreed. He said that Litvak's legacy at Mass General is that the hospital continues to use operations management research heavily to improve performance.[57] Slavin elaborated on Litvak's legacy, "He demonstrated here in a very powerful way that these tools, which have been used in factories, hotels, and other businesses for years, are very relevant to the healthcare environment and can make it safer, better, and more efficient."[58]

Litvak said he couldn't blame Slavin for Mass General's failure to adopt his methods. "Most of our work was done while Slavin had gone to Barnes Jewish. He asked me to examine this problem and left shortly after this. Jim Mongan was president and most of our work took place under his watch," he said.[59]

Early in 2000, Mike Long retired, leaving Mass General after decades of practicing there and leaving Litvak alone. "Mike said I should think about what I will do. No one ever told us they wouldn't implement our program. Mike realized it and then he decided to retire. But it never sunk in for me. I would have continued another five years pushing if my consulting contract had not expired. Once Mike left, I knew my time at Mass General was limited. I saw the writing on the wall and understood I alone would not be able to change this. I kept lecturing and doing operations research, but began exploring other opportunities."[60]

He said they showed Mass General a clear way to implement operations management techniques and educated them about implementing this process. "What we learned was beneficial to them," he said. "And what they did with that afterwards was up to them. Later I was delighted to learn that they had adopted some of our approaches to managing variability."[61]

■ ■ ■

Litvak said that hospital overcrowding was a big public issue at the turn of the millennium. Many hospitals were spending millions of dollars to build new hospital wings and add new emergency room beds – at a capital cost of $1 million to $2 million per bed to solve their overcrowding issues. (Today the per bed capital cost in

The Litvak Method: A Massachusetts Hospital Became His Test Lab

California is $3 million.) And Litvak conceded that strategy worked – for a while. What hospitals weren't doing was dealing with the real issue: patient flow and the barriers the hospitals themselves erected to block and upset that flow.

Harvey Fineberg, MD, might be described as Litvak's fairy godfather and benefactor, a mentor and friend who has supported the immigrant's career for nearly 30 years dating to Fineberg's tenure as dean of Harvard's School of Public Health and beyond.

In 2013 Litvak and Fineberg published a piece in the *New England Journal of Medicine*, titled "Smoothing the Way to Health Quality, Safety, and Economy."[62]

Fineberg said Litvak possesses "a far-sighted brilliance grounded in years of math and logical thinking. He has an ability to rapidly and seemingly intuitively reach the right solution."[63]

Litvak said he explained how variability impacts hospital patient census at Mass General to Harvey Fineberg. He said that the one week of the year when emergency departments are not overcrowded is Christmas week. That's because surgeons take that week off and hospitals do not schedule surgeries, hence there is no competition for OR rooms.

"The worst time to schedule a surgery or suffer an emergency hospital admission is within the first few weeks of the new year," Litvak said. "Most surgeons are not salaried employees of hospitals, but operate independently. They are paid by the number of procedures they perform. So if they're not working over the Christmas holidays, they have to catch up to make money again. Mike Long used to repeat a common surgical saying: 'You only eat what you kill,' (meaning surgeons don't get paid unless they perform surgeries). Weekends are another important parameter, because, by Monday, the surgeons need to catch up."[64]

■ ■ ■

In 1997 Litvak reached out to William Pierskalla, a guru in the operations management world. Pierskalla is well-versed in process management tools like Toyota's Lean and General Electric's Six Sigma. He is the former president of Institution for Operations Research and the Management Sciences (INFORMS), an international association for operations research and analytics professionals.

"I placed a cold call to him and introduced myself," Litvak recalled. "He was particularly interested in healthcare, and I told him I was getting frustrated. He said it's a very difficult field to change. He was very encouraging to me. I needed spiritual and moral support that I was on the right track, and he reassured me that I was and advised me to be patient."[65]

Pierskalla is one of the giants of the operations management world, the people who study system processes and improve them. He served as a distinguished professor emeritus and former dean of the UCLA Anderson School of Management and was the director of the Huntsman Center for Global Competition and Leadership and the chairman of the Health Care Systems Department at the Wharton School of Economics at the University of Pennsylvania. Litvak knew Pierskalla's work, even while he was still living in the USSR.[66]

"Eugene is very analytical and looks deeply at the causes and effects of practices and how to change and improve the system. This is a systems thinking approach to life. We look at problems, understand them, and try to find out how to fix them. He's very good at that. Eugene is less of a theorist in the abstract sense and more of a seeker of answers to real problems," Pierskalla said.[67]

Pierskalla said that the science of operations management has been overlooked in hospitals until the last decade. He said major healthcare systems have invested in operations and systems research and management. They include the Mayo Clinic, the Cleveland Clinic, and Kaiser Permanente. But he said today too few small- to mid-size hospitals have explored the potential of operations management tools. "They didn't need to. Until recently, they've never seriously needed to cut costs. And operations management was not a skill set familiar to hospital administrators, wasn't part of their background or training. So it was not natural for them to think about this," he said.[68]

Pierskalla said one of the main reasons for that inertia has been the way that hospitals have been paid by private and government insurance plans. He said physicians and the procedures they perform drive hospital revenue. And historically, the more tests, operations, and procedures doctors completed, the more they earned, and the more money hospitals made.

"The physicians run the show and the CEOs are figureheads. The doctors are good at what they do, and they bring in the money, so there's no real pressure from administrators to change this. The administrators' job is to make the doctors happy. That's where the power is. If they don't make the doctors happy, the doctors will go elsewhere, and they'll be out of a job. Eugene runs into this all the time. His biggest problem is persuading physicians to change, particularly when they don't want change."[69] Most of the time, even if there are problems within the hospital, the doctors are happy with the status quo and appreciate their independence and institutional power, Pierskalla explained.[70]

Don Berwick, MD, the former CMS administrator and quality improvement innovator, said in a 2000 story in the Harvard Medical School *Focus*, that Litvak's work is of profound significance for healthcare. "It is extraordinarily important that we attempt to apply it," he said. "Everyone knows that Litvak and Long are right. If we are able to engage the issue they are challenging us to, then the potential for creating lots of winners is huge, because we will be able to mobilize resources that can be reinvested where they are needed."[71]

Litvak said Berwick invited him to lecture at the Institute for Healthcare Improvement (IHI), a not-for-profit organization that aims to disseminate proven ideas to improve healthcare quality. IHI sponsored conferences and educational sessions for hospital managers and clinicians. "I started teaching some of my ideas about operating rooms." In 2000 he called a meeting at a Cambridge hotel and invited a select group of people to explore how patients move from one department to another. Prior to that, patient flow was not a widely used term.[72]

Berwick said he knew Litvak while he was working at Mass General. "He showed that OR demand was controlled by elective surgeries, not the ED schedule. Nobody else had ever thought of that. He wasn't a physician or healthcare policy person. Yet he was showing results through his research that were so counterintuitive that they captivated me. They came from totally out of the blue."[73]

He said Litvak identified improper design as a root cause of many healthcare system problems. "I've always been open to the idea that design and engineering hold many answers to the problems we encounter in healthcare," Berwick said.[74]

He called Litvak a "world class expert" genuinely trying to make things better. "He saw things he didn't like in the USSR and that left him with a social conscience and a strong sense of duty to improve things," Berwick said. "He's courageous and speaks his mind, partly because he cares and knows so much and has such a forceful personality. He's not shy about doing that."[75]

■ ■ ■

In 2000 Litvak moved from Harvard to nearby Boston University, where he established a program for the management of variability in healthcare delivery. He held the position until 2009, when he established the nonprofit Institute for Healthcare Optimization (IHO). At BU he conducted research while teaching courses on managing patient flow at Harvard's School of Public Health.

Litvak believed that the years he spent at Mass General instilled the conviction that his ideas were sound and could be applied to other hospitals, and that the problems facing Mass General's OR and ER were not unique, but widely shared by thousands of American hospitals. "We didn't confirm this until I moved to Boston University. We understood it was true but did not yet have proof."[76]

Mass General was the laboratory where he and Mike Long tested the core of their ideas. But it would be at BU where he could prove those ideas worked. In 2009 Litvak founded IHO, which succeeded BU's Program for Managing Variability in Health Care Delivery.

"At first I was alone at the program at BU, the prince and the bottle washer, a program of one," he said. But once business picked up there, he brought in his former student, Michael McManus, MD, and Abbot Cooper, and Mike Long also returned.[77]

The band was back together. "I was no longer alone. We had quite a team. For me that was a really big deal, but also an extra burden on my shoulders because I had to provide paychecks to all those people. (The original deal with BU was that Litvak was to support himself and the program without university financial assistance.) And the media continued writing about our work."[78]

After launching IHO, Litvak hired Sandeep Green Vaswani, who served with him until 2019. Litvak said he chose to make IHO a not-for-profit, patterned after Don Berwick's IHI. He ignored suggestions to operate as a for-profit model, understanding that Harvey Fineberg, then president of the Institute of Medicine, could not serve on the board of any for-profit organizations. So he opted for the not-for-profit tax-exempt status, which would allow Fineberg to sit on his advisory board. He couldn't surrender the opportunity to benefit from Feinberg's vision, guidance, and support.

Almost one decade later when Litvak published research about their findings at the Boston Medical Center, he ran into a Boston journalist who had written about his groundbreaking work in local hospitals. The journalist, Scott Allen of *the Boston Globe*, told Litvak he couldn't believe he'd been banging his head on the wall for all these years without seeing broad adoption of his methods.

"Even in Russia it took less than 20 years to become aware of what Stalin was secretly doing. With me it's been 25 years, and it's still swept under the rug," Litvak observed. "That's still really amazing to me and really frustrating. The media's job is to explore what's wrong with our healthcare system, but it's not doing its job."[79] Litvak had discovered the cause of an underlying problem afflicting hospitals, as well as a solution. But, he admitted, finding a solution isn't enough if no one is listening.

A New Research Center as Emergency Department Overcrowding Grows: Finally, the Media Notices

The new millennium saw a confluence of Litvak's previous efforts in teaching, research, and consulting finally begin to bear fruit. His work as a hospital consultant, as always, was fueled by his research.

In the early 2000s he continued to publish important research on patient flow and the consequences of failing to manage it, demonstrating his methods of successfully applying it throughout hospital departments and in hospitals of different sizes and locations. He continued to teach a course at Harvard's School of Public Health about operations management in healthcare and began lecturing through Don Berwick's Institute for Healthcare Improvement. Hospitals began showing interest in his ideas and their potential to improve patient care and reduce costs.

And after years of contacting journalists to promote his ideas, news organizations finally began to take notice, producing dozens of stories about this strange Ukrainian mathematician roaming hospital hallways and finding the roots of problems no one was addressing.

"What drove me was the same thing that compelled me to fight for a decade to obtain an exit visa from the USSR – to me, the benefits were absolutely clear and worth the consequences. I had no doubts. I had evidence that these methods save lives and huge amounts of money and led to better patient care and higher patient satisfaction. Anger probably was driving me. I didn't know how to act differently. So I kept at it. Was it good for the public? Yes. Was it good for hospitals' bottom lines? Yes. Some hospitals adopted the program and it worked, benefiting patients and improving hospital profit margins."[1]

Litvak's "program" was a series of steps and interventions implemented within hospitals after extensive data collection, lengthy staff interviews, and training. He applied complex math concepts that included graph, reliability, and queueing theories – ideas commonly accepted and successfully applied to improve efficiency in industries ranging from manufacturing and hotels to telecommunications, computing, and banking. Somehow, due to the way hospitals were paid (cost plus reimbursement), these innovations had not been adopted in healthcare. His method involved scheduling and staffing changes and even how to make appointments and room reservations.

These steps all serve to improve the journey of patients through the hospital, an industrial term called "throughput," that measures the amount of material or products moving through a system. While it originated on manufacturing lines, the term "throughput" has been adopted in the computing and telecommunications industry to describe the rate of data processed or delivered. Throughput comes down to this: what is the best, fastest, simplest, and most efficient way to get from A to B? What are the barriers and how are they overcome? What steps can be eliminated and how can the overall process be improved?

Litvak's methods aim to improve efficiency in the same way he had earlier smoothed the hills and valleys to construct new Soviet railroad lines whose grades were elevated or flattened to smooth the journey of trains. He understood that the same variability in the earth posed problems of quality and efficiency, slowing down for every

Hospital, Heal Thyself

bump or hill, then quickly sliding downward into a basin. During this period, Litvak saw great career opportunities arising from his research and nascent hospital consulting work.

After moving to Boston University in 2000, Litvak said Don Berwick, his Harvard colleague and the founder of the Institute for Healthcare Improvement (IHI) offered him "a big microphone" when he asked Litvak to teach about the relatively new concept of "patient flow" at IHI.

"Failing to achieve hospital-wide patient flow – the right care, in the right place, at the right time – puts patients at risk for suboptimal care and potential harm," an IHI white paper concluded. "It also increases the burden on clinicians and hospital staff and can accelerate burnout."[2]

Achieving good patient flow requires an understanding of the hospital as an interconnected, interdependent system of care, Berwick said. While Litvak was a master at understanding process, he was still learning how hospitals function. But he learned fast. "I finally had my moment. All of a sudden people wanted to learn from me. These ideas were resonating. People are tribal creatures. We want recognition from the tribe. Things improved for me. Emotionally, it was extremely rewarding. I engaged with more and more hospital people and figured out how to get my ideas out. I thought finally I broke the wall. I was absolutely confident."[3]

For several years Litvak taught healthcare clinicians and executives at IHI. "Don (Berwick) opened this floodgate. When you teach hundreds of people sometimes a few become interested," he said, citing multiple students – clinicians and hospital executives – whose hospitals became clients.[4]

Though he was then in his 50s, he worked even longer hours. "It was a rare weekend when I didn't work."[5]

He described the current state of America's healthcare system as, "Demand currently exceeding capacity, given the way that capacity is being managed. To state it even more boldly, demand exceeds mismanaged capacity."[6]

On a business trip to Sydney, Australia, the general director of New South Wales Health asked Litvak to present to his organization throughout Australia's most populous state.[7] For nearly two weeks Litvak made daily presentations to hospital executives and boards, physicians, and nurses about patient flow. "I was working like a farm horse and had a hard time adjusting to driving on the opposite side of the road."[8]

On an earlier business trip to Great Britain, Litvak worked with leaders at Great Ormond Street Hospital in London. From those cultural immersions in the UK and Australia he prepared an answer to a frequently asked question.

"People often tell me that implementing this program calls for a pretty big cultural change. They ask, 'Can we just apply this gradually, to just one hospital surgical service line, say cardiology or neurology, without touching the others?' Then I tell them about an imaginary meeting of British transportation officials. One official points out, 'It's not good that the rest of the world drives on the right side, while we drive on left. We should change.' Another official yells out, 'That's a hell of a project. Can we do it gradually?'"[9] Litvak maintained that it is possible to adopt his program if a hospital offers a particular surgical specialty, such as orthopedics, its own OR and its dedicated beds where patients go after surgery. Then his program can be applied to only one surgical specialty.

"The problem is that normally ORs do not belong to just one service line – except in giant hospitals. The ORs are often shared between neurology or cardiology and others. So you cannot optimize resources by sharing them, because one group will take advantage of it. *You* might be frugal, while *I* gamble. To me adopting this a little bit is like being a little bit pregnant."[10] His audience needed to understand that the hospitals function like an ecosystem.

Hospital, Heal Thyself

Litvak's Methods Find a New Home and Hospitals Come Knocking

Shortly after arriving at Boston University's School of Management, Litvak set up his Program for Managing Variability in Health Care Delivery, then, a one-man organization dedicated to researching and solving patient flow problems. Later he was able to hire more staff to join him.

His advisory committee included Charlie Baker, the future governor of Massachusetts, who then served as CEO of Harvard Pilgrim Health. This "Murderers' Row" of healthcare heavy hitters included Berwick; Harvey Feinberg (then president of the Institute of Medicine); Dennis O'Leary, president of the Joint Commission; Margaret O'Kane, president of the National Committee for Quality Assurance; Gregg Lehman, CEO of the National Business Coalition on Health; and the presidents and CEOs of the region's biggest and most powerful hospitals and health systems. "I was told that our advisory board was a list of Who's Who in healthcare." The group's first meeting was held September 14, 2001, three days after the 9/11 bombings that shook the world.[11]

While Litvak had a new shingle, great expectations, and a new address and sponsor, he still had no paying hospital clients. That would come soon enough. That year a fellow IHI faculty member, Roger Resar, MD, a pulmonologist and assistant professor of medicine at the Mayo Clinic School of Medicine, approached Litvak with questions. Resar, whose actual official hospital title then was "Tremendous Change Agent and Global Innovation Seeker," is now a senior fellow at IHI. Back then he told Litvak he'd like to implement his ideas at the Mayo Clinic's Luther-Midelfort Hospital in Eau Claire, Wisconsin.[12]

"I told him the right things to do, then Roger and the hospital did everything themselves. He told me that one of the surgeons left after

A New Research Center as Emergency Department Overcrowding

Luther-Midelfort implemented Litvak's system," Litvak recalled. "But Roger said the overall results were so good it was worth it. He was surprised, but I was not. I was impressed with the job they did."[13]

Local media took notice. A November 1, 2002, story in the *Boston Business Journal* cited the early success of Litvak's methods at Luther-Midelfort. According to data the hospital provided to the *Journal*, the time that the three-hospital system spent on ambulance diversion fell from 12% to under 2%, while the number of patients placed in a bed within one hour after arriving in the ED rose from 23% to 40%. Nursing vacancy rates dropped from 10% to 1% in that one-year study period, while revenues also rose an average of $200,000 per month (nearly $2.5 million).[14]

Christina Dempsey, the OR manager for St. John's Regional Health Center in Springfield, Missouri, attended one of Litvak's lectures, and in 2002, at Dempsey's behest, the hospitals hired Litvak. Years later, Dempsey told a reporter in a July 5, 2006, story in the *News-Leader* that St. John's had been facing a crisis impacting patient safety and quality.[15]

The story described Litvak's intervention as "a better way to schedule surgeries so patients had fewer delays and were moved to the appropriate floor for recovery. The overall goal of the project: reduce complications or patient deaths due to hospital errors."[16]

The scheduling process for elective surgeries then created unpredictable and excessive staff overtime and caused recovering (surgical) patients to be placed in beds on the wrong floors. That alone jeopardized staff's ability to provide safe, postsurgical care, Dempsey told the *News-Leader*.[17]

She said that St. John's adopted Litvak's recommendation to staff a separate OR for emergency cases and later to persuade surgeons to perform operations more frequently on other days of the week. "It made a huge difference. It did create a better flow for add-on (emergency) patients and let scheduled volume (elective surgeries) process without delay or bumps," she said.[18]

After Dempsey posted the results of the changes, other hospitals within the IHI hospital collaborative took notice. IHI reported the success of the program in a report, pointing out that by designating one or more ORs to serve unscheduled cases, St. John's decreased waiting times for patients and even increased revenue for participating surgeons using this method. IHI said St. John's recorded a 5% increase in surgical case volume, a 45% decrease in surgeries performed after 3 p.m. (late night surgeries were becoming a problem), an all-time low in OR overtime costs, and a 4.6% increase in revenue. They also recorded increased patient satisfaction.[19]

"Eugene took me under his wing, and we continued collaborating after the creation of the add-on OR room," recalled Dempsey, who was promoted to vice president of perioperative (surgical) and emergency services. "We started leveling out the surgery schedule to get rid of the peaks and valleys in the scheduled surgery volume and that made a difference and allowed better staffing in the OR and staffed units," she said.[20]

Dempsey said the accomplishment was not achieved without resistance. "To upend a surgeon's schedule is very difficult to do. You get pushback," she admitted, noting that some surgeons threatened to leave the hospital and take their patients with them. "But it made sense when you think of ORs and EDs vying for the same beds."[21]

She said the problem manifests itself within the ED, which is why many hospitals erroneously focus improvement efforts exclusively there without tracing back the problem's roots in the hospital OR. "You could see the temperatures of ED doctors going down when they realized I knew that this was not an emergency department problem, but a system problem."[22]

She said one reason hospitals are reluctant to adopt Litvak's program is the perceived impact on surgeons. Litvak and Dempsey, now the chief nursing officer for South Bend, Indiana–based hospital survey company Press-Ganey, presented their findings at a Joint

Commission presentation. Dempsey said that the biggest challenge she faced was persuading surgeons to change their work schedules, not just when they operated, but also their office hours and clinics. "We worked to help them get there."

She said Litvak's system is "definitely replicable." After she left St. John Hospital in late 2007, Dempsey continued to work with Litvak to improve patient flow in other hospitals.

"St. John's improved efficiency without reducing quality," Litvak wrote in a chapter in a *Joint Commission Resources* book. "The OR saw an increase in its ability to accommodate 10% annual surgical volume growth for the previous two years."[23]

After St. John's implemented Litvak's ideas, the reporter wrote: "The next time you or a loved one are spared a long, agonizing hospital wait before emergency or scheduled surgery at St. John's Hospital in Springfield, you can thank a Boston-based, Russian professor and statistician named Eugene Litvak."[24]

The Institute of Medicine (formerly IOM, now the National Academy of Medicine) included St. John's results in its report, "The Future of Emergency Care in the United States Health System." IOM reported a 45% reduction in wait times for emergent and urgent surgical cases; an increase in appropriate inpatient placement for orthopedic patients, from 83% to 96%; a 59% increase in inpatient capacity (excluding the intensive care unit) without the addition of a single staffed bed; a 33% increase in surgical volume; and a reduction of 2.9% in OR overtime.[25] The success of Litvak's methods was spreading.

His approach was adopted at nearly the same time in 2004 at Elliott Hospital in Manchester, New Hampshire, which then boasted the largest obstetrics ward in the state. Maternity Center Director Susan Leavitt Gullo, RN, had attended one of Litvak's IHI seminars on patient flow and wondered if the same principles that had worked in

ORs and EDs could be applied to hospital labor and delivery units, often called maternity wards.[26]

Litvak, too, was curious. While he believed his program to improve patient flow could be applied throughout a hospital's many departments, he needed proof. So he agreed to help, pro bono. He said Elliott's maternity ward was stressed and requested more staffed beds and nurses.

He explained that there were two streams of patients competing for the same resources: scheduled deliveries, women who planned to be induced with drugs to deliver their babies, or planned caesarean deliveries; and unscheduled deliveries, expectant mothers who knew they would be delivering, but sought natural births.

"There were pregnant mothers waiting to get beds and relatives arriving, and it was stressful for patients and nurses and hospital leadership," Litvak said, noting that many were sent home to deliver their babies another day, their deliveries pre-empted by unscheduled deliveries.[27]

He said there were constant bottlenecks in the labor and delivery unit. More expectant women were requesting to schedule their deliveries (either by induction or caesarean) and getting bumped by the unpredictable deliveries, or normal births.

"We studied this and found if we separated scheduled and unscheduled births, fewer deliveries would be bumped."

Armed with Litvak's data and recommendations, Elliott Hospital set aside half the maternity beds (four of the unit's eight beds) for scheduled deliveries and slated the other half for unscheduled deliveries. Mothers seeking planned deliveries were instructed by their obstetricians to call at 4 p.m. the day before to book the room. Within weeks the maternity ward saw results. Fewer scheduled deliveries were postponed, and patient satisfaction scores rose.

"At first the hospital's administration really did not believe in this. But after it happened, they were teaching its success story at a Joint Commission conference," Litvak said.[28]

A *Boston Globe* story chronicled the improvements. "It was a morning ritual that nurses at New Hampshire's busiest obstetrics ward dreaded: calling expectant mothers to tell them they couldn't come in to deliver their babies after all. Doctors had become so eager to schedule surgical deliveries and labor inductions first thing in the morning that Elliot Hospital often couldn't fit everyone in, especially when there was a surge in the number of women going into labor naturally. So nurses often had to call women at 5:30 a.m. to reschedule deliveries," the *Globe* reported.[29] "Some obstetricians told patients to go to the hospital anyway, triggering unseemly jostling for beds at the desk, and making women even madder when they were sent home."[30]

The *Globe* story explained that Litvak advised nurses to set aside half the beds for scheduled deliveries and decide each afternoon who would use them the next day. Women pursuing natural childbirth were allocated the other half of rooms.[31] "Almost immediately, obstetricians began spreading deliveries through the day, the morning chaos disappeared, and an issue that had festered for years was resolved."[32]

Litvak was on a roll. Starting that same year, he enjoyed even greater success at the Boston Medical Center (BMC), Boston's safety net hospital, which included New England's largest Level 1 Trauma Center at the time, which treats more than 130,000 patients annually.[33]

BMC's John Chessare, MD, the hospital's chief medical officer, had attended one of Litvak's IHI lectures and sought his help. The hospital committed to implementing Phase 1 of the program: separating scheduled surgery patients from unscheduled (emergency patients) by providing a separately staffed OR for ED cases.

"John said if this project fails, he could find himself unemployed," Litvak recalled. "He understood that for him to succeed, he would have to change surgeon behavior, and if he didn't succeed, he'd lose his job. That put a big burden on my shoulders."[34]

Litvak said BMC's emergency department was constantly overloaded because of OR scheduling.

They began in the step-down unit, the hospital ward that acts as a buffer between the intensive care unit (ICU) and the medical/surgical unit, where patients ideally ended up after surgery when there were few complications.

BMC's step-down unit suffered large swings in patient volume, particularly between Tuesdays and Thursdays. On those peak days of large volume, he said the unit lacked open beds. Staffing was challenging. Some days there would be one scheduled patient and some days nine. After adding a separate OR and later, convincing surgeons to spread out their surgeries over five weekdays instead of two or three – a process Litvak calls "surgical smoothing" – the average census in the step-down unit remained at four to five patients.[35]

Niels Rathlev, MD, was the vice chairman of the ED in the early 2000s when Litvak was working with the hospital to improve patient flow. Rathlev, who now chairs the department of emergency medicine at the University of Massachusetts School of Medicine–Baystate, in Springfield, said Litvak wanted to smooth the surgical schedules in the ORs at BMC.

Word began to spread. In an Aug. 10, 2005, *Wall Street Journal* story, BMC reported fewer delays and the near elimination of canceled elective surgeries, recording just three between April and September 2004, compared with 334 in the same six-month period the year before. It also opened up beds for more patients admitted through the ED.[36]

"A large part of this had to do with the charisma of Eugene and John [Chessare] and their commitment to doing this. They won people over. The solutions were difficult, but they didn't make anyone operate on Saturdays or Sundays, and nobody lost money. Surgeons want to operate, and they offered surgeons incentives to operate more and spread those surgeries out, rather than piling them up on one day."[37]

After implementing Litvak's methods, BMC reduced variability (the size and frequency of the peaks and valleys) in the step-down unit by 55%. By decreasing nursing hours per patient day by 30 minutes, BMC realized annual savings of $130,000 on wages alone, according to a Joint Commission paper Litvak wrote.[38]

BMC's experience continued to serve as an example for other hospitals. Rathlev, who collaborated with Chessare and Litvak on a research paper published in 2018 in the *HSOA Journal of Emergency Medicine and Surgical Care*, said Litvak encountered some pushback.[39]

"Redesign of the operating room resulted in a 99.5% reduction in the number of postponed and canceled cases. It was associated with reductions in direct nursing hours (5.7%), overtime pay on nursing floors, and ED time from decision to admit to departure for admitted patients (18.5%)," the 2018 study found.[40]

"What do crowded ERs have to do with Litvak?"

At the turn of the 20th century the United States was facing a resurgent crisis in emergency medicine, one that its hospitals had grappled with for decades. Long emergency room waits sometimes exceeded one day. Hallways were overcrowded with patients awaiting treatment or emergency patients lying in gurneys waiting to be admitted into the hospital, a practice called boarding. Ambulance diversions began to grow in popularity and frequency. Ambulance diversions occur when a hospital emergency department (ED) becomes overcrowded and is unable to accept new patients. The hospital contacts the local emergency services network to declare they are on diversion status and must redirect ambulances to nearby hospitals.

While Litvak said the intention is noble – to relieve the pressure on a stressed ED, diverting patients is not only ineffective, but can harm patients requiring immediate treatment. He said diversions reroute ambulance patients to other hospitals, often miles out of their way while wasting valuable minutes. The practice fails to cure the overcrowding problem that ignites it, studies have shown.

Yet another symptom of ED overcrowding occurs when patients treated in the ED are admitted to the hospital but assigned beds in inappropriate hospital units because beds in the right unit for their condition are unavailable. So neurology patients may be sent to a general surgery unit, with nurses on those units not always trained to spot symptoms of decline. This practice tragically claimed the life of Lewis Blackman, the teenager whose death sparked a movement described earlier in the book.[41]

"This is the new normal," Litvak said. "People have come to accept it. I called a few state health departments asking how many complaints they receive from patients who waited too long or were placed in the wrong bed. The answer was, 'None.'"[42]

But the problems are not new. Similar issues have plagued American hospital EDs since the 1980s.

Litvak pointed out that every five or 10 years, something bad happens in an ER somewhere. Someone dies unnecessarily or is terribly harmed and there is a big public scandal with investigations and news stories and outrage from politicians. "Then someone appoints a commission to look into it, and we forget about it and pretend it went away," said Litvak. "It doesn't get better, but our attention moves onto another crisis. People lose interest."

Lurid stories of patients dying on gurneys awaiting admission to overcrowded hospitals continue to appear, as well as sad tales of ambulances driving miles out of their way because they've been diverted from overcrowded local hospitals while patients wait for lifesaving treatments. And angry, irritable patients continue to wait unsafely for long hours, sometimes days, to be treated or admitted. These problems continue to escalate.

Patients like Bill Cameon, 81, a Highland, Indiana, electrician and trade school instructor, are not rare. On November 28, 2018, after routine blood tests revealed elevated enzymes signaling a possible heart attack, Cameon's family physician urged him to go immediately to the emergency room at Community Hospital of Munster (Indiana). Because the ED there knew Cameon could be having a heart attack, he immediately received a cubicle room in the ED. There he lay all evening, overnight, and into the next morning. Finally, 23 hours later, a cardiologist entered his room and said that the young physician who referred Cameon to the ED was perhaps a little overzealous because his enzyme levels, while slightly higher, were not severe enough to indicate a heart attack.[43]

Cameon, a quiet, laconic man, took the news in stride. "The hallways were crowded with patients on stretchers. I felt guilty for having a room because most of them were sicker than me," he admitted.[44]

Amid the ED chaos and noise he couldn't sleep all night and missed work the next day. "But it sure beat the last time I went to the ER."[45] He explained that on May 1 of the previous year his girlfriend drove him to the same ED for an emergency appendectomy diagnosed by the same young family physician.

"She was right that time," he chuckled.[46] Surgeons in the OR removed his burst appendix and part of his colon and cleaned out the poisons that leeched out into his abdomen. He was heavily dosed with painkillers, prophylactic antibiotics, and stool softeners. In the middle of the night he was moved from his comfortable room in a surgical unit to a cold and spare observation unit bed in a room without a toilet. He said the hospital and the ER were crowded that night. He was connected to a heart monitor, a urinary catheter with a urine bag, and an IV bag and cart. And he was left alone.

"I'll never let anyone treat me that way again," he swore. "I had to go to the bathroom and buzzed the nurse, but nobody came. So I rolled my monitors and equipment and IV cart down the hallway wearing an open gown and never felt so embarrassed in my life."[47]

■ ■ ■

Government regulators and researchers were noticing the looming crisis. In 2009 the Government Accountability Office (GAO) released a study examining the impending disaster in American emergency medicine.[48]

For example, the average wait time to see a physician for emergent patients – those patients who should be seen in 1 to 14 minutes – was 37 minutes in 2006, more than twice as long as recommended for their level of urgency.[49]

In its "Strategies Related to Emergency Department Output," the GAO recommended, "The strategy will streamline elective surgery schedules to make elective daily admission volume even and increase the opportunity for emergency department admissions."[50] A 2005 study from the Robert Woods Johnson Foundation found one hospital frequently boarded some patients for as long as 48 hours.[51] The 2006 IOM report that Litvak helped produce explained that while many causes contribute to overcrowding and the conditions it aggravates, the primary driver of the chaos is poorly managed patient flow, a condition Litvak diagnosed one decade earlier. The authors wrote that ambulance diversions place patients at greater risk and recommends eliminating diversions in all but the most extreme circumstances.[52]

"The emergency department is the canary in the coal mine," explained Charlotte Yeh, MD, a former ED physician now serving as chief medical director for AARP, an advocacy organization for older Americans.[53]

Litvak said that typically emergency departments steer more than one-half of all hospital admissions. Elective admissions, primarily after surgery, typically account for 30% to 35% of the remaining hospital admissions, while the rest are due to transfers from other hospitals or nursing homes and physician referrals. In October 2002, Litvak and his new colleagues at Boston University's School of Management Program for the Management of Variability in Health Care Delivery, Michael McManus, MD, and Abbot Cooper, published a paper under a grant from the Massachusetts Department of Public Health that examined the source of problems in the emergency departments of two Massachusetts hospitals.[54]

Their "Root Cause Analysis of Emergency Department Crowding and Ambulance Diversion in Massachusetts" validated Litvak's theory that "the number of scheduled admissions is more variable than the number of admissions through the ED. Although previously neglected in healthcare, this counterintuitive pattern suggests that variability control of scheduled admissions may provide a significant opportunity to increase hospital throughput and access to care." In other words, Litvak confirmed that one of the primary drivers of ED overcrowding, long waits and ambulance diversions, could be found upstream in the hospital operating rooms.[55]

That finding was further validated by a study the following year at Boston Children's Hospital. In that June 2003 study that appeared in the medical journal *Anesthesiology*, Litvak, McManus, and colleagues found that almost 70% of ICU diversions at the hospital were associated with variability in the scheduled caseload. That meant that on days when surgeons scheduled the most procedures – usually Monday through Wednesday – the hospital's limited number of

Hospital, Heal Thyself

intensive care unit (ICU) beds were quickly occupied, leaving no room for incoming emergency patients, who were diverted from the ICU and the hospital and transported elsewhere.[56] "The graph shows that whenever we have a peak in demand in scheduled admissions, we usually have a peak in diversions from the ICU, with all of the consequences that brings in terms of quality," Litvak told *OR Manager* in a November 2003 story.[57]

This was a significant finding that aroused public discussion. The year after the "Root Cause" study, Massachusetts formed a task force to study ED overcrowding in the state. Joining him on the task force was Yeh, who was not only an ED physician, but also an outspoken patient safety advocate. Yeh then was a well-known emergency physician who had participated in several significant public health initiatives, including reducing long ER waiting times and ambulance diversions and the common practice of hospital EDs boarding patients. Litvak said the task force members held high hopes that they could improve the worsening ED crisis. "The miracle didn't happen," he conceded.[58]

However, in 2009 Massachusetts became the first state in the country to prohibit ambulance diversions. Litvak said while Massachusetts banned its hospitals from requesting diversions, the practice remains problematic in many other states.[59] "In California, hospital diversions are a big deal. People suffering emergencies might be taken too far away, because their hospital might be on diversion," Litvak said.[60]

Litvak and other researchers have proven that ambulance diversions, which are intended to reduce the flow of emergency patients to a hospital's ED, cause many adverse effects on patients and hospitals, while failing to achieve the goal of reducing patient intake to the ED. "Here's what typically happens. If you're a hospital CEO in a market with multiple other hospitals and at least one of your competitors goes on diversion, what should you do? If you're the last hospital not on diversion, you are prohibited from going on diversion status. So the game is to go on diversion sooner and not be the last hospital, which then has to take all the diverted patients. Often hospitals will reject patients prematurely and go on diversion status, just to make sure they're not the last not to divert."[61]

Litvak said ambulance diversions are a means for hospitals to reject patients that they cannot treat in a timely way. "I don't blame them for wanting to divert patients when they are overcrowded. I do blame them for not solving their problem of overcrowding. The bigger and more prominent the hospital, the more chance for overcrowding. And sadly, the media only talks about ambulance diversions when something terrible happens."[62]

He said most people don't complain that they won't live 300 years, because nobody expects to. Mortality is a part of life. "Now hospital overcrowding has become a part of life. We condition patients to accept these long waits, even as we declare that we are patient-centered. We would rather accept negative outcomes than change the culture. Now that's a taboo."[63]

Litvak said hospitals are under increased pressure to discharge patients early, even those who may not be healthy enough, to open new patient beds. That practice could put patients at risk, but keeping them hospitalized longer costs the hospital money under today's complicated reimbursement system.

"In Ukraine we have a saying: 'Sleep faster. Somebody needs your blanket.' That's what we're doing. Patients are coming back to hospitals after being discharged. Many hospitals are being disciplined for high rates of patient readmissions for problems they're ignoring."[64]

Pain and Suffering: The New Normal

Litvak said hospitals complain loudly about the readmissions penalties they face from CMS, the federal agency that administers Medicare.

"But if everyone is readmitting patients, well, they can't punish everyone. This is becoming the new normal. And it is absolutely unnecessary. It's all because of hospital culture."

Litvak said that instead of grappling with the real issue, many hospitals are introducing a variety of interventions to reduce hospital occupancy, such as expanding primary care services. "And most of these are good ideas. But they are Band-Aids. Emphasizing them while failing to deal with the primary cause of overcrowding, a problem that hospitals can solve, is just beating around the bush."[65]

Former ED Physician Yeh agreed. "Right now, sadly, the ED continues to be viewed as a cost center. That's a problem. We are missing the opportunity to view ED as part of the solution, to take advantage of what EDs are: a 24-hour safety net."[66]

Yeh called emergency rooms "the most egalitarian place in healthcare, the only place in our healthcare system where you are guaranteed to be seen, whether you're homeless or the president of the United States, you will be treated."[67] She said that hospital overcrowding exacerbates existing ED problems. "When the canary passes out, mine owners are supposed to prevent incoming miners from entering to avoid casualties. But EDs can't turn away patients coming in. Who gets hurt in the process when we don't have the capacity to admit those ED patients into the hospital? The patient and the family."[68]

While Yeh admitted she hasn't worked as an ED physician in years, she continues to monitor the field in her current position at AARP. And she echoed Litvak's observation. "I think people have gotten used to it. Hospitals believe they can take care of this with more discharge lounges and staff shakeups and by adding new ED beds. But it still goes on."[69]

Yeh said stress, delays, and long waits also harm patients. "No one talks about the burden on patients. If you're sitting in ED for 10, 20, or more hours, which is not uncommon, what is your personal

A New Research Center as Emergency Department Overcrowding

cost and time loss? How are the waits affecting your condition? That should be evaluated as well," she said.[70]

Then there is the burden of care on families. The Mayo Clinic has attempted to calculate the cost of long patient waits. "We do know for geriatric patients that the longer they wait immobilized on beds, the greater chance they'll end up in rehabilitation centers [nursing homes] instead of going home. And nobody wants to talk about the cost of medical errors, which can be expensive, life-threatening, and personally devastating."[71]

Jesse Pines, MD, a nationally renowned researcher, emergency medicine physician, and George Washington University professor, called ambulance diversions a house of cards. "If you have four hospitals and three are on diversion, that fourth hospital is getting killed. As the only remaining hospital in the market that hasn't gone on diversion, it can't refuse the ambulances because it is the only option left," Pines said. "So it gets swamped with patients."[72]

He said the benefit of Litvak's method is that it's comprehensive, a combination that improves efficiency, lowers costs, and improves quality of care, which increases access. "That's 'The Iron Triangle' of healthcare. Few interventions can impact all of those. But it's difficult to administer."[73]

Richard Wolfe, MD, chief of emergency medicine for Beth Israel Hospital in Boston, said hospital overcrowding has been a problem for a long time, particularly in big city hospitals and academic medical centers. Wolfe said the poor have historically utilized the ED, which has always been treated as a financial loss leader and less supported by hospital owners. He conceded that Litvak's methods offer better use of hospital capacity, but said surgeons like the traditional surgery schedule of Monday to Wednesday.[74]

"And when it comes to a question of personal lifestyle versus optimal functioning, surgeons win out. They are important commodities for hospitals and can always choose to vote with their feet. It's just that simple. Recruiting star surgeons is a high priority strategy for any hospital CEO. They are willing to take the financial losses that come with the failure to do surgical leveling over losing high performing surgeons."[75]

James Augustine, MD, is vice president of the Emergency Department Benchmarking Alliance (EDBA) and chairman of the national clinical governance board for U.S. Acute Care Solutions, a company that operates hospital emergency rooms. "We began Alliance in 1994 because of the growing difficulty of managing EDs. He said the EDBA has evolved into an organization dedicated to sharing best practices across all categories of EDs. More than 2,000 EDs contribute data, including many freestanding EDs owned or managed by hospitals. We represent more than half of the EDs doing business today in the United States."[76]

Augustine agreed there were more bottlenecks delaying the admission of ED patients into hospital beds. When hospitals can't admit patients in a timely way, he said, it dramatically impacts how long patients have to wait in EDs. "We're having ED nurses taking care of patients who should already be in hospital beds. The result is they suffer worse outcomes, longer lengths of stay and long, long waiting times," he said. "All this makes the job even more stressful and at times leaves you feeling like you've been abandoned."[77]

Augustine said the most recent survey results from the Alliance indicate that ED overcrowding is "clearly growing. Boarding times and the length of time an admitted patient remains in the ED have not changed since 2013 since the federal government has been monitoring boarding times. It's disappointing that we've not been able to decrease the amount of time patients spend in the ED. In many cases those waiting times have increased."[78]

Seth Trueger, MD, an emergency medicine specialist who practices at the ED of Northwestern Memorial Hospital in Chicago and works at the *Journal of the American Medical Association*, said he believes the problems plaguing America's emergency departments "have grown worse on a bigger scale."[79]

Trueger, an assistant professor of emergency medicine at Northwestern's medical school, said American hospitals continue to expand and add new beds. But he pointed out that hospitals aren't facing a capacity problem, but a flow problem. "It's like prioritizing cleaning the blood off the floor instead of treating the patient whose arm was just chopped off. Too often we focus on the wrong problem."[80]

Trueger explained that ED wait times are terrible for many reasons. "They discourage people from coming to get care in the first place. Nobody wants to come to the ED. It is a hassle, scary, and expensive. The time costs are substantial for many people. And boarded patients aren't just taking up space, but also nurse and physician time, and making it impossible to take care of their other patients."[81]

He said when the ED is overcrowded patients receive worse care. "That means that some of these patients aren't receiving the antibiotics, stroke care, or cardiac treatments they need," Trueger said. "If you're sitting in a hallway waiting for 10 hours, that's a miserable, potentially dangerous place to be."[82]

The 2020 coronavirus pandemic further challenged hospital resources, taxing not only the limited supplies of ventilators and specialized quarantine equipment, but also hospital capacity and staffing. In China, where the pandemic began, many of those early casualties were healthcare workers, nurses, and physicians.

Some ED physicians and researchers say until hospitals learn to better manage patient flow, they will be unable to handle the huge patient loads of mass casualty disasters or epidemics. "Nobody prepares for disasters like 9/11 until they happen," Litvak said. "After 9/11 a few people asked me what kind of resources and how much should they prepare for such disasters. My answer was a question:

'How could a disaster help you to determine your hospital and ED capacities if you don't know this now even without a disaster?'"[83]

After 9/11, US hospitals went through extensive risk assessment and preparation for handling mass casualty events like terrorist bombings. But Litvak said most hospitals never attempted to control their badly managed patient flow. "And this is in the best of times," Litvak said. "What happens if we are operating at peak capacity and there is a mass casualty event or disaster? They are completely unprepared for that."

Eric Goralnick, MD, an ED physician, was working at Brigham and Women's Hospital after the 2017 Boston Marathon. Goralnick published a piece in the *New England Journal of Medicine* about how his ED treated mass casualties transported there after the bombing in 2017. He said that some symptoms of ED dysfunction have not improved in hospital emergency rooms since the Boston Marathon bombing.[84] "Boarding hours have only increased over the years. I think our boarding hours and waiting times have only grown since then."[85]

Goralnick, the medical director of emergency preparedness at Brigham Health and an associate professor of emergency medicine at the Harvard Medical School, said mass casualty incident demand outweighs even his hospital's supply of services. "We have to provide the best care we can and understand the limitations on resources. When hospitals are busting at the seams and a disaster is laid on top of that with a massive influx of patients, we do what we can."[86]

Peter Viccellio, MD, a renowned ED physician and vice chair of the department of emergency medicine at the Renaissance School of Medicine at Stony Brook University in New York, partially blames state and federal regulatory agencies for allowing overcrowding to grow. "When we know things are dangerous and people are being harmed and that there are fixes, what do the regulatory agencies do?"[87]

Viccellio explained that during a recent inspection his ED was overcrowded, with every room filled and unmonitored patient gurneys swarming ED hallways, clearly a problem. But a state inspector observed all that, then walked over to a glass-enclosed fire extinguisher and cited the hospital for an expired device. That was the extent of the ED inspection, he said.[88] "They examine every bit of minutia and ignore the rest. The hospital responds by purchasing a new fire extinguisher, and the inspectors approve the hospital and show the public they are watching out for patient safety, while the hospital gets to boast it was approved by the regulatory agencies. It gives the public the illusion and appearance of safety without addressing the real issues of safety."[89]

Viccellio said his hospital ED has gone from boarding five patients to more than 50 in a 66-bed ED. "We are defining deviancy down and now everyone just gets used to it."[90] He said his ED implements well-meaning, but ultimately ineffective solutions to a big problem it refuses to address. "What we're doing is polishing shiny little turds."[91]

He said unless the public complains, hospitals won't do anything about long waiting times, ambulance diversions, or boarding patients. "We know what works, but many hospitals don't do it and the state won't enforce it. I'm very frustrated. Regulators don't want to do things that are unpopular. Everyone is already conditioned to believe this is the way things are and there's nothing we can do about it."[92]

Viccellio said CMS requires hospitals to report their ED turnaround times. "But there's no requirement to act on them."[93]

A study by Viccellio and his colleagues at Stony Brook confirmed for the first time widespread variability in hospital census on a statewide basis. An analysis of nearly 1.7 million New York state hospital patient admissions in 2015 found almost 1.1 million patients were admitted to the hospital from EDs and nearly 600,000 admitted through other pathways. On Sundays, Mondays, and Tuesdays, there were more admissions than discharges, causing overcrowding and

ED boarding, "likely due to an increase in elective admissions in the beginning of the week," the study found.[94]

Viccellio and his co-authors concluded that, "There are significant variabilities in admissions and discharges throughout the week," recommending that "Hospitals should evaluate ways to smooth elective admissions throughout the week while deploying resources to increase discharges on weekends."[95]

That endorsement served as a state validation of the theories posited by Litvak and Long almost 20 years after they first published. The authors also examined mortality data for the study, confirming that more patients die on weekends. "The mortality rate was twice as high on weekends," Viccellio said. "No surprise to ED physicians."[96]

He said the message is clear: "You can get sick or injured seven days a week. We'll only be there five days a week."[97]

While EDs and hospital ICUs are open daily, patients arriving on weekends with ruptured aneurisms or severe heart attacks may not find the appropriate physician specialists in the hospital. "It might take them 30 minutes to an hour to get to you. ED physicians see this all the time during off hours and weekends. Patients need the doctors there now, but they're not. The care for them is not arranged for the needs of the patient, but for the convenience of the staff. That variability that threatens quality care is because of the doctor, not the patient."[98]

Mary Lou Buyse, MD, a physician and geneticist, served with Litvak on a state commission looking into emergency care. Buyse, was president of the Massachusetts Association of Health Plans in 2003 and said Litvak had a bold and different approach to improving patient safety and outcomes and reducing costs. "He had a unique solution to solving our problem of ambulance diversions," said Buyse, who currently serves as the chief medical officer and senior vice president for the Smithfield-based Neighborhood Health Plan of Rhode Island.[99]

Mark Smith, MD, served with Litvak on the committee of the Institute of Medicine (now the National Academy of Medicine) to explore "The Future of Emergency Medicine," a 2006 report that endorsed Litvak's approach.[100] Smith, the president of the California Health Care Foundation from 1996 to 2013, still practices medicine and treats HIV patients. He had read Litvak's papers on queueing and reducing ambulance diversions and recommended that the foundation fund his work.

Smith sees the application of the scientific study of variability as part of a broader movement to bring modern operations management techniques to problems in healthcare. Smith said Litvak is dedicated to his mission to improve the quality and efficiency of America's healthcare system. "He has the persistence of a scientist who understands the importance of this work. That's what it takes. Few scientific advancers become heroes. It often takes 20 years. Eugene is a great example of someone who keeps pushing and pushing his ideas until everyone else can understand their importance."[101]

But the problems with ED overcrowding Litvak uncovered two decades ago continue, confirmed by recent studies, regulatory agency reports, and media investigations. A 2019 series on ambulance diversions by the *Milwaukee Journal Sentinel* found at least 21 deaths after patients were turned away from hospitals, "though that number is likely just a sample, given how widespread the practice is," and likely underestimates the total.[102]

Milwaukee County ended ambulance diversions in 2016, seven years after Massachusetts ended that practice. "Two-thirds of the largest 25 cities allow diversion or practices similar to it, including nine of the top 10," the series revealed, while noting: "Numerous studies have found diversion doesn't solve overcrowding and puts patients at risk by delaying care."[103]

A study of ambulance diversions among 14 San Francisco hospitals by that city's Emergency Medical Response, its 911 system, found the average percentage of time spent on diversion has grown from 6% in 2011 to 16% in 2019. However, within that cadre, there was wide variation. Chinese Hospital, which reported being on diversion status 40% of the time in 2013, dropped to zero by the end of 2019 and has remained under 10% since. But Zuckerberg San Francisco General Hospital, the city's only trauma center, reported diversion status 27% of the time in 2011, rising to 70% in 2021 and 2022.[104]

Litvak said those diversions sometimes portend dire consequences for patients, leading to greater complications and even death.[105]

Litvak: The Unlikely Media Darling

Litvak said it took him a while to recognize the power of the American media to drive discussion, influence elected leaders and regulators and spur business. "I thought that the media was the force that would bring my ideas into the public domain. After a few years of calling reporters, it began happening."[106]

Word spread. "The media started calling us and I welcomed that. There was coverage of our research and some of the hospital success stories in *Forbes*, *the Boston Globe*, and even *the Wall Street Journal*."

One example of Litvak's persistence in the face of resistance might be his pursuit of the healthcare journalist, editor, and author Susan Dentzer. In the late 1990s Dentzer was a prominent television healthcare reporter for public television's *PBS NewsHour with Jim Lehrer*.

"I called quite a few journalists, with mixed results. But Susan was responsive and asked about my work. I practically called her every month or two from 1997 until 2005 about developments in healthcare."[107]

Finally, in 2005 she came to BU with a crew from *PBS NewsHour* to interview Litvak. "I waited until he had enough research published and projects underway that I thought the story was worth telling,"

Dentzer said. "We taped it and the story worked out well. It was PBS, which has an intelligent audience, and it attracted attention."[108]

She said in the early 2000s the response of hospital administrators to ED overcrowding was to expand the ED and build more beds. "That was gospel. We, as a nation, and Boston as a city, just did not have enough ED capacity, we were told," Dentzer recalled. "And we're also having too many patients show up at the ED because they lacked insurance coverage. The issue of diversions was gaining some prominence. There was an underlying sense that diversions were bad for patients. But nobody had studied it, so there was no proof that patients were dying."[109]

She said Litvak did study emergency departments and took a more analytical and systemic approach, tracking the patient journey like an engineering process, which she said was anathema to physicians and hospital CEOs. "Litvak said if you analyze like an engineer, you see that the problem is not the ED, but the rest of the hospital. He was able to show that was the problem. A small coterie of ED physicians rallied around him then. He was able to pinpoint the problem that in many instances, hospitals were prioritizing elective surgeries over everything else."[110]

She said most people then believed that ED use was completely unpredictable: who could possibly know the number of injuries and accidents on a given day? "But his research showed that belief was wrong, that over time you could predict it pretty accurately."[111]

Dentzer said Litvak's contention that poor scheduling in hospital ORs caused ED overcrowding "so completely contradicted conventional wisdom on every front that it became the 'man bites dog' story. He got all the predictable pushback when someone like him contradicts conventional wisdom. But he was able to prove that if hospitals can smooth out their elective surgeries, they could not only become more efficient and perform more surgeries, but also save money. And if they could convince surgeons to operate every day of the week, they could reduce or eliminate ED overcrowding."[112] Litvak says that focusing on ED performance to reduce hospital overcrowding always reminds him of a joke: "Near midnight, a drunk man is walking in circles around a streetlamp. A policeman approaches him and asks what he's doing there. 'I am looking for my wallet,' the inebriated man replies. 'Where did you lose your wallet?' asks the policeman. The man pointed to the dark end of the street. 'Well, why are you still looking for it here?' the cop asks. 'Because there is more light here.'"[113]

■ ■ ■

Litvak said he was flying from Boston to Cincinnati with a business colleague on June 7, 2005, the day the Dentzer story would air on PBS about 30 minutes after their arrival. The two stopped in an airport bar to watch the show, perhaps the first time anyone has ever rushed into a bar and requested a PBS show. "I was particularly delighted," he recalled. "Because as soon as Susan finished the story, an interview with then British Premier Tony Blair aired. I thought I was in good company."[114]

The first televised airing of his ideas disappointed Litvak in one way, however. "When they were taping me, they suggested going outside on a bench beside the Charles River to shoot it, so I could compare patient flow to the traffic on the opposite side of the river, and all I had were these transitional lenses that grew darker outside. They made me look like a mafioso, and I had no other glasses, so she asked me to remove them. I looked like an idiot without my glasses."[115]

Vanity, thy name is Litvak. But he was thrilled by the exposure and the story. "By nature, I am an optimist. Every time something happened I thought, 'This will be a breakthrough. Now that it's been on PBS, I will have to fight hospitals off with a stick.' I thought I'd

A New Research Center as Emergency Department Overcrowding

finally made it. But that didn't happen. I was naïve," he said. "While these stories were good for my business and sometimes attracted potential new clients, they did not move the needle on hospital practices. I am still looking for who has the power in this country to do that."[116]

■ ■ ■

Litvak said he really began to recognize patterns between the pushback he faced when introducing a new HIV blood screening tool and the resistance from hospitals to his methods of controlling patient flow. "It was two different fields, but with many similarities," he explained. "My rose-colored glasses became a little clearer."[117]

He felt that resistance, but thought that the main reason his ideas were not more widely implemented was because of surgeon complaints. However, he later discovered that surgeons could be persuaded by data that his methods really do improve patient care and safety, as well as their work conditions.

"I came to believe that hospital CEOs were preempting the surgeons. They believed the surgeons would revolt and overreact, too fearful of taking risks. The government responds similarly. In both cases, I believe they are wrong."[118]

Nearly everyone who has worked with Litvak admires and agrees with his methods of improving care. But few hospitals have embraced his ideas. "Nobody has challenged me to say that what I propose is wrong," he said. "They just don't do it. After teaching at IHI for several years I sounded like a broken record."[119]

Sometimes, he said, hospital administrators remind him of another Russian joke: "A Soviet man on the street was asked if he has his own point of view. He said, 'Yes, but I disagree with it.'"[120]

Litvak said that literature teaches us that actions are driven by character. "I don't plan to stop fighting," he vowed.

Chapter 7

Physician Burnout and More Hospital Successes

By the mid-2000s Litvak believed his program for improving patient flow was "one step away from national adoption. I truly believed we were on the road to doing that," he said, citing projects in prestigious hospitals that included London's Great Ormond Street Hospital and at Johns Hopkins University Hospital, Greater Baltimore Medical Center, and the Mayo Clinic in Florida. "I believed if it was so good, everyone would jump in. I was embarrassingly wrong for my age. It just shows I don't learn."[1]

He said a friend who knew him from the time he arrived in the United States asked Litvak: How do you feel now about living in America? "I told him that I still like and admire many things here," he said. "But I am seeing some things similar to what I didn't like about living in Russia. Sometimes I feel as if I'm back in time and reliving my life again and again, like I know what's going to happen tomorrow. It's like that movie *Groundhog Day*, a weird déjà vu feeling that I know what will come next."[2]

Frustration seemed to follow every success. His disappointment stemmed from the glacial pace of change, but derived chiefly from the failure of hospital leaders to implement steps that would reduce medical errors, nurse stress – particularly severe during the COVID pandemic – and save patient lives and healthcare dollars.

Eugene Litvak's goal in the mid-2000s was to implement his methods of improving hospital patient care nationwide. He continued trying to reduce variability and improve patient flow in hospitals in the United States and abroad, focusing on problems and bottlenecks in healthcare delivery. He published research and discovered that his methods can reduce nurse and physician stress and burnout, conditions that harm patient care, lead to more mistakes, and drive clinicians from the field.

Now, Litvak points out, as US hospitals continued to confront the variations of the coronavirus, "they would rather cancel elective surgery than smooth it." Litvak said the coronavirus and the COVID disease it spread exposed hospital vulnerabilities just as periodic patient surges taxed staff resources. It is tough being a prophet in your own land, even in your adopted land. For two decades Litvak has tried to warn hospitals that if they are harming patients now, during routine spates of overcrowding, even without seasonal flu patients, waves of RSV (a less deadly, but still sometimes fatal condition, Respiratory Syncytial Virus) and those suffering from COVID, they need to confront the problem of mismanaged patient flow and implement the solution. "If they're not listening now, when will they?"

Political Leaders Supported Litvak

He was "only" the chief executive of one of New England's biggest health plans. But his success in the healthcare world in a progressive and sophisticated state like Massachusetts propelled Charlie Baker into the governor's seat. Today Governor Baker is the president of the National Collegiate Athletic Association (NCAA).

In a 2005 *Boston Globe* story, Baker, then the top leader of Harvard Pilgrim Health Care, said that when he first grasped the significance of flow management, he thought, "Oh my God, this is big!" Baker served on the advisory board of Litvak's BU Program for the Management of Variability in Health Care Delivery.[3] Baker also found space for Litvak at Harvard Pilgrim to teach his courses on variability and patient flow.[4]

Litvak was also writing to elected officials attempting to explain his ideas and enlist their support, meeting with, for example, US Rep. Barney Frank, D-Boston. "He [Frank] was very receptive," Litvak recalled. "But did nothing."

Litvak Examines Rapid Response Teams

After Don Berwick's Institute for Health Improvement began encouraging the establishment and deployment of Rapid Response Teams (RRTs), also known as Medical Emergency Teams (METs), in its 2004 "100,000 Lives" campaign to reduce hospital deaths, hospitals around the country began creating and deploying specialist teams to save the lives of patients on hospital units outside of the Intensive Care Units (ICUs).[5]

"An RRS (Rapid Response System) is a coordinated and organizational-wide approach to care for patients in crisis by getting the right resources and services to the patient as quickly as possible to prevent adverse patient outcomes," a 2015 *Joint Commission Journal on Quality and Patient Safety* survey explained, noting the groups "have the potential to improve both patient and broader organizational outcomes."[6]

RRTs are small groups comprised of physician and nurse intensivists who travel – sometimes from the ICU – to hospital rooms and intervene when patient conditions deteriorate quickly. "Simply put, the purpose of the Rapid Response Team is to bring critical care expertise to the patient bedside (or wherever it's needed)," according to the Institute for Healthcare Improvement.[7]

Litvak expressed skepticism about the care teams. In a September 2010 issue of the *Journal of the American Medical Association*, he co-authored a commentary paper on "Rapid Response Teams" with Peter Pronovost, MD, one of the nation's leading medical researchers and innovators, then with Johns Hopkins University Medical School in Baltimore.[8] "It was a very popular intervention then and deservedly still is. But it is being used more often than needed," Litvak said. "Teams of intensive care specialists are sent from the ICU to hospital floors to direct that care. Conditions deteriorate when a patient is placed in the wrong unit and provided with an inadequate level of care. And the patient is placed in an inappropriate unit because of overcrowding, because beds in the right unit were not available."[9]

While Litvak conceded that RRTs save lives, he calls them a "Band-Aid solution, and a costly one. In my lectures I tell my students, hospital executives, and physician leaders that they could save even more lives if they placed the patients in the hospital parking lot and sent RRTs out there. They would save more lives because they would endanger more lives in the first place," he said. "The solution is to address overcrowding, not place Band-Aids over it."[10]

"If a pilot was told there was inclement weather and was ordered not to fly, but did not heed the warnings, took off anyway, and still landed safely, should we reward the pilot for that?" Litvak asked, paraphrasing the JAMA piece. "That is exactly what is going on. In Ukraine we used to say, 'We create our own problems so we could successfully solve them ourselves.' This variability in patient flow has many ramifications on cost and quality throughout the hospital."[11]

Pronovost, a critical care physician who was named one of the 100 Most Influential People in the World by *Time* magazine, was a recipient of a MacArthur Foundation Fellowship. Pronovost, now the chief clinical transformation officer for University Hospitals of Cleveland, Ohio, said their 2010 *JAMA* study attempted "to get the field to look deeper for solutions that are highly effective, rather than quick fixes that may not be as effective as you thought. One of the challenges when people are dying needlessly is it causes moral dissonance. You want to look for quick solutions, and that innovating spirit is great. But when you stick to something that may not be effective, you give wind to it. What that piece did was help us to think like a systems engineer as we approach this and examine how all the parts fit together."[12]

Pronovost's 2010 book, *Safe Patients, Smart Hospitals: How One Doctor's Checklist Can Help Us Change Health Care from the Inside Out*, documented how using his basic checklist of evidence-based practices to prevent catheter infections saved 1,500 lives and $100 million in a project with the Michigan Health & Hospital Association.[13]

"What changed was the narrative," Pronovost said. "We used to see these things as inevitable. Now we say they are preventable and it's my social responsibility to fix them. So we have to change the narrative, aim for zero infections and connect people to learning groups to improve their ability to implement practice changes. We have to align around the narrative of zero harm and design interventions to get them to zero."[14]

Pronovost believes that healthcare is grossly under-engineered, particularly relating to systems engineering. "Systems engineering has the greatest potential to drive value, lower cost, and improve care. If we apply what we know works, we could dramatically improve value in care. But healthcare didn't grow out of the engineering discipline, but an apprentice system. People like Eugene and me shine that lens on healthcare," he said, pointing out that operations management and systems engineering are well-grounded sciences accepted in every other discipline.[15]

"He [Litvak] brings state of the art science to healthcare. The science of smoothing and flow demonstrate over and over again that these things work and improve outcomes and save lives and a ton of money."[16]

Mandatory Nurse Staffing Laws

In 1999 the state of California passed a law after heavy lobbying by the state's largest nurses' union, the California Nurses Association, requiring mandatory minimum nurse-patient staffing ratios. To date, California's law, which took effect in 2004, remains the only state law mandating nurse staffing ratios. But in 2019, similar proposals failed passage in Illinois and Massachusetts. But as recently as 2021, a national nurse staffing law was introduced into the US House and Senate and other states continue to debate the issue.[17]

Pronovost said there is evidence that adequate nurse staffing improves outcomes. If hospitals in New Jersey and Pennsylvania equaled California's nurse-patient staffing ratios in the medical surgical units in those states, then New Jersey would have experienced 13.9% fewer patient deaths and Pennsylvania 10.6% fewer deaths in 2006, according to a 2010 study by the University of Pennsylvania's Linda Aiken, PhD.[18] In her study, Aiken surveyed responses from more than 22,000 nurses in 600 hospitals in those three states, noting that if those two states alone had adopted California's nurse staffing ratio, they might have saved the lives of 486 general surgery patients over two years just by staffing more nurses. "California hospital nurses cared for one less patient on average than nurses in New Jersey and Pennsylvania . . . and an average of two fewer patients on medical and surgical units."[19] The study concluded that "better nurse staffing is associated with better nurse and patient outcomes."[20]

Pronovost agreed the evidence is solid that adequate nurse staffing matters in hospitals: It saves lives and money. But he has two problems with a legislative mandated approach to resolving the issue. "Nursing ratios are impacted by many other things, like support staff numbers, the presence of nurse practitioners, and various tech support staff. Mandating staffing ratios takes this complex system and legislates one component of it without controlling for other variables," he reasoned. "Even more problematic, legislation is too slow and blunt of an instrument to keep up with the rapid advances of science and would anchor us to poor practices."[21]

Pronovost said implementing Litvak's methods to improve patient flow and smooth surgeries, as well as new technologies like wireless monitoring, could reduce the need for legislated staffing mandates. Litvak opposes mandatory nurse staffing laws, except as a last resort if patient flow is not managed optimally.[22] "But if you tell me my choice is between maintaining the status quo and legislation, I choose the latter. Why are nurses demanding ratios? Because they need them. Their patients need them. Almost 10 years ago I said we'd never get rid of this problem: nurses are demanding staffing ratios because they cannot safely take care of the surges of patients thrust upon them. Sooner or later, if hospitals do nothing to improve patient flow, staffing ratios will be legislated."[23]

But Litvak warned that legislated mandates can produce unforeseen consequences. "Imagine being a hospital CEO. Legally, you have to provide a set number of nurses to care for a certain number of patients. So if you have more patients and don't have enough nurses, which patients would you reject? You have to reject someone. So you'll turn away the patients who pay less, those who come in through the ED. California has some of the highest rates of ambulance diversion. The mandates may explain that."[24]

What Does Patient Flow Have to Do with Nurse Stress and Burnout?

Litvak organized a conference at Boston University on nurse staffing and quality issues. "It was so successful that they had to return checks to some prospective attendees because they couldn't accommodate the demand, which was unusual," he said, noting that almost 300 attended. "Everybody was receptive, and the conference received the highest evaluations I ever got. The sessions dealt with staffing, burnout, and variability in patient flow and the audience was comprised of nurses. We documented that surgical flow is one of the main, if not *the* main determinant of overcrowding. They were surprised and happy that we documented the cause."[25]

He said that dozens of publications have demonstrated how nurse staffing affects quality of care, readmissions, and mortality. "That was new. And then we showed the solution. What was happening reminds me of a joke. It's a reflection of what's going on with nurses and healthcare in general."

"Soviet Premier Joseph Stalin was riding in a train when it stopped. An aide approached him and told the volatile leader there were no more rails in front of the train and their journey was halted. Stalin said, 'Execute whoever is running the train and the minister of transportation.' The same situation confronted Premier Nikita Krushchev. 'Take the rails from behind the train and reset them in front of the train.' Leonid Brezhnev advised, 'Let's close the curtains on the windows and shake the train to pretend that we're moving.' Finally, Mikhail Gorbachev said, 'Comrade: Open all the windows and scream as loud as you can that there are no rails in front of train.'"[26]

"We ignore our problems in healthcare. If you go into any other industry and do something wrong, they're embarrassed about it and try to fix it. In healthcare, we take our wounds as a matter of pride."[27]

Litvak said in the early 2000s, he began to read new research in medical journals linking nurse staffing shortages to adverse events. Those studies pointed to a variety of serious problems impacting patient care and nurse retention. He understood that his methods to improve patient flow, bolster staffing, and shrink overcrowding would also reduce nurse stress and the errors it causes.

"The media jumped at this issue shortly after the state of California passed its mandatory nurse staffing law. These peaks and valleys in patient flow affect everything in hospitals. I was trying to connect my ideas with a focus of public attention. Nobody cared about ED overcrowding, I thought, so maybe they'll care about mortality rates. I was wrong again," he admitted. "In 2020 to 2022 we had this coronavirus and yet they [hospitals] still didn't want to smooth patient flow, which would have expanded their capacity to treat more patients and reduce staff burnout. I do not know what else it would take to get their attention. A biblical Sodom and Gomorrah?"[28]

Litvak said there are several ways to staff a hospital with nurses to meet the patient demand. "First, you staff at the peak [highest] patient census. All these problems would disappear if you did that. The only problem is nobody has the money or nurses to staff at the peak because occupancy doesn't reach the peak every day. So that is not feasible, though hospitals did that for decades when their reimbursements were high and they didn't have to worry about money."[29]

He said the second solution is to create a dynamic pool of nurses, so when there is a peak in demand those nurses can be summoned to work. "The problem with that is bed occupancy in different wards changes every hour or two and for nurses to react in a timely way, they'd almost have to live in the hallway. Because, by the time they come in from their homes, that peak could have dropped into a valley. Then you waste money."[30]

The third option is mandatory nurse staffing laws like California's, which require hospitals to staff some legislated minimum ratio, for example, one nurse for every six patients, depending upon the severity of the patient condition. That potential solution also brings other problems.

He said the fourth possible solution is the most prevalent one. "Most hospitals create nursing task forces or committees to look into it," he said. "Nothing changes, but later they can say they formed a committee. The only outcome is the scheduling of the next committee meeting."[31]

Litvak said that most hospital executives staff to the average daily patient census, which doesn't resolve the dilemma of peaks and valleys. What's left? "Controlling patient flow. Smoothing those peaks and valleys. These five possibilities cover every conceivable option. When I ask hospital executives: which option do you choose for your hospital? The answer I get is the equivalent of 'Take a hike.' Because nobody wants to answer [that question]."[32] Because, he said, then hospital executives would have to admit that they are putting their patients at risk.

Nurse Stress and Burnout Are Costly and Harm Patients

The mounting evidence Litvak cited of a strong association between nurse staffing and patient quality care grew stronger in the early 2000s. Healthcare quality organizations, researchers, and provider associations released membership surveys and studies exploring the harms of nurse understaffing.

A 2001 survey found that the primary motivation for nurses to leave patient care positions (besides retirement) was to find decreased stress and less physically demanding work (56%). Respondents in that Peter D. Hart Research Associates study identified the biggest problems with nursing was understaffing (39%) and the stress and physical demands of the job (38%).[33]

One year later a report from the Joint Commission (formerly the Joint Commission on the Accreditation of Healthcare Organizations) revealed that nursing shortages pose risks to patient safety and contributed to nearly one-quarter of the Commission's sentinel events – unanticipated and preventable events that result in death, injury, or permanent loss of function – reported to the Commission in the previous five years. No hospital wants a sentinel event: wrong site surgeries, falls, suicides, and medication errors are embarrassing, harmful to reputation, and costly in legal fees and settlements. "Higher acuity patients plus fewer nurses to care for them is a prescription for danger," the report stated.[34]

"We now have clear data linking nurse staffing levels to quality of care," said Dennis O'Leary, MD, then president of the Joint Commission. "We didn't have that before."[35] The report found that the nursing shortage "is putting patient lives in danger and requires immediate attention."[36]

More evidence of higher mortality risks was bolstered by another study by the University of Pennsylvania's Linda Aiken and colleagues writing in 2002 for the *Journal of the American Medical Association*.[37] The authors found that when nurses cared for more patients than recommended staffing levels, the risk of dying grew exponentially for those patients. If the patient census grows more than 25% over the staffing level, those new patients face a 14% increase in mortality rates.[38]

Each extra patient per nurse was associated with a 7% increase in the risk of dying within 30 days of admission and a 7% increase in the odds of failure to rescue. But patients were not the only victims. The researchers also found that each additional patient per nurse was associated with a 23% increase in the odds of nurse burnout. "In hospitals with high patient-to-nurse ratios, surgical patients experience higher risk-adjusted mortality and failure to rescue rates and nurses are more likely to experience burnout and job dissatisfaction," the authors found.[39]

Hospital executives have also been aware of this crisis for decades. In a 2001 American Hospital Association survey of hospital executives, respondents reported that the nursing shortage caused a flurry of problems in their hospitals, including emergency department overcrowding (38%), diversion of emergency patients (25%), reduced numbers of staffed beds (23%), and cancellations of elective surgeries (10%).[40]

A different study seemed to demonstrate the efficacy of improved hospital staffing. "Nurse-Staffing Levels and Quality of Care in Hospitals," published in the *New England Journal of Medicine* concluded that more hours of care and higher proportion of care delivered by registered nurses was associated with better care for hospitalized patients. It showed shorter hospital stays, lower rates of both urinary tract infection and upper gastrointestinal bleeding, lower rates of pneumonia, shock, or cardiac arrest and "failure to rescue" (defined as death from those conditions), or sepsis and deep vein thrombosis when hospitals staffed registered nurses and allowed them more time to spend with patients.[41]

Marilyn Rudolph, a retired surgical services director with VHA and faculty member with Don Berwick's IHI, said Litvak's methods offer hospitals and clinicians the ability to achieve far more predictable scheduling in contrast to the ups and downs common to every OR she's encountered. That variability is the crux of many quality and financial issues.[42]

"More predictable scheduling impacts staffing and allows hospitals to get patients through the system while accommodating emergent and urgent patients. His methods hands-down make far more sense than anything I've encountered throughout my career. My eyes were opened when I learned about managing patient variability and the impact they have on quality and how we delivery healthcare."[43]

She said Litvak's methods help hospitals deliver the right care in the right setting at the right time. It takes the variability, which can cause chaos, out of the system. It is based on data. "You cannot manage without data. His method identifies where the trouble spots are and shows how to work through those trouble spots to bring predictability between emergencies and the day-to-day OR flow."[44] Litvak participated in some of the research, co-authoring a 2005 paper for the *Joint Commission Journal on Quality and Patient*

Safety, finding that "Increases in adverse clinical outcomes have been documented when hospital nurse staffing is inadequate."[45]

The study revealed that "Since most hospitals limit nurse staffing to levels for average, rather than peak patient census, substantial census increases create serious potential stresses for both patients and nurses. By reducing unnecessary variability, hospitals can reduce many of these stresses and thereby improve patient safety and quality of care."[46] The authors blamed "system stress introduced by demands for nurses to care for more or sicker patients has been shown to be a leading cause of adverse patient outcomes."[47]

"Preventable medical errors and excessive mortality rates will continue to occur, therefore, as long as the health care system in the United States fails to mitigate the stresses that contribute to operational dysfunction," the authors wrote. They found that "a fundamental cause of error and injury in health care is stress, which appears in turn to reflect variation in workload" and recommended a better understanding and management of that variation.[48]

The Mayo Clinic Signs Up

The Mayo Clinic is arguably the most famous medical center in America. It is the first and largest integrated not-for-profit physician group practice in the world, employing 3,800 physicians and scientists and more than 50,000 allied health staff, serving more than 1.1 million patients annually at 18 hospitals and scores of clinics. The clinic dates to the 1880s when the brothers Will and Charles Mayo joined their father's medical practice in Rochester, Minnesota. Since then, the Mayo Clinic has expanded services to multiple US states. The Mayo routinely attracts patients from around the world, from royalty to foreign heads of state to celebrities and billionaires, lured by the high-quality medical care, "team" concept of treatment, and reputation for innovation. So it was no surprise that the Mayo, one of the most innovative health systems in America, hired Litvak to improve patient flow.[49]

Denis Cortese, MD, one of the most influential and progressive voices in healthcare and an advisor to US presidents, was the former president of the Mayo Clinic Health System. Cortese served on the advisory board of Litvak's IHO. He is currently the director of the Center for Healthcare Delivery at Arizona State University and teaches health policy there.[50]

Cortese, who worked for the Mayo Clinic for 40 years, said the organization is steeped in systems engineering. "When I got there, I understood that the system makes everyone better," he said, pointing out that the clinic staffed a department of systems engineers.[51] "They were like Eugene: always thinking about how to best manage change and workflow," he recalled, noting that in the 1990s he edited a book on systems engineering in healthcare, which was how he met Litvak.[52] "Litvak and our team were able to achieve improvements in our Jacksonville OR, even though we were already doing quite well. Mayo always likes to make things better," he said.

According to Cortese, "The kind of work Litvak does is aimed at producing the results that patients want. They don't expect to come into a hospital and die. They don't expect medical errors or injuries to happen. His system is designed to reduce errors and mistakes. Patients will have positive experiences without complications or errors made. Their care will be delivered in a timely way, and they will go home smoothly."[53]

He said under Litvak's system, physicians experience fewer delays in getting medication to patients and fewer delays getting patients into operating rooms. Nurses have better experiences with patients. "Just having the food delivered on time will make a big difference," Cortese said. And hospital administrators will see more income and patients flowing through their hospital more smoothly, fewer problems with billing and an improved hospital reputation. If the hospital manages it correctly, there is a win-win all around."[54] Cortese said one barrier to achieving better healthcare results is that the United States lacks a common vision of what constitutes high-value healthcare.[55]

"If you want better health outcomes, link payments to better outcomes and services," he said, noting that many things happen to sick people in hospitals that go unexplained: mistakes, do-overs, providers performing more procedures and more highly paid specialist fees.[56]

Cortese said that hospitals are grappling with how to respond to changes in the healthcare marketplace and navigate two different payment systems reimbursing them for care, reimbursements that incentivize different hospital behaviors. The fee-for-service (FFS) system pays hospitals and physicians by the service or days spent in the hospital: the more operations, tests, and days in the hospital, the more everyone is paid. However, for nearly one decade, the healthcare system has been transitioning toward a "pay for value" reimbursement system, wherein government and private health plans pay hospitals and clinicians for quality care. This system serves to keep members healthy while managing their care outside of hospitals when possible, preventing complications and delivering and managing their care as safely and efficiently as possible at home. "We need a key commitment from the government to change the way payments are made. Because whatever Medicare does, the whole country follows," Cortese said. "We can easily reduce the amount of money we spend on healthcare in this country by $1 trillion. But we have to pay providers differently to make that happen and work to keep people as healthy as we can."[57]

He said Litvak is really trying to change the system. "I was skeptical whether he could do much at Mayo, but he did. If people can learn from him and do it themselves, there is a big chance this process can accelerate, particularly if new payment models are accepted to drive change. If those come out in the marketplace, he won't have to look for customers," Cortese predicted. "They'll come to him."[58]

In the early 2000s former IHI faculty member, Dr. Resar, worked at the Mayo's Luther-Midelfort Hospital in Eau Claire, Wisconsin. With Litvak's support, Resar employed his teacher's methods to improve patient flow there. Time spent on ambulance diversion dropped from 12% to under 2%, while the number of patients finding beds within an hour after arriving in the ED rose from 23% to 40% and revenues increased by $2.5 million annually. Luther-Midelfort's CEO then was William Rupp, MD, who replaced Denis Cortese at Mayo Clinic in Florida when Cortese was promoted to head the entire Mayo Clinic Health System.[59]

Leading the Jacksonville implementation was C. Daniel Smith, MD, a board-certified general surgeon now at the Esophageal Institute of Atlanta, Georgia. In the late 2000s, Smith was surgeon-in-chief in Jacksonville.

"I became a serious student of Eugene's methodology and the role variability plays in our healthcare system. What I learned from Eugene was how to gather and analyze day-to-day operations data and put it back together in a more rational way to manage this variability, then hypothesize how it could translate into performance metrics in healthcare," Smith recalled.[60]

Smith said patients and their families are clueless about the impact of overcrowding in hospitals until it happens to them. "If there is overcrowding, but no complication, they will remember it only as an inconvenience. It's only when there is a complication that it becomes an absolute outrage. And not many patients experience that directly. As a surgeon, though, I see it 100 times more than the average person. We need to help people understand how inappropriate this is and how preventable it is."[61]

Smith said he was proud of the work he and the Mayo team did. His title as Mayo's surgeon-in-chief was not an honorary, but a command position with authority over the entire surgical practice, which produced $250 million annually in revenue. He described himself in the early 2000s as "a student of change, a career long agent of change," even dating back to his administrative residency at the Mayo Medical School, when he received the "Winds of Change Award."[62]

"I got hired in Jacksonville to guide change," he said. "When Eugene came along with this idea, it was a natural platform for change for me and I was well positioned to do it. I have since learned why change doesn't happen. Things don't change because most people (85% to 90%) don't want to change. They seek comfort, and change is not comfortable. But then there are the 10% to 15% of people who are just the opposite and cannot settle for the status quo. They have to change. That's Eugene."[63] He said both he and Litvak arrived at Mayo a little naïve.

"We thought the Mayo Clinic was the perfect place to implement his program because the surgeons there were employed and fully integrated throughout the delivery system," Smith said, explaining that Mayo doctors are paid salaries, not compensated by traditional fee-for-service metrics like productivity and performing more surgeries.[64]

They spent more than one year planning and gathering data and redesigning the OR schedule. He said Mayo's surgical case volume grew by 4% and utilization improved by 5%. At the same time OR overtime staffing dropped by 37%. Annual staff turnover costs fell by $1.07 million, and the hospital's annual OR net revenue grew by $5 million.[65]

Smith said the difficulty of implementation, even in the face of proven benefits, is high. "The other cost to the healthcare system is of not doing it. And while those costs are measurable, they are not costs that make it into the boardroom when the CFO presents his financial report," he explained. For example, patients forced to

Physician Burnout and More Hospital Successes

sleep in hallways when no beds are available might end up with longer lengths of stay. Nurses who care for patients over multiple shifts might burn out and leave the hospital. He said the absence of those difficult-to-quantify financial conditions might partially explain why hospital boards aren't pressuring CEOs to resolve these problems.[66]

Johns Hopkins Improves, Too

Johns Hopkins Hospital is a fabled teaching hospital and research center for the Johns Hopkins School of Medicine in Baltimore, Maryland. The 130-year-old hospital attracts some of the best physicians and researchers in the world, and the hospital is usually ranked as one of the nation's best.

Julie Freischlag, MD, is the current chief executive officer of Wake Forest Baptist Health and dean of the Wake Forest School of Medicine. But she was a professor and the chief of surgery at Johns Hopkins Hospital when Litvak was hired to improve patient flow there.

"Julie was one of the few surgical chairs who really got engaged in the activity. She anticipated the resistance and knowingly pushed for this intervention. I experienced this resistance only behind her back. She's very quiet and very calm. But somehow, she made this resistance disappear," Litvak recalled, noting that the hospital was in transition and opening new OR suites.[67]

He said Freischlag accomplished that by seeking consensus to achieve buy-in from all the related parties, surgeons, anesthesiologists, nurses, and administrators, meeting and listening and integrating what she learned into the process. "Most of our hospital clients would say, 'Let's wait until we build new OR suites or implement EPIC' [the most popular electronic medical records program]. The bottom line for most of them is 'tomorrow is better than today.' But she used the knowledge she acquired during the transition to the ORs."[68]

Freischlag, who has led education and training programs at top medical schools in her roles as professor and chair of surgery and vascular surgery departments, said Litvak presented to a group of 25 Hopkins' nurses, surgeons, and anesthesiologists.[69]

"We were trying to change the culture and facing huge skepticism. He studied our data and kept hammering on us every week for months. He showed us where to release (surgical) block times and we saw that it started to work. It made us able to do emergency and urgent work more efficiently and helped us to illustrate what we needed to build," she said. "That work predicted the future for us and still works very well."[70]

She said surgeons typically 'hit and run and leave,' moving on to the next procedure once they complete the previous operation.[71] "They [surgeons] worried if they gave up their block times, they'd lose cases and lose money," said Freischlag, a past president of the American College of Surgeons. "Some would book cases under false names or not show, wasting manpower and resources. The focus was not on the patient, but on the surgeons then. I was that way, too, when I did surgery. It was all about me, not the patient. This made us think which patient should go next, not which surgeon. We changed the culture to patient-centered care. Eugene proved it with data, got things done, made it about the process, which is about the patient."[72]

And Hopkins reaped the rewards. The teaching hospital saw wait times for emergent/urgent surgical cases decrease by 39%. Physicians could treat an additional five cases per day in the main hospital ORs and four cases per day in the outpatient facility, Freischlag said. Overtime decreased by 6.6%. And the increase in surgical volume netted an additional annual $4 million revenue.[73]

■ ■ ■

Johns Hopkins and Mayo Clinic in Florida achieved significant results by only partly implementing Litvak's methods for improving patient flow. To date, just one hospital – the Cincinnati Children's Hospital – has totally embraced his program throughout the hospital's many departments, reaping huge financial rewards and substantial gains in quality, improvements that have lasted more than 15 years and benefited thousands of patients.

Eugene Litvak's paternal grandparents, Jacob and Faina Litvak, around 1953. Jacob Litvak was hung by drunken soldiers seeking gold. His life was saved by a thick coat collar, which kept him from strangling until he was rescued.

Litvak's maternal grandmother, Lisa Shachnovich, early 1930s. Litvak's maternal grandparents and great grandparents were moderately wealthy, but their property was confiscated by the Bolsheviks and they died poor.

Anton Shachnovich, Litvak's maternal grandfather, playing his violin. Shachnovich was a gifted musician. Litvak did not inherit this gene.

Litvak's father, Israel Litvak (bottom left), recovering with other wounded soldiers in a Kyrgyzstan hospital in 1941 during World War II. He met his future wife, Anna Shachnovich, at the hospital, where she worked as a nurse and helped him recuperate.

Litvak's maternal grandmother, Lisa Shachnovich, early 1930s.

The Litvak Family: Israel and Anna and Eugene (lower), circa 1952–1953. Litvak's parents listened illegally to Voice of America, even at the height of the Cold War.

Litvak on the balcony of the family's Kiev apartment with his mother. Before the Russian Revolution the apartment was occupied by one family. By the late 1940s, five or six families—as many as 15 people—occupied that apartment.

Litvak's first day of school in the uniform he wore proudly, 1956.

Zhenya Litvak's musical career lasted one week. His school orchestra assigned him the baritone horn, but tenants complained so loudly about his playing that Litvak was forced to return the instrument.

Eugene Litvak standing before the Winter Palace in Leningrad (now St. Petersburg), USSR, December, 1966. Though he earned top grades, Litvak seldom attended classes and after three years was expelled and returned home to Kiev in humiliation.

Litvak at his desk in the Reliability Lab of the Kiev Branch of the Soviet Central Institute of Telecommunications in 1976. By the late 1970s Litvak's research was gaining worldwide acclaim.

Litvak and his wife, Ella, at their favorite Soviet vacation spot, the Lithuanian city of Druskininkai, 1976. Druskininkai is a spa resort near the Polish and Belarussian borders.

Litvak with Claude Shannon of the Massachusetts Institute of Technology at Shannon's home outside of Boston. Shannon was a towering figure in international mathematics and telecommunications, a World War II cryptographer, and the "Father of Information Theory."

Litvak with some of the "Gods of Math" at his first American apartment outside of Boston in 1993. Boris Gnedenko, a giant in international mathematics, visited the U.S. that year. (Left to Right) Judith Chernoff, wife of Herman Chernoff; Litvak's wife, Ella Litvak; Herman Chernoff, a world renowned statistician; Gnedenko; Litvak's Ph.D. advisor, Igor Ushakov; Gnedenko's son, Dmitry Gnedenko.

Eugene Litvak, Ph.D., at his office at the Institute for Healthcare Optimization (IHO) in Newton, Mass.

The Harvard School of Public Health's Department of Biostatistics, December 1993, which hosted Boris Gnedenko (center), Soviet mathematician and physicist Akiva Yaglom (right), who emigrated to the U.S. from the USSR in 1992 and taught at MIT. (Litvak is left.)

Litvak's nonprofit Institute for Healthcare Optimization attracted some of the top names in healthcare for its Advisory Board. From left to right, they are: Sir Cyril Chantler, chairman of the University College London Partners Academic Health Science Partnership; Benjamin Chu, president, Kaiser Permanente–Southern California; Mark Smith, president and CEO, California Healthcare Foundation; Sandy Schwartz, Leon Hess Professor of Medicine and Health Management and Economics, School of Medicine and the Wharton School, University of Pennsylvania; Eugene Litvak, president and CEO, IHO; James Tallon, president of the United Hospital Fund of New York, chair of the Kaiser Commission on Medicaid and the Uninsured and Secretary/Treasurer of the Alliance for Health Reform; Helen Darling, president and CEO, National Business Group on Health; Richard Umbdenstock, president and CEO, American Hospital Association; Susan Dentzer, former Editor in Chief, Health Affairs; Glenn Steele, president and CEO, Geisinger Health System; Michael McGinnis, senior scholar and executive director, Institute of Medicine; William Pierskalla, professor and former dean, Anderson School of Management at University of California Los Angeles and former president of the International Federation of Operational Research Societies.

Chapter 8

The Rest of the Hospital and Healthcare

As we've seen in earlier chapters, Litvak's program for smoothing patient flow has worked in hospital emergency rooms, operating rooms, maternity wards, and stress labs, in community hospitals, giant academic medical centers, teaching hospitals, and children's hospitals. But in the last decade it also has been adopted successfully in hospital telemetry units and even outside of the hospital, in a community health center, a federally funded outpatient clinic that treats the poor and uninsured.

Litvak has seen that his program can save money and lives in many healthcare settings, both inpatient and outpatient. He pointed out that there are at least four problems caused by the ineffective management of patient flow: emergency department overcrowding and limited access to care, nurse understaffing and overloading, diminished quality of patient care, and unnecessarily high healthcare costs.[1]

A 2010 Institute of Medicine report, "Best Care at Lower Cost: The Path to Continuously Learning Health Care," found that nearly 30% of healthcare expenditures in the United States ($760 billion to $935 billion then, well over $1 trillion now) is wasted. Litvak, who served on the committee that issued this report, believes – and numerous studies have confirmed – that his program to reduce variation reduces that waste and benefits patients as well, including decreasing harmful overcrowding.[2]

A 2013 survey of hospitalists (internal medicine physicians whose practice is confined to serving hospitalized patients) published in *Journal of the American Medical Association Internal Medicine*, found that 40% of hospitalists reported that their typical inpatient census exceeded safe levels at least monthly, and 36% of those reported a frequency greater than once per week.[3]

Patient Flow Matters in Telemetry

Telemetry is a hospital unit where patients are admitted or transferred, often in critical condition, requiring constant electronic monitoring. Telemetry units also require low nurse–patient staffing ratios (a typical telemetry unit staffing ratio of one nurse to three patients) because of the amount of care and monitoring the patients need. It's also a high-cost unit because of all the sophisticated and expensive monitoring equipment required. But leaders in one hospital saw an opportunity to reduce costs and improve care in this unit.

In 2013 IHO was hired by the New Jersey Hospital Association on a federal hospital quality improvement program called "Partnership for Patients" through the Centers for Medicare and Medicaid Services (CMS). The program, funded through the Affordable Care Act, was an effort to support hospitals undertaking quality improvement initiatives. One of the 14 hospitals that contracted with IHO was Newark (New Jersey)–based Beth Israel Medical Center, where Robert Lahita, MD, served as chairman of medicine and vice president from 2007 to 2017.

"I have to give him [Lahita] big credit for what was done at Newark Beth Israel," Litvak said. "When we started, they had 90 telemetry beds and the average wait in the emergency department to get into a hospital telemetry bed was 15 hours. We discovered that they often placed patients in telemetry beds who shouldn't have been there and then were slow to discharge them, causing bottlenecks, long waits, and high costs."[4]

Litvak said that the results of IHO work at Beth Israel far exceeded his expectations. He said the hospital changed its admissions, discharge, and transfer practices and developed consensus for what vital signs and diagnostic test results should be required to meet telemetry medical admissions standards. For example, a patient should be sent home as soon as that patient is ready to go and only patients that meet the right medical criteria should be hospitalized.

"If you rely on common sense, that's a big mistake, because common sense is not compatible with our healthcare delivery system. If I give you a choice: Do you want to drive a Lamborghini or a Ford Escort, given that I'm paying for it? A doctor, like anyone else, would say the Lamborghini. A doctor would always prefer a telemetry bed for his or her patients, even though it is not always an appropriate choice."[5]

He said Beth Israel lacked protocols for determining when a patient should be admitted to a telemetry unit. And because many patients were unnecessarily admitted there – they didn't meet guidelines – it became more difficult and a longer wait to admit patients who truly belonged there. Litvak said he talked with Lahita about prioritizing telemetry beds and the hospital adopted it. With IHO help, the hospital developed patient admission and discharge criteria at the telemetry unit.[6] "It was a huge amount of work on Bob's shoulders. He personally checked and did rounds and as a result of that, the hospital discovered it only needed 64 telemetry beds (instead of 90). Because of that intervention, their 15-hour average waiting time dropped down to 3 hours. Their length of stay was reduced by one full day and their profit margin in telemetry improved by over $10 million per year."[7]

Litvak said that since the hospital reduced the need for telemetry beds, it freed up nurses for other hospital units, dropping from 30 nurses to 21. After careful review, Beth Israel began placing more patients in regular hospital beds, where constant high-tech monitoring

The Rest of the Hospital and Healthcare

is not as vital, and where the nurse-patient staffing ratio is 1 to 5 – lower than in the telemetry unit. "You're adding nursing resources without added staffing, without spending a penny," Litvak said.[8]

Lahita, a rheumatologist specializing in auto immune diseases, now serves as chairman of medicine at St. Joseph's Healthcare Patterson, New Jersey. He said Beth Israel's administration supported his efforts in the one-year project that launched in 2013–2014.

Lahita said Beth Israel chose telemetry for the Litvak project because those beds are among the most expensive to staff and operate within hospitals.[9] "I went to the ED daily to review patients admitted to the hospital and would downgrade patients to keep them from being automatically sent to telemetry. I cut that admission rate to telemetry by 50%: not by turning them away from the hospital, but by redirecting them to the appropriate bed for their condition. We managed to save millions of dollars and decrease our length of stay to an all-time low," he said.[10]

But Lahita conceded that the process was labor intensive at Beth Israel. It required the creation of a list of telemetry bed admission criteria, which were codified on laminated cards and distributed to doctors. Then a nurse collected data, and argued with physicians whether their patients were appropriate for telemetry unit admission.

"Our data showed the majority of backups in our ED centered on bottlenecks relating to telemetry beds. A telemetry bed request can keep you in the ED for hours and even days if a bed is not available. After we implemented Litvak's methods, 90% of the time in Newark those beds were made available much sooner."[11]

Lahita, who earned a PhD in microbiology and molecular genetics, said at his hospital and many other urban, public, and teaching hospitals, most patients now are admitted through the emergency department, what he called "the front door of the hospital." He said as much as 40% of hospital patients don't belong in the hospital and can be safely and more cost effectively treated in other care settings.

Plus, the failure to discharge patients early in the day costs hospitals and health plans huge amounts of money.[12]

"If your Hilton hotel said check-out time is at noon, you would comply with that rule," Lahita said. "But try to do that at a hospital, where the average cost of a room is $3,000 per day. For length of stay rounds, we spent an hour on specific floors each day and worked with nurses to get patients discharged in a timely way. If you could solve that problem [of unnecessary hospital stays], you could save hundreds of billions of dollars nationally."[13]

Betsy Ryan, president and CEO of the New Jersey Hospital Association, said that a 2012 program that 14 Garden State hospitals participated in with Litvak saw big gains in hospital capacity. The NJHA found 11,800 to 17,300 additional patients that could be treated without adding inpatient beds or operating rooms, 20,000 additional patients that could be accommodated in hospital emergency departments, and a range of between 21% to 85% decreases in wait times for emergency department patients to be admitted to hospital beds.

"The results are consistent with the goals of the Affordable Care Act – to reduce healthcare costs through improved efficiency," Ryan said in a 2013 article. "But each of those efficiency standards also yield important results in improved quality and safety for patients."[14]

■ ■ ■

Healthcare Experts Agree: The Future Has Arrived and It Looks Like Litvak

John Halamka, MD, trained as an emergency physician, but is a man of many interests. He is one of the world's leading experts in poisonous mushrooms, treating 900 patients annually around the globe remotely through his Harvard telemedicine clinic. He is best known, however, as an information technology guru who served as chief information officer for the Harvard Medical School and as the chairman of the Healthcare Information Technology Standards Panel, which set standards for electronic health records (EHRs).

Halamka, a vegan who, with his wife, operates an organic produce farm, accomplishes so much partly because he does not sleep, but only naps a few times a day. He calls Litvak's work in improving hospital operations "extraordinary," noting that several Harvard-affiliated hospitals have adopted Litvak's methods to improve patient flow and reduce wait times and delays. *Modern Healthcare* reporter Joseph Conn, once needing a deadline interview with Halamka, conducted it via phone while the versatile physician was dangling from climbing spikes on the face of Yosemite National Park's climber's mecca, El Capitan.[15]

"I could argue that the United States doesn't really have a healthcare system, but a lot of disconnected pharmacies, clinics, and hospitals," Halamka said. "Amid that kind of chaos, expecting a precision Swiss watch is not what you're going to get. There isn't a lot of consistency."[16]

However, Halamka said, the health system is moving – perhaps too slowly – to a value-based system that compensates healthcare providers based on the quality of their outcomes. "In an environment like that, hospitals would spend money on workflow," he predicted.[17]

He said in his 25 years in hospital administration he's learned that standardizing processes reduces costs. "If you standardize hospital workflow, emergency department workflow will be faster, patients won't be boarded on gurneys in hallways and will be admitted to the right hospital room. Physicians and nurses will feel less stress because there will be less variation in patient census, fewer peaks and valleys. Patients won't get unnecessary tests and drugs," he explained. "By taking the waste out of the system, hospitals will have more capacity, higher throughput at a lower cost and will become more profitable."[18]

He said as the US healthcare system moves to value-based purchasing, hospitals will be given economic incentives to deliver wellness and quality care, as opposed to payment for "heads in beds." Halamka said that widespread adoption of Litvak's methods is a function of alignment of incentives.

Halamka cited the science fiction author William Gibson, whom he said nailed one of the primary problems plaguing US healthcare. "Gibson said, 'The future is already here, it's just not very evenly distributed.'"[19]

"If you look at the Mayo Clinics, Geisinger Health Systems, Johns Hopkins, and Kaiser Permanente Health Systems, they share long and successful histories of aligning incentives, and those places are more profitable than the hospitals choosing the status quo."[20] He conceded that many of Litvak's recommendations aren't adopted by hospitals because they present political challenges. "One challenge he faces is that you can't expect revolutionary outcomes unless his recommendations are put in practice. I've learned in the world of IT that adaptation is 80% people, 15% process, and 5% technology. The technology is already here, but convincing people how to use it and putting in policies to make it appropriately leveraged are challenging. You have to get nurses and physicians behind these changes and because many doctors working in hospitals are independent contractors, getting them aligned on any change is hard."[21]

Halamka said that electronic health records are now widely used, but much of the potentially useful data is not collected. For example, hospitals don't always time and date-stamp patient movement through the hospital, so it's difficult to know how long patients may be waiting and give situational awareness about every patient in the hospital and ED.[22] "That kind of data is not easily available on most EHRs," Halamka said.[23]

The Rest of the Hospital and Healthcare

He said hospitals' core competency is care delivery, not data analysis. "And finding experts is hard. In Boston where I hire people to work in hospitals, we compete with Google and Facebook, who pay MIT grads starting salaries of $500,000 or more. We can't compete with that."[24]

He said insurers that pay healthcare providers for care provided should use their financial clout to achieve better outcomes. "What if an insurer refuses to pay for a three-week hospital stay for a congestive heart failure patient if that patient was readmitted soon after to the hospital? Suddenly that hospital would send a visiting nurse to give Lasix [a diuretic drug to treat water retention and eliminate salt through urine] and go through the patient's kitchen to throw out salty foods," said Halamka, who added that some hospitals are already taking those extra steps to prevent hospital readmissions.[25] In essence, he said, hospitals would be working harder to keep patients healthy if they had more financial skin in the game, such as incentives for improving patient health.

■ ■ ■

Helen Darling has lived, breathed, and preached healthcare quality for decades. Darling is the former interim president and CEO of the National Quality Forum, a not-for-profit organization that works to implement improvements in healthcare. She is the former president and CEO of the National Business Group on Health, a national nonprofit group representing large employers seeking both improvement in healthcare quality and more affordable prices.

Darling said Litvak is a driver and a leader in the healthcare quality improvement community. "I have not met many people as smart, talented, and driven on these topics as Eugene," she said. "His faith in operational management research methods is rigorous. I know few others who have stayed committed to the kind of work he's done. If he was just looking out for himself, he might have done much better financially. But he's set his mind to this challenge and applied his passion, persistence, and energy to making hospitals safer for patients."[26]

Glenn Steele, Jr., MD, spent 14 years as president and CEO of Geisinger Health System, the Danville, Pennsylvania–based integrated not-for-profit healthcare system known for its quality of care and innovation. Geisinger, which operates 12 hospitals in Pennsylvania and New Jersey, treats more than three million patients annually. Steele was the vice chair of the Health Transformation Alliance (HTA), an employer health-purchasing alliance that included giant US companies.[27]

Steele said innovation is very different than scaling, the adoption of new ideas and methods outside of laboratories into real world application in multiple settings. "What I'm doing now in my post-hospital career is focused on scaling, replicating what we did at Geisinger and figuring out how to scale it," Steele said.[28]

Steele was surprised to learn that 40 to 45% of healthcare costs don't benefit patients.[29] "That turned me onto re-engineering. I'm driven to see how much of those 40% of costs could be removed and how that value creation could lead to better outcomes for patients and insurance company members, but also serve as a really good business model."[30] He pointed out that many community hospitals and private physician practices cannot continue to exist independently. "They're getting so squeezed that they have to become bigger and when that happens it becomes easier to re-engineer or be re-engineered," said Steele, who described Litvak as "aggravatingly persistent."[31]

Steele said he found common ground with Litvak's approach for process improvement. "As a surgeon I looked at very concrete events and always tried to understand whether when I did something to a patient, did it end up helping or not helping, or did it hurt that patient," Steele said. "Eugene has both an evidence-based and an engineering approach. It's not just taken on faith. He focused on very concrete rate limiters: such as the flow in pre-op holding rooms, operating rooms, or post-op discharge strategies. That enables the organization he's working with to tell in an extra compact way whether what he's pushing is working or not. He's focusing on real problems."[32]

Steele said many hospital consultants pitch technology solutions or proprietary software platforms even when it's sometimes unclear what problems they would solve. "Eugene is much more focused on solving problems that every hospital CEO is aware of. He's persistent, forceful, articulate, and immutably focused on his gospel. Those qualities are important to his success."[33]

Rich Umbdenstock, former president and CEO of the American Hospital Association, who now serves that trade and lobbying association as president emeritus, said that for decades hospitals and hospital leaders had been known as builders, with a crane in every parking lot, building greater bed capacity to care for more and more patients.[34]

"That made sense at the time," Umbdenstock said. "My parting message since I retired was that we have to fall out of love with our overhead. Today as we attempt to reduce costs and utilization and keep people out of hospitals, the thing you want to do is not add unnecessary capacity and bottlenecks to your throughput process. That's where Eugene's work is helpful."[35]

He said today hospitals are increasingly avoiding building additional beds, "which you continue paying for decades later and which works against you. We have to think of ourselves in different ways." He said relying on remote monitoring and greater use of technology and electronics can reduce the need for bed capacity in a central hospital location.[36] "Eugene's work is consistent with that, specifically helping in operating rooms and emergency rooms to make better use of what you already have," Umbdenstock said.[37]

He doesn't view this change in approach as rocking the boat. "I have the stature and credibility and a contract with a severance agreement, and I am encouraged to make these tough calls. In any area of business or life, the 'Valley of Death' lies in crossing from the status quo to the new frontier. Litvak's program doesn't find adoption easily in large, conservative organizations like hospitals."[38]

But Umbdenstock said two things are changing significantly that could help Litvak's program find more fertile ground in hospitals. First, he explained, more organizations are taking on financial risk and being paid in some sort of reimbursement arrangement in which every cost comes out of that payment. Those risk-based payments encourage providers to do more things more efficiently, unlike the traditional fee-for-service (FFS) payment system, when hospitals and physicians were paid by the procedure, not by the quality of the care they provided.[39]

Second, he said, the traditional separation between doctors and hospitals has diminished. An April 2022 study prepared by Avalere Health for the not-for-profit Physicians Advocacy Institute found that almost 75% of US physicians were employed by hospitals, health systems, or corporate entities as of January 1, 2022, up from 69% the previous year. The report, "COVID-19's Impact on Acquisitions of Physician Practices and Physician Employment 2019–2021," found that more than half of all physicians, 52.1%, were employed by hospitals as of January 1, 2022.[40]

Umbdenstock said, "Now they're both on the same team, so a policy initiative has to be a win-win or a lose-lose. Both sides are encouraged to work together. More physicians have been selling their practices to hospitals and becoming employees. And most hospital CEOs see where this is headed: better clinical and financial outcomes. And that's what everyone is striving for."[41]

Umbdenstock said Litvak is passionate about his work and finding results that will change the healthcare environment. "He knows

The Rest of the Hospital and Healthcare

it works and has seen it happen in other sectors. He knows it can happen in healthcare, too. You have to admit that he is swimming upstream and single-handedly struggling to overcome decades of cultural inertia."[42] "I love the way he goes after it and has not been daunted by the resistance and stays on task. Eugene is a terrific messenger for this process improvement. He needs more disciples and mentees to spread the message across this tough sector."[43]

Litvak served on the AHA National Advisory Committee for improving quality, patient safety, and performance and invited Umbdenstock to join IHO's board. At a closed-door session for board members, Litvak asked, "How should we introduce our methods to hospitals so they would open their minds to this program?"

"Rich had an immediate reaction: 'as a survival kit.' Later he sent a memo to every hospital CEO under his leadership. He believed in it and was doing a lot to promote it."[44]

Umbdenstock said the good news is Litvak's results show this is a win-win-win set of results for hospitals, physicians, and patients. "It achieves significant cost savings, the quality of care is positively affected, and patient and clinical satisfaction improves. Those happen to be the things hospitals are being measured on and compensated for," he said. "It shows that expertise and techniques from other industries can apply in healthcare as well."[45]

Litvak knows that science can't cure racism, but it can alleviate some of its worse healthcare symptoms. He said his interventions for reducing variation in patient flow not only make patients safer and hospitals more efficient, but also expand access to care, which can decrease healthcare disparities and racial inequities.

When asked, Mark Smith, MD, an HIV/AIDS specialist and healthcare policy expert, said he believes science can address some of those disparities caused by racism. "Absolutely," responded Smith, the founding president and CEO of the California HealthCare Foundation and former vice president of the Kaiser Family Foundation.[46]

He conceded that healthcare lags behind in the application of innovations like Litvak's that can make healthcare more efficient and reliable. "Many branches of industrial engineering, or management science operations research, are widely accepted in a variety of industries. But in healthcare the adoption of these is relatively recent and thinly applied. Litvak and a few leading clinics and health systems are the exceptions in increasing reliability and reducing waste while producing higher-quality care at lower costs. Litvak's methods will improve healthcare outcomes of everyone in the healthcare system, particularly those most challenged by bad quality and higher costs. Patients should not suffer because of irrational variations of care. The modern management sciences should be part of the struggle to reduce healthcare inequities and disparities."[47]

Smith said that Litvak's methods should be broadly applied in outpatient settings like federally qualified community health centers (FQHCs), a safety net model of care that treats all patients regardless of their ability to pay. "Those findings ought to be more widely known. It's incumbent upon those who support community health centers to help these clinics learn this and apply these methods."[48]

Smith said in healthcare, "we come to accept things when we're forced to. Many things in healthcare happen not because of principled decisions, but because that's the way we've always done things. Ignaz Semmelweis, the Hungarian physician, proved 150 years ago that we could reduce the transmission of disease by washing our hands. Yet we still have healthcare providers failing to wash their hands. Old habits die hard. To some degree, the COVID pandemic has shaken things up. We're starting to adopt measures that have been technologically possible before, but were not adopted earlier because of inertia or habit."[49] He said that longtime practices were profoundly disrupted by the pandemic, which he predicts will be viewed as an accelerant to speeding change.

The Rest of the Hospital and Healthcare

Numerous studies confirm a wide variety of racial disparities in healthcare, disparities that have continued throughout the pandemic. In a study published in the March 2021 issue of the *American Journal of Preventive Medicine*, researchers found that, "Potentially avoidable hospitalizations are disproportionately experienced by racial and ethnic minorities and expose these groups to unnecessary iatrogenic harm (including the risk of nosocomial COVID-19) and undue financial burden," concluded the study of nearly 5,000 patients admitted to the UCLA Health hospitals before and during the COVID pandemic in 2019 and 2020.[50]

The study found that potentially avoidable hospitalizations decreased by 50.3% among non-Hispanic Whites, but only by 8.0% among African Americans.[51] "Given that the pre-pandemic rates of potentially avoidable hospitalizations were already higher among racial and ethnic minorities, especially among African Americans, this finding should cause alarm and lead to further exploration of the complex factors contributing to these disparities."[52]

In a March 26, 2021, Los Angeles Times story about the study, one of the co-authors said that "Black patients may be getting poorer access to outpatient care – the kind that could have helped maintain their health and prevented it from deteriorating so much that they landed in a hospital bed," according to Richard Leuchter at UCLA Health, one of the study's lead researchers.[53]

Ronald Wyatt, MD, vice president and patient safety officer for MCIC Vermont and fellow with the Boston-based healthcare quality group, the Institute for Healthcare Improvement, said he was asked by IHI's founder Don Berwick, MD, to visit St. Thomas Clinic of New Orleans and meet with Donald Erwin, MD, CEO.

"In the United States, race is an independent risk factor for health. I wanted to speak with Dr. Erwin about the independent, non-medical determinants of health. It's the one thing that's killing people that no one wants to talk about," recalled Wyatt.[54]

He said working with IHI changed the trajectory of his career and further motivated him to speak out about the role of racism in healthcare. At an annual IHI forum in Atlanta, Wyatt told attendees: "Until we address racism, how can we move forward with any of these other strategic ideas for improving care?"[55]

Wyatt said that Litvak's methods of smoothing patient flow can reduce racial disparities in care by expanding access. "I think there's something to it. When we think of these topics, we need to think about the things that continue to separate black people from high-quality healthcare. How is that flow interrupted for different patient populations?"[56]

Wyatt said the healthcare system serving African-Americans was already on life support before the pandemic hit. "We cannot fix this until there's a concerted effort to show how racism operates in this system. At least now it's being talked about."[57]

Litvak agreed that, while it's a start, "That is not enough. There must be action. You cannot change people's minds overnight either," he said. "But scientifically, we can help those less fortunate healthcare providers to compete with richer and stronger competitors who have more money. And those financially poorer entities cannot compete without improving their efficiency. They have no other option. The only way to improve healthcare for poor people is to provide them access to quality healthcare. You either have to manage patient flow or you throw money at the problem. And throwing money at it only solves the problem in the short term if you even have money to begin with. In outpatient clinics, becoming more efficient means seeing more patients and increasing revenues that will allow you to remain in business and care for your patients."[58]

The Rest of the Hospital and Healthcare

Chapter 9

The Clinic Was Going to Fold

In February 2014, after more than 25 years of serving some of New Orleans's poorest and sickest patients, the St. Thomas Clinic was about to close. "We began to realize we wouldn't make payroll that July. Many organizations don't ever successfully grapple with that financial challenge and either close, merge, or make bad decisions that affect quality. It's hard not to," said Don Erwin, MD, the founder and leader of the federally qualified community health center (FQHC), a federally subsidized outpatient health clinic that primarily serves the poor and uninsured.[1]

"We contacted IHO and told them we would probably go out of business if they didn't help us. They arranged a March–August consulting contract that totaled $75,000, far less than they normally charge."[2]

The safety net clinic was in dire straits, seeking revenue wherever it could and trimming costs to the bone. And residents of the St. Thomas public housing project, where the clinic is located, were so upset about the potential closing that they publicly demonstrated their support for what they saw as a vital community asset.

"Everyone took 25% salary decreases. We were cutting costs all we could. Our administration team took bigtime cuts. We heard about IHO and wondered how we could afford it, but decided: How could we afford not to do it? We were at a really critical juncture."[3]

St. Thomas serves a poor area hard hit by Hurricane Katrina. "Our staff is truly committed. They took pay cuts. We didn't want to be the biggest," Erwin said. "We just want to be the best in our community to meet our patients' needs."[4]

To afford IHO, Erwin and his wife wrote personal checks for $30,000 because the clinic didn't have the cash available. Clinic administrators contributed $1,000 each. Erwin said the clinic was originally founded by two nuns in 1987 to serve residents of the St. Thomas Housing Development as an alternative to the local Charity Hospital. The nuns left two years later, but Erwin remained, committed to the survival of this safety net provider.[5]

In 1991 the clinic constructed its own building and in 2007 changed its status to a FQHC, a designation that allows it to collect higher levels of Medicaid reimbursement and purchase drugs at a discount in exchange for treating all patients that show, regardless of income or insurance status. That higher reimbursement arrangement allows the physicians there to provide low-cost, high-quality primary care services. One bonus for physicians working there is relief from the high cost of medical malpractice insurance and forgiveness of medical school loans. "We agree not to turn any patients away for financial reasons. We assess what people can afford to pay and charge them on a sliding fee payment structure," Erwin explained.[6]

After the 2010 passage of the landmark Affordable Care Act (ACA), Louisiana refused to expand its Medicaid program and the clinic lost some funding. "The uninsured rate among our patient base rose from 18% to 35% in less than two years. We'd had a business model since 1987 built on grant support and we lost much of that. What it meant was that we also lost providers (doctors and nurses) and for a while couldn't accept new patients. At the same time, more patients needed us."[7]

Erwin, 82, a native Virginian specializing in nephrology (kidney specialist), was chairman of the department of medicine and chairman of graduate education at the prestigious Ochsner Clinic in New Orleans and was able to bring medical residents from Ochsner to work at St. Thomas. Before IHO's 2014 intervention, St. Thomas employed a staff of 65. Today it has grown to 150 while serving many more patients. "Having patient visits rise by 25% really spurred the growth," Erwin said. "To offer same day/next day access, we continue to hire new providers so we can have open schedules. That's why our business has grown so much. We had three clinic sites then and today we staff six."[8]

How Did IHO Help St. Thomas Clinic to Turn Around?

Erwin said five IHO staffers, including physicians and statisticians, consistently worked in that six-month period on St. Thomas's account, interviewing staff, collecting data, and training and educating clinic telephone operators, physicians, and other providers and administrative staff. "This was Greek to us. I wouldn't have imagined it could work. It's a pretty sophisticated evaluation. IHO took an intelligent, scientific approach to the data that brought us along in a way that we could understand it."[9]

Erwin said St. Thomas providers were skeptical at first, but all agreed to try out the new system without complaint. "There was no real resistance and once we did it, within a month we could see a difference in our bottom line (profit) and utilization (efficient use of resources), and our providers understood this would be a good business model."[10]

Litvak said IHO was used to dealing with large hospitals and health systems. It can take 18 months or more to implement IHO-recommended changes. "They were amazed to see results within a month," Litvak said.[11] Erwin said every day before IHO's arrival the clinic reported that one-quarter of its patient appointments were no-shows, patients with appointments who never arrived. At the same time other prospective patients waited for weeks to secure appointments. St. Thomas never even approached the 75% to 80% utilization of the appointments it did book.[12]

The clinic once took around 400 phone calls a day for appointments. "But we weren't approaching the appointment-making process with academic or scientific rigor," Erwin said. "We started measuring how many unanswered calls, how many appointments and missed appointments we saw. IHO pointed out how many operators we would need if we wanted every phone call to be answered within one minute of picking up the phone. We decided that our community niche would be same day/next day service."[13]

IHO told Erwin that their research shows that 70% of people who call in would rather see someone that day rather than wait to see their own provider. "They recommended that our practice adopt open access and start filling our daily appointment schedule at 7:30 a.m. each day. We stopped taking advance appointments and told everyone to call on the day they wanted to be seen, and we would see them that same day or the next day. If you were elderly or disabled and needed transportation, we would accommodate that. We then noticed that we filled up everyone's schedule almost immediately."[14]

Erwin said that once the clinic learned about queuing theory from IHO, its leaders reassessed how to deploy their operators and scheduled more of them to work during periods when calls came in clusters. "Typically during those times, if you didn't have enough operators, you would have many dropped calls, phone calls that were not answered, which meant fewer appointments. That meant that some of our patients left to go someplace else or were not treated at all. We would never have had the wisdom to forsake advance appointments and use open access. It took IHO's knowledge and data. We were flying by the seat of our pants and knew it wasn't working out."[15]

Erwin said he learned that the world is moving toward "open access appointments," seeing an available provider when a patient needs one versus waiting longer to see a regular family physician. In addition to switching to an "open access appointment" model, Litvak's team also showed St. Thomas how to better use the space it had. And by applying Litvak's methods, IHO showed St. Thomas leaders how long patients would wait to be seen by a provider. "They bring science to their practice and recommendations are based on solid data. The brainpower in the room was pretty impressive."[16]

Erwin said two things made the project successful. "First we were starting from a less than optimal position," he admitted. "We had nowhere to go but up or close."[17] He said the other relevant factor in the IHO success was the medical staff's support for open access appointments. "They were behind us 100%," he recalled. "It was a leap of faith, like jumping from a burning building. Frankly, we didn't have much choice. But we felt God's hands in our clinic. Litvak was clearly a blessing to us. IHO helped us with a lot of good metrics."[18]

Practice revenues rose from $317,000 in March of 2014 to $438,000 per month by January 2015, an increase of $120,000, or 38%, per month. The clinic also increased appointments by 35% and patient visits by 25%. By August 2019, monthly practice revenue had risen to $876,000.[19]

The clinic now employs seven or eight health coaches whose job is to telephone patients every month to remind them of their appointments, find rides for them if necessary, and help them to comply with their medications and scheduled tests and vaccines. "Having open access appointments means you can bring people in to get preventive tests, which is harder to schedule if you're waiting two to three weeks for an appointment," Erwin said.[20]

Erwin said providing high-quality, standardized care across multiple clinic sites is challenging. "But the improved revenue has

The Clinic Was Going to Fold

helped us to hire health coaches and establish better practices across our clinic system."[21]

He said that in 2016 a newly elected Democratic governor expanded the state's Medicaid program. "Our Medicaid population went up from 25% of all patients we saw to nearly 60%. And because we're paid on an augmented basis, that extra revenue helps us to subsidize the patients we treat for little or no reimbursement. Patient satisfaction relating to appointments has been very good. They're happy to be seen in one day. Ultimately, they realized if they wanted to see a particular provider they could, but not necessarily that day."[22]

Erwin said much has changed since 2014. "We had 12 providers [physicians and physician extenders like nurse practitioners and physician assistants] then and have 26 now. We've more than doubled our capacity and greatly expanded our revenues, from $2 million to close to $16 million this year." And he said that's enabled the clinic to expand staff and service sites to treat even more needy patients.[23]

Erwin said he believes there are few barriers to adopting Litvak's methods in community health centers. "I really think there is a market in the FQHC arena that CMS should bring Dr. Litvak into," Erwin advised. "I think the primary barrier is arrogance: most clinics don't think they need it. Few FQHC clinics know about Litvak."[24]

As of May 2022, there were 17,890 FQHC satellite sites and FQHC lookalike clinics in the United States, according to *Definitive Healthcare*.[25] And those clinics serve a crucial role in America's healthcare safety net.

"In 2021, health centers achieved a historic milestone of serving more than 30 million people (roughly one of every 12 Americans). Health centers deliver primary health care to the nation's underserved individuals and families, including one in three people living in poverty and one in five rural residents," according to the federal Health Resources and Services Administration (HRSA), a branch of HHS that funds community health centers.[26]

Erwin said if every FQHC adopted Litvak's methods, those centers could better serve more patients and be more financially stable, while saving huge amounts of money for our healthcare system. He said that because hospital services are increasingly provided in outpatient settings, the real market for Litvak's ideas about patient flow should be in large physician clinics.[27] "There are plenty of good-size clinics that will soon be faced with a substantial need to provide fewer tests outside of hospitals. The insurance world is saying to them that the way you've been getting your revenue isn't the way you're going to be getting your revenue in the future. You'll be rewarded for quality outcomes, not more tests and services. That's where it's heading. Being efficient is going to be increasingly important for healthcare providers. We must learn how to provide more efficient care. It will become more necessary to spend less money and learn where the waste is and how to eliminate it."[28]

Erwin said he hired two new physicians last summer. "When I add a new provider, it's not long before that provider is fully utilized and booked. We are guests in this community within a housing development and we want to provide for their healthcare needs. But you can't do that by operating in the red. It's easier with a stable bottom line. We were taken off the critical list, and IHO did that for us. We consider it a real godsend to have had IHO."[29]

An added benefit of Litvak's interventions is that providers can expand healthcare access, thus treating more patients and reducing inequities. Erwin concurred that applying Litvak's methods, while not curing or addressing the underlying root causes of institutional racism in American society or its healthcare system, can reduce disparities through a different pathway.

"We strongly agree with the position that being able to provide more efficient care to larger populations of patients is, in our opinion, clearly anti-racist behavior," said Erwin. "With the guidance of IHO, St. Thomas has been able to both see more patients, and also to see them when they need to be seen – same day service when needed. Our board takes this capability very strongly as we have in our bylaws that we will try to provide our healthcare using an anti-racist model."[30]

Erwin said 90% of St. Thomas patients are African-American, with the same percentage living under 200% of the federal poverty levels.[31] And before Louisiana expanded its Medicaid program, many didn't qualify for Medicaid assistance. "So they lacked access to care," he said. "Our failure to perform and survive as a clinic to serve those patients would have dramatically impacted this population."[32]

Erwin said Litvak's interventions helped St. Thomas to serve its mission in treating its patients. "If you can operate efficiently it's not rocket science. You can not only survive, but thrive, and complete your mission. We wouldn't have been in business without Eugene Litvak. When he goes down in the annals of science there probably won't be a marker noting that he saved St. Thomas in New Orleans. Because outside of this community, not a lot of people give a shit about St. Thomas Clinic. What he did was that in spite of systemic racism, he helped us to improve our clinic and the quality of care we can give to our underserved population."[33]

Erwin noted that for all Litvak has done, it has not changed the racial dynamic of local healthcare. "What IHO did for us was really important. Because African-Americans get less of what we'd call good medical care and more bad care, more amputations of limbs than revasculations. Their prostate cancers will be treated more with castration than hormones. When our clinic first opened in 1987, well-meaning local doctors sent us their expired drugs. They did not want to give them to their own patients, but they were probably good enough for ours. Still today, African-Americans will get more of the things we consider inadequate care in hospitals. But what Eugene Litvak did in this environment is all the more amazing because he did it. We were really presiding over a sinking ship."[34]

He said IHO enabled the clinic to avoid threatened extinction and adaptation and ultimately thrive. "We record about 85,000 patient visits per year now, and we would not have survived 2014 had it not been for the benevolence of Eugene Litvak. In our view, Eugene Litvak did the epitome of real anti-racist work – he helped us rethink how we practiced medicine and allowed us to offer high-quality health-care to an ever-enlarging, but chronically underserved, population. This is something rarely done in our country. It is easier to get a photo op or write out a check, rather than to dig in with someone and help them to deliver a high-quality care product to an under-served population, and do so on a consistent basis. Providing the highest-quality care is maybe the most anti-racist thing we can do."[35]

IHO to the Rescue

Hakmeng Kang is a vice president at IHO who helps manage the University Health Networks project in Toronto, a system-wide optimization project. Kang also assists Litvak with IHO business development and marketing. Kang was a physical therapist who later earned an MBA at Babson College before joining IHO. He worked closely with Dr. Erwin and staff at St. Thomas.

"They were in financial trouble then due to a lack of funding from the government and operational issues. They were trying to think of ways to be more efficient and provide better access for the uninsured in that New Orleans community," Kang explained.[36]

To better understand the clinic's problems, IHO studied how St. Thomas operated as a service provider, how it ran its practice on a day-to-day basis and scheduled and treated patients. Kang said IHO's goal was to help the clinic become more efficient, improve patient access to care, and allow providers to see and treat more patients.[37] The team went to New Orleans and did a time study, examining the flow of patients and tracking them each step of the way on their journey through the outpatient clinic, while chronicling that process from an operations perspective. "The biggest issue was how they [St. Thomas] schedule provider time and patient appointments. It turns out that they were often overbooked and sometimes under-booked, with doctors having to cancel patients and reschedule. No-shows were a huge problem for them. We showed them tools they used to get more patients to come to their appointments on time and offered recommendations for better communications tools."[38]

One example was setting reminders, either through cellphone texts or home phones calls, and working with clinic receptionists to make daily reminder calls. The project team tracked these cancellation rates in a database so that St. Thomas could see and report on them.[39]

IHO also recommended that the clinic hire another phone operator to work a different shift when appointment calls came in greater volume. They scheduled operators on certain days at certain times when call volumes were high, so no potential appointments were lost to unanswered calls.[40]

"It's important to look at that pattern," Kang said. "It's like a restaurant. You staff up for the lunch or dinner rush when you're busiest."[41]

Litvak's team also recommended staggering physician schedules to accommodate patients coming in at different times of day. They also suggested allowing other providers to treat patients who needed appointments right away.[42]

"We worked with them for about six months. It was new territory for us to work at a community health center in an outpatient setting. We discovered that operations management tools can be applied anywhere to different models of care and make a big impact on healthcare," Kang said.[43]

He said the challenge in working with St. Thomas was the clinic didn't make much money on their patients in their old business model. And because of reduced government reimbursements and the no-show appointments and cancellations, they faced a dim future. Kang said it's all about resource utilization.[44] "The demand was there, but they weren't using resources efficiently to get the volume they needed to expand access and services. In a hospital setting, the revenues are in the billions and there's a lot of waste in the system, but they can get away with it because of the amount of revenue the hospitals bring in," he explained. "For St. Thomas, which relies on government funding and provides care to underserved populations with little or no money, it can be challenging if you don't utilize your resources properly. It's like a restaurant at dinner hour with empty tables and a lot of fixed costs. You can't survive that way for long."[45]

For the past two years Litvak has volunteered to assist St. Thomas to improve quality of care and efficiency. He said he would welcome working in other healthcare settings, such as nursing homes, home healthcare, mental health centers, outpatient surgery, and dialysis centers and pointed out that the future of healthcare services is moving away from hospitals into homes and less intensive care settings.[46]

Chapter 10

The Rest of the World Comes Knocking

For nearly two decades Litvak has worked with hospitals and health systems throughout the world, mostly in the United States, but also in Australia, Canada, England, and Scotland. "When I started at St. John's Hospital in (Springfield) Missouri, I was chief cook and bottlewasher. I did everything. When the number of clients increased it was no longer feasible. I found I could not do everything and gradually started moving away from the technical site meetings. For the Mayo Clinic, Johns Hopkins, and Cincinnati Children's Hospital projects, I worked full-time with only a few colleagues," he recalled. "But with Scotland I was not there. Mike Long inserted the culture of research. When people do very sophisticated analysis, frequently they forget about the goal. I repeat to people when we work with a client that when they pay us, they should get a return multiple times and after that I welcome any research. Research alone isn't enough. At the end of the day, the hospital wants to know how much they got for what they paid. Our ROI should be at least double the amount they paid annually."[1]

In the early 2000s Litvak headed a patient flow initiative for his friend and colleague Don Berwick's Institute for Healthcare Improvement (IHI), teaching courses there that attracted physicians and hospital executives from around the globe.

A Boston Yankee in King Arthur's Court

Litvak's reputation, heralded by healthcare influencers like Harvey Fineberg and Don Berwick and trumpeted in research journals, healthcare business press, and newspapers was spreading internationally. Elite hospitals of the United States, Canada, and Great Britain were seeking his services. One of the most prestigious was a 172-year-old children's hospital.

Litvak's first trip to London was spurred by an invitation from Peter Lachman, MD, a physician then practicing at the Great Ormond Street Hospital. The pediatric hospital dates its origins to its founding in 1852 as the Hospital for Sick Children, the first hospital offering inpatient beds for children in England. Lachman and Jason Leitch from the Scotland National Health Service were Litvak students at IHI in Boston. After attending Litvak's course, Lachman, then the deputy medical director for patient safety at the Great Ormond, said he would like to implement Litvak's methods there.[2]

On his first visit to the hospital, Lachman introduced Litvak to Martin Elliott, Great Ormond's leading heart surgeon. Elliott served as Great Ormond's co-medical director and professor of pediatric cardiothoracic surgery at University College London. Elliott is a distinguished looking man with angular features, white hair, and clear, blue eyes. While he speaks like an erudite professor, there is little pomp and plenty of self-deprecating humor, a trait he shares with Litvak, who arrived from the airport unshaved and looking a little ragged to meet the eminent surgeon with his deputy. Litvak explained his theories and the methods for implementing them and told Elliott that Great Ormond's elective surgeries were less predictable than the hospital's unscheduled admissions.

"His reaction was, 'This sounds like nonsense,' which is typical," Litvak said. "What was not typical was that when he was shown the data, he not only acknowledged that it was true, but wanted to make changes at the hospital. The hospital was very supportive of the efforts in the cardiac ORs, but was not ready for hospital-wide change, which is always a problem."[3]

Elliott has earned a reputation, both in the United Kingdom and around the world, as a relentless seeker of quality improvement. He has consulted with leading experts in the airline and hotel industries and even worked with the luxury carmaker Ferrari in his search for process perfection.

"Moving a patient from the OR to the ICU carries significant risks, in many cases, as many as the operation," explained Elliott.[4] He said a team from Ferrari taught his cardio group how they conduct pit stops and the Ferrari team learned how to move babies. "We reduced errors by four times and learned from that the importance of process. Whenever you are managing flow it's about the deep importance of process, however small that process is. In my experience, few hospitals understand the importance of flow process," he said. "Culturally, it had a big impact for us. Quality is what we were looking for. We knew we would have to be better next year. Nobody jumps higher by lowering the bar. You have to keep getting better."[5]

The results from implementing IHO's patient flow program more than satisfied hospital leaders. Its cardiothoracic theatre (OR) saw an average increase of 2.2 procedures performed per week, which translated to an increase in annual revenue of £1.72 million ($2 million). That meant the OR could treat more children needing specialist surgery. The OR saw a decrease of 2.5 stress-related nursing shifts lost per week, which saved more than £30,000 ($35,000) in nurse agency costs. OR cancellations dropped by 2.3% weekly and utilization rose from 60% to 80%.[6]

"He helped us think," Elliot said. "After that you have to work as a group to find what's valuable to you, and in times of stress, go back to things he taught us."[7]

Peter Lachman has so many credential consonants behind his name you'd swear there was a national vowel shortage. He is a pediatrician with a master's in public health who later became CEO of the International Society for Quality in Health Care (ISQua), a worldwide organization dedicated to improving healthcare quality. The South African native was a Health Foundation Quality Improvement Fellow at IHI when he attended a Litvak session in 2006.[8]

Lachman said Litvak represents a threat to the healthcare establishment, particularly those benefiting from the status quo. He is "one of the smartest men I know. One of the problems is that he has a solution and knows the answer, but there are too many vested interests too big to allow the adoption of his methods to happen. He's asking people to change the way healthcare is delivered and that goes against the power base in the healthcare industry. Even if you know what is right, getting others to do what is right is another thing entirely."[9]

Attending Litvak's IHI course, Lachman learned how variability affects patient flow and how patient flow can improve or clog hospital systems. "I said, 'I've seen the light.' For the next three years I translated what he [Litvak] said. He was theoretical and I was clinical. We were there to take concepts, like queueing and variability theory, math that no one else understood, and help others understand what both sides were talking about. When translated, Eugene's program became very powerful. I really think he has the answer to many of the problems afflicting healthcare today, but it calls for total redesign," Lachman said.[10]

He said that Litvak has demonstrated that his program can work.

"And that's great," he said. "But now you must deal with humans: not so great. He brought it to Great Ormond, collected and analyzed our data, and came up with a solution. The solution was complex and that's where the trouble began. The CEO had to decide whether he wanted to keep his job. There are many vested interests in a hospital. So rather than a full implementation, we ended up doing a semi-implementation."[11]

Lachman, who speaks with a faint South African accent diluted by his years in England and Ireland, said that the problems afflicting US hospitals are the same plaguing hospitals around the world: Healthcare delivery was designed by, and around, individual doctors.[12]

Where Are the Air Traffic Controllers?

"Think of an airport," Lachman challenged. "What would happen if all airplanes wanted to arrive at the same time, or if all flights were scheduled to take off at once? Of course, no one would do that. But in healthcare that's exactly what we do. The people in control are the doctors, and they decide this schedule for surgeons. The surgeons own the time in the hospital operating rooms, not the hospitals. The surgeons decide when it's convenient for them to operate. But when that happens, the hospital goes into stress. Nobody decides which patient needs which surgery the soonest. And this is the normal practice worldwide. Doctors control healthcare, but not always with the patients first in mind. Hospital managers and administrators may think they have the power, but it's the doctors holding the real power."[13]

Lachman said Litvak is challenging the core problem of healthcare and the power balance within the system. "Even before you bring Eugene in with the solution, you need buy-in from the clinical staff to change and the assurance that the new system won't affect the doctors' relationships with patients."[14]

Lachman said that when Great Ormond applied Litvak's methods to cardio-thoracic surgery, the hospital saw outcomes improve. "It worked and made a big difference," he said.[15] He attributed that to its hospital champion, Elliott, the top pediatric cardiac surgeon in

Great Ormond's most important department, which owned its CT scanners, laboratory, and operating rooms. "It worked there because cardiothoracic surgery could control everything, whereas in the rest of the hospital, there were more competing fiefdoms and interests, and it would be more difficult to implement."[16]

Lachman said physicians and surgeons need to change how they work. "But without a champion like Martin [Elliott], it won't work," he said. "I would concentrate my focus on implementation. Eugene is the theoretician. He needs clinicians to sell it for him. If he gets enough physicians to believe in it, things will change."[17]

Lachman, who splits his time between Dublin and London, pointed out that: "It's all about the local context, understanding who the local power brokers are and working with the local teams."[18]

Lachman said he is a realist who believes in Litvak and his ideas, but recognizes that the barriers he faces are difficult to change. "Moses never made it to the promised land. He saw it from a distance, but was not the one to take his people there. I would say it will take years for this to be adopted. But it will happen."[19]

Scotland National Health System

Jason Leitch is another of Litvak's former students. Leitch, director of clinical quality for the National Health Service (NHS) of Scotland, said the nation's health service contracted with IHO in 2014 as part of Scotland's improvement projects, seeking the best international advice in the world. To date, it is the first nation to implement Litvak's methods throughout its system of hospitals, though not every hospital has adopted Litvak's programs entirely.[20] Leitch said the NHS believed its hospitals could benefit from improvements in flow quality, which it believed could accelerate the pace of other hospital improvement programs. He said a handful of the nation's hospitals sought to choose from three different IHO interventions.[21]

In the beginning, there were no numeric outcomes. The value was broader than just money, Leitch explained. "We were seeing a waste of bed days (patients unnecessarily hospitalized for too long). Utilizing resources may not always save money, but it's given us value for the pound we're spending, value in the broadest sense. It's making our work flow better for patients and families and for the workers, making work smoother for all participants."[22]

Leitch said Scotland's NHS did achieve success. "The simple answer is yes, but it's not as binary as that. There was clinical engagement in the work. The numbers went in the right direction. We saw improvements in utilization and assessing people for surgery and medical flow. There is definitely something in the methodology that has driven improvements."[23]

Leitch said the clinical engagement within the program was stronger than he'd hoped for or could predict. And he said NHS was grateful that Litvak and IHO were willing to share their methodology and learning and help Scottish hospitals build those tools into the system's capacity. Adopting IHO's program across an entire national health system was daunting, Leitch conceded.

"There are competing priorities. You can't do everything, everywhere, all at once," he said, pointing out that vaccinations, mental health services, and other improvement projects are underway by the NHS's 168,000 employees.[24]

"You have to set priorities nationally to decide which to undertake. To make this go faster, we had to sacrifice some of the other programs because there is only a limited amount of resources," Leitch said, explaining that IHO is one among a tapestry of health improvement programs throughout Scotland.[25]

He said those included: better utilization and improvement in patient flow and surgery and patient flow on the medical side of hospitals, with options within each category, such as categorizing surgical cases and finding the right beds for the right patients at the right time. Scottish hospitals, which are grouped in systems they call boards, pursued options they chose. IHO did the earlier training and education, but the NHS and the nation's 14 hospital boards performed the work, using clinical leaders and analysts IHO trained.[26]

Leitch said the nation's 14 boards oversee 25 to 30 large hospitals and a few hundred smaller ones, some staffing as few as six beds on remote Scottish islands. "To get to some of these rural and remote hospitals you have to land on a beach. The hospital might be run by a single family physician," he said, "more like Alaska than New York. But all of the hospitals are linked and the physicians are employed by NHS. There is no private healthcare in Scotland."[27]

He said Scotland's NHS emergency departments collectively perform better than the other three UK countries, but noted that there remains wide variability across the country by season, time of the year, and geographic location. "Some are doing well year-round, while others are struggling and need work. One of the challenges of hiring IHO in a publicly funded health system is that the priorities have to be by necessity slightly different. We have no alternative but to treat everyone within a fixed budget."[28]

He said Scotland has a long track record of healthcare improvement. "We worked with IHI on several big projects testing new methodologies and measuring the results. What IHO brings is crucial. Sharing across an entire system helps."[29]

Leitch said that implementing the IHO program "was a slog. It's hard work. We knew that. Getting it to work is difficult. There are many challenges. But if you put time into it and are really dedicated, there is a real benefit. People saw the results and got very enthusiastic."[30]

Leitch said the early results are promising.[31] "More work needs to be done, but our data tells us that applying these methods to Scottish systems of hospital care appear to improve patient flow and outcomes and reduce costs. We're seeing shorter waits as well," he said.

Hospital, Heal Thyself

"The jury is still out on how we can do this on a big broad scale across the system. I do think it's sustainable."[32]

Ottawa Hospital, Canada

Litvak was giving an annual guest lecture on patient flow at the Harvard School of Public Health for physician executives earning master's degrees, a course he teaches every July to between 20 to 25 doctors. Mark Walker, MD, a physician who worked in Ontario's Ministry of Health attended and reported back to Jack Kitts, MD, the president and chief executive officer for 1,200-bed Ottawa Hospital.

"Mark reached out to me and said there could be some interest. I was invited to give a lecture to their executive committee in May 2011," Litvak remembered. "After that they invited IHO."[33]

At Ottawa Hospital Litvak met with hospital executives, nurses, surgeons, intensive care unit (ICU) staff, and anesthesiologists. "I met with each group for about an hour, gathering information and listening. After two days of meetings we frequently experience finger pointing. If only not for the surgeons, we could do miracles here," Litvak said, repeating a common excuse hospital CEOs use to explain why hospitals have difficulty adopting his methods. "I ask questions about whether there is anything their group can do to improve, which forces them to slow down their grievances. Then I ask if I could perform miracles, could they give me three miracles they'd like me to do in descending order. This is very helpful because I begin to understand their priorities, what people really want. Then I tell them how they can do this and explain why the miracles are impossible unless things change."[34]

Then Litvak asked how those goals can be achieved if nobody knows how many surgeries will be performed tomorrow. "So, to get a carrot they must change something. With hospital executives, it's a little different. I tell them that the miracles will not happen without them being hands-on. Miracles won't happen independently."[35]

Kitts, an anesthesiologist who has spent decades in operating rooms, said Walker knew "my search for the unicorn was how to manage surgery flow through ORs more effectively.[36] Kitts said Litvak formed a strong first impression, but admitted that he was skeptical. "He said to achieve high performance in your OR, it will require disruptive change in the way your surgeons, anesthesiologists, and nurses are working today. You will have to introduce disruptive change. Are you willing to lead that change? I said if you show me the data, I am willing to lead that change. Then he said that change could require us to open emergency ORs, in addition to the elective ORs we currently operate, to have two distinct patient streams."[37]

Kitts said applying IHO's data and guidance, Ottawa Hospital was able to reduce the variability of elective surgeries and smooth out the peaks and valleys of its daily patient census. "We opened dedicated ORs to separate the elective from the emergency surgeries. But we failed to implement seven-days-a-week surgery," he conceded. "I was unable to convince the surgeons and anesthesiologists to accept that. But as Meatloaf [the late American rock star whose actual name was Marvin Lee Aday] sang, 'two out of three ain't bad.'"[38]

Kitts said the hospital made great inroads in the first three months, reducing mortality rates and waiting times, improving access to care and safer care for patients with greater efficiency and a better patient experience. Kitts said Litvak didn't need to know how to perform surgery to improve Ottawa Hospital's surgery programs. "He applied research to a health challenge as he would a challenge in any other business. He applied proven methodologies to solve the patient flow problem and wasn't afraid to try those in the healthcare world. He had the courage of conviction to go into healthcare without a healthcare background and do things that have never been done before," Kitts said. "He thinks completely outside of the box, and he does it standing on his feet."[39] Kitts said even the partial adoption of Litvak's methods saved millions of dollars and scores of lives.[40]

Litvak called Kitts "a unique and strange kind of hospital CEO. He actually feels embarrassed if his hospital does not do the right thing. Many others don't. And that pushes him to improve patient care."[41]

Prioritizing Elective Surgeries to Save Patients and Hospitals

IHO's work has already produced results for Toronto's largest hospital system, the three-hospital University Health Networks (UHN), whose Toronto General Hospital is routinely ranked one of the world's best. Before the pandemic, IHO recommended UHN surgical units create eight categories of elective procedures and determine how long patients could safely wait for each operation, ranging from 45 minutes to 14 days.

His team "helped us to prepare for the flu and coronavirus," said Shaf Keshavjee, MD, UHN's chief of surgery. Keshavjee also worked with IHO to improve patient flow in surgery at UHN, where he serves as surgeon-in-chief, directs the Toronto Lung Transplant Program, and is a professor in the Division of Thoracic Surgery at the University of Toronto.[42]

"Our institution is light years ahead because of what we've learned from IHO and the steps we've already taken ourselves," he said. "We know what resources we need, how and what needs to be fixed, and what's needed to do it. It's still a work in progress."[43]

The combination of systems UHN already adopted and IHO's data gathering and real time tracking enabled the hospitals to separate their elective surgeries. "Everyone knew exactly what we were talking about."[44]

Keshavjee said Litvak's process reinforced that "the way we've done things for the last 100 years wasn't working."[45] He said Litvak's method of surgical smoothing reduces many problems surgeons have faced for many decades. "Planning a surgery and then finding the OR room that was assigned was canceled because of overnight emergency admissions is frustrating for the surgeons, staff, and most importantly for the patients," Keshavjee said. "Sometimes the hospital assigns you OR time when you're not available. Or an OR room was booked by a surgeon who wasn't using it. It's all demoralizing."[46]

He said Litvak's method of assigning ORs exclusively for emergency cases solves some of the problems as well.

"That leaves us room for emergency cases. Fewer scheduled surgeries are canceled. It also has led to fewer cancellations due to a lack of resources, having no hospital beds, OR rooms, or equipment available when needed," Keshavjee said. "Being more organized in our approach to surgery and recognizing the many forces influencing our ability to deliver care has helped us to modify our environment and change our practices. IHO helped us to prepare for the flu and coronavirus. They helped us to use our data to prepare our hospitals for other events, disasters, and epidemics."[47]

Litvak discovered long ago that clustering elective surgeries in the morning and early in the week proved disastrous when sudden rushes occurred in the ER. They led to ambulance diversions, intensive-care-unit overload and staff burnout, along with higher rates of medical errors and more preventable deaths.

When Susan Brooke, a former management consultant and bank executive, heard that the UHN of Toronto was seeking input from patients as it undertook a patient flow program from IHO, she was interested in participating. Brooke has personally battled health issues for nearly 30 years, ranging from heart valve problems and heart failure to Marfan Syndrome, a connective tissue disorder. After her most recent major surgery in 2016, she agreed to join UHN's Patient Partnership Program.

"I've always been passionate about our healthcare system and wanted to do my part to help make the system better," Brooke said, explaining that UHN assigns patients to different projects according to their interests and skills. She has participated in UHN's strategic plan to improve patient flow through surgical smoothing and reducing variability.[48]

"This is the most interesting one and feels the most actionable," Brooke added. "Because it is so focused, it is the most likely to have a significant impact, both in terms of cost and experience."[49]

She said as a patient she was aware of the process of patient flow. "I thought it was a fascinating problem they were grappling with, but assumed hospitals were already doing that kind of analysis," said Brooke, whose strong business background exposed her to operations management techniques decades earlier in different industries. "I was surprised to learn they weren't. At the end of the day, hospitals are kind of a manufacturing business. But for them, just gathering the data was a new endeavor."[50]

She said reducing the time patients spend awaiting surgeries is itself a noble goal. "Not canceling surgeries is important on many levels. As a patient, you're so vulnerable at that time, your emotions are so raw. My family came from other parts of the country for my procedure. And when they told me they were canceling my operation, I was in tears."[51]

She once waited sleeplessly in a hospital ER for 50 hours before a hospital room was available so she could be admitted. "And I should point out that I am over six feet tall, so those ER stretchers, uncomfortable at the best of times, were no match for my stature. Spending over two days in the ER when you are already badly depleted is soul-crushing and detrimental to recovery," Brooke said. "Anything you can do to shorten the time a patient spends in the ER is invaluable.[52]

The Rest of the World Comes Knocking

During a 2016 hospitalization, a man in the bed next to her was scheduled for cardiac surgery. "He was prepped and hungry because he couldn't eat before the procedure. They gave him an enema so he wouldn't have a bowel movement during the surgery. And then, at the last minute on a Friday afternoon, they canceled his surgery because his surgeon was needed in an emergency case. I felt so bad for him. He would have to wait until Monday."[53]

For her second open-heart surgery Brooke said she was weakened and scared. "The emotional build-up to my surgery was intense. I needed to update my will and powers of attorney; I needed to prepare my family. We had some difficult conversations. Sometimes anxiety got the better of me. There were tears. I had special outings with friends and a family dinner the night before surgery. My 80-year-old father traveled from Ottawa; my brother came from Vancouver. Emotions ran high. This is what happens when you're preparing for major surgery.

"Now imagine what happens when, 10 minutes before departing for the hospital, I received a call telling me there is no bed. I can't adequately convey the psychological and physical impact of this. It's like hitting a wall at 100 miles per hour – you're on autopilot and it suddenly disengages. Surgery itself is tough enough; the preparation can be emotionally draining. A delay increases the anxiety exponentially."[54]

Luckily, she said, hours later the procedure was moved up. "There are many uncontrollables in healthcare," Brooke said. "But where there is opportunity to improve, I think it's up to each of us – patients and providers – to do our part to make it happen. Ultimately, opportunity lies in smoothing patient flow to reduce variability."[55]

Chapter 11

Making Change Happen: How to Speed Hospital Adoption of Litvak's Methods

Eugene Litvak's goal of introducing operations management tools to control patient flow and reduce or eliminate its artificial variability across America's hospitals is unlikely to be achieved without outside intervention. Litvak believes it will take a grassroots, patient-based movement to demand such changes in US hospitals.

Others have suggested that different options could speed the adoption of Litvak's methods. Some of healthcare's brightest luminaries and deepest thinkers have weighed in on what it would take to make that occur. Some recommended legislative mandates requiring hospitals to adopt these proven methods to improve patient safety. Others suggested some mixture of incentives, financial "carrots and sticks," rewards, and punishments for improving patient flow. Still others believe health plans or hospital accrediting agencies should leverage their purchasing power or regulatory clout to persuade hospitals to change.

Julie Freischlag, CEO of Wake Forest Baptist Health; dean of Wake Forest School of Medicine in Winston-Salem, North Carolina; and the former chair of surgery at Johns Hopkins Hospital, said that healthcare is delivered differently state by state. "We're heading to a national hospital landscape where we'll have big systems that can make money and afford to do Litvak's methods. Many academic systems are already using bits and pieces of this, partly because of CMS readmission policies [punishing hospitals for higher-than-average readmission rates and rewarding them for lowering those rates]."[1]

Freischlag said teaching operations management in medical schools could help. "You have to teach the teachers. Having medical students do rotations in operations management might be a good idea. They need to learn that," she said.[2]

Longtime Litvak collaborator Mike Long, MD, a retired Massachusetts General Hospital anesthesiologist currently living in Portland, Maine, said that introducing their methods of controlling variability to student physicians in medical schools could achieve broader adoption.[3] "I don't know any medical school programs that even consider operations management tools to improve hospital practices," said Long, who worked with Litvak over two decades. We thought if we outlived the older generation that seemed opposed to these changes 10 or 20 years ago that we could reach people more amenable to change. But that didn't turn out to be true. We thought if hospitals employed surgeons, the hospitals would have enough leverage to implement IHO ideas. And that didn't work. Maybe we have to get to them as babies. I don't know of any medical school that does this, though. They barely teach surgeons how to deal with patients."[4]

William "Bill" Pierskalla, a retired distinguished professor emeritus and former dean of the UCLA Anderson School of Management, said he doesn't have much faith in government to oversee the adoption of Litvak's methods.

"The only successful government department has been our military. They're really good at logistics and they've built good infrastructure," which is needed, said Pierskalla, formerly president of the Operations Research Society of America and of the International Federation of Operational Research Societies.[5]

"I would like to think the government could do something like that. But look how long it's taken the government to do anything in IT [information technology]. Hospitals know little about making management systems decisions. I don't know how they could mandate it, because they don't know how to do it themselves. Outside of military and a few other organizations, they're not trained to think this way and don't understand the capabilities."[6]

He said many healthcare organizations hire consultants to teach them how to implement Six Sigma and Lean ideas for improving efficiency. "But those people keep changing and evolving and often that learning doesn't stick without infrastructure. Without basic staffing, it just dies. Nurses and doctors don't know how to do it. You need to build infrastructure like the Mayo or Cleveland Clinic, who keep working on it and do better than everyone else. You need people in command at a high level, a connected chain of interest up the line so they get the authority of people at the top wanting to do it and interested in continuing it. What Litvak is trying to do is basic improvement. If they don't have people to carry forth, it can disappear. Because leadership changes and you lose champions."[7]

Harvey Fineberg, MD, the president of the Gordon and Betty Moore Foundation and chair of the Standing Committee on Emerging Infectious Diseases and 21st Century Health Threats for the National Academies of Sciences, Engineering, and Medicine (NASEM), said the hospital accreditation process is a good avenue to spur widespread implementation of Litvak's methods.[8] "Every hospital has to be accredited on standards of safety and operational quality," said Fineberg, a former Harvard provost and president of the Institute of Medicine. "There are many standards of design and construction and many issues of safety in the accreditation process. I think it would not be a giant leap for accreditation agencies to attend to matters of quality and efficiency in patient flow, to make this a standard of accreditation. If that were to be possible, that would automatically bring this to the attention of every facility. That could make this a standard of performance so that it's unthinkable for a hospital not to have it."[9]

Fineberg said if Litvak's ideas were adopted, it could save tens of billions of dollars and significantly more in operational and capital savings. He said it would fit in with the long-term trend of treating patients outside of hospitals. "The best patient flows in hospitals are the patients who never enter the hospital," he said. "The movement to do more outside of hospitals also involves flow and increases the efficiency of hospitals."[10]

Richard Umbdenstock, the former president of the American Hospital Association, who served on IHO's advisory board, said the $64 billion question is: How do you spur widespread adoption?

One influential group that holds sway over hospitals is the credit rating organizations like Fitch, Moody's, and Standard & Poor's, firms that assess the credit risk of hospitals seeking short- and long-term bonds, usually used to pay for new construction or medical equipment. They assign ratings codes that determine the level of interest rates charged, offering upgrades or downgrades and assigning positive or negative forecasts.[11]

Umbdenstock reasoned that if credit rating agencies assessed hospitals' ability to safely expand capacity and operate efficiently, that could convince hospitals to adopt methods like Litvak's to make those changes. If the credit ratings firms penalized hospitals that failed to improve patient flow by assessing unfavorable ratings and costing them more in interest payments, hospitals would look for ways to improve efficiency.[12]

"When a hospital's credit rating organization tells them they need to expand, that agency could run tests to see if capacity is being maximized. We change, but only when we absolutely have to," he said.[13]

He said the key players in adoption are the clinicians. "It takes a champion, someone out of managerial or clinical leadership, and a group of strong supporters to get this done. It might be smart to focus on clinical audiences, like the American College of Surgeons, the Operating Nurses Association, and demonstrate to them the results of this in simplifying their lives, de-stressing their lives, improving the satisfaction of colleagues and patients, and champion that to management."[14]

Glenn Steele, MD, the former president of Geisinger Health System who also served on the IHO Advisory Board, said he opposes mandates. "If mandates are very granular and detailed, they become invitations to work-arounds. I've never seen anything failing to motivate human ingenuity like mandates. I think what Obamacare did was good, a huge amount of it. But the main reason there was so much pushback was mandates. People don't like mandates," he said.[15]

"Here's the solution: You change the reward system. We're moving towards payment for outcomes for specific bundles of care or better care for type 2 diabetics within a population. That's the way to go. Let those paying for treatment choose the way. Some hospitals will choose IHO, or Lean, or other methods best suited to their needs."[16]

John Halamka, MD, president of the Mayo Clinic Platform, said three practices could speed adoption of Litvak's program by physicians. "You can pay them more for something; promise a better quality of practice life – with less stress and more predictable working hours. Or you embarrass them by publishing their quality outcomes and scores in local news media," Halamka said. "That would motivate them to participate and speed adoption."[17]

Helen Darling, the former interim president and CEO of the National Quality Forum, said that hospitals are incredibly powerful politically and are almost always the biggest employers in their communities. Almost every city or town of a certain size has a hospital, and they are often beloved institutions in their regions. Darling said it would require a consumer movement to spark real change. She said consumer and public health movements brought about reductions in smoking and opioid use and focused national attention on issues like

Making Change Happen: How to Speed Hospital Adoption

suicide, addiction, and gun control and could shame hospitals into adopting patient flow practices.[18]

Darling said a country of America's size and complexity requires more of a community-by-community approach, noting that Litvak's successful implementations employed that strategy. She stated, "It's so dependent upon leadership. How do you make it happen? Much of what happens at a national level happened first in a community or state sector where it worked. It will have to happen area-by-area, institution-by-institution. It takes leaders to pick up on it and lead."[19] Ideally, she said, organizations with strong leaders bring along regional hospital association or regional Blue Cross plans.[20]

Retired surgeon Fred Ryckman, MD, said if none of the financial "carrots and sticks" appeal to physicians, then hospitals should appeal to their sense of duty.[21] He said, "You're hired to do the right thing, and this is the right thing to do. CEOs should show doctors the door if they threaten to leave, because they will do that again and again. Nobody is irreplaceable. If a hospital implements a safer, higher-quality, and more efficient system, surgeons will want to work there"[22]

He said hospitals should implement the program, not just in the OR or ED, but throughout the entire hospital organization.[23]

Denis Cortese, MD, the former president of the Mayo Clinic Health System, said America's healthcare delivery system has fully adjusted to maximize the way hospitals and physicians are paid. "I know the delivery system can change. What is one lever you could pull to change the whole system? Pay for what we want. Pay for value and link payments to quality of care," said Cortese, now a professor at Arizona State University. "Every other current stakeholder is fighting this tooth and nail. But if providers were paid in such a way so they could stay in business by keeping people healthier, that would make Eugene's program more attractive and more in demand. We need a key commitment from government to change the way payments are made. Because whatever Medicare does, the rest of the industry follows."[24]

Peter Lachman, CEO of the International Society for Quality in Health Care, said: "If he [Litvak] really wants to see wider adoption, he needs to have more clinical salespeople on his staff. I would call them interpreters and advise him to step back, review his theories, and see what people could do in stages. Translate it into a how-to guide. I think Eugene is well ahead of his time and has answers that people aren't ready to hear."[25]

Peter Pronovost, MD, the chief transformation officer at Cleveland-based University Hospitals, said there are many levers to spark national change, including enlisting the national general media to create peer pressure and ask local hospitals why they are not undertaking this program. Pronovost said appealing to clinicians could work, enlisting them to ask, "'Why aren't we doing this?' There is no debating the science. It's a matter of will."[26]

Pronovost said that insurers could exert financial pressure on non-participating hospitals. He said that improving patient flow is a primary benefit of adopting Litvak's methods. "It's managing throughput flow throughout an organization, trying to optimize flow and cost. We need a systems engineering approach. What Eugene has done is just the tip of the iceberg in applying systems engineering in healthcare. It's spot on. The checklists work, but there are checklists for many harms. And we need a more comprehensive systems approach to integrating them into our care delivery system."[27]

Pronovost said that for more than 20 years he and others have been frustrated by the failure of the healthcare system to track the number of medical errors in hospitals and enumerate the deaths and other harms they cause. "Nobody does that. I view errors as the process, harm is the outcome. Balancing those two is a real key link. The harm estimates vary from 50,000 to 500,000. The biggest indictment of the field is that we've been at this problem for 20 years, and we still

Making Change Happen: How to Speed Hospital Adoption

don't have deaths per medical error statistics. It's largely voluntarily reported and the threshold for reporting varies widely. We should be able to measure the harms throughout."[28]

Don Berwick, MD, the aforementioned founder of the Institute for Healthcare Improvement, said systems engineering is so foreign to hospital leaders. "They think managing is an art," he said.[29]

Berwick also said that the payment incentives are probably not strong enough now to compel hospital administrators to adopt Litvak's methods. "The political hassle of getting physicians to change OR schedules is not perceived to be worth the pain. Now that hospital margins are decreasing, however, hospitals are going to need to grow productivity, and this program is a poster child for that."[30]

Berwick, whose IHI has worked for more than 30 years to convince hospitals and physicians to adopt evidence-based practices to improve patient care and safety, said many healthcare leaders are ineffective at change management. He said Litvak's program has a technical component and an adoptive component, two elements that require buy-in.

"Doctors may not want to change right away. Most change management components fail – something like 95% fail – because of the adoptive component. There are tips and tools for that, adoptive change tools. The time is right now to see this more broadly implemented."[31]

Berwick said he would not support more regulatory requirements for hospitals. "They're already laboring under too many."[32] He said that the hospitals' move away from traditional fee-for-service payment incentives toward capitated payments "should be a tonic for growing this kind of program." He doesn't think that the average hospital executive or board of trustees have been trained in systems thinking. "For a long time I've believed that the leaders of complex systems need this kind of training."[33]

He said more hospitals should hire industrial engineers and incorporate them into systems operations. "I don't think the engineering professions have been wedded to healthcare. I think we should do more to make sure those skills are embedded in hospitals."[34]

C. Daniel Smith, MD, the head of the Esophageal Institute of Atlanta and former chief of surgery at the Mayo Clinic in Florida, said government or public groups must convene a think tank consortium with a budget and dollars allocated to pursue Litvak's methods in a more organized fashion.[35]

Smith said, "I believe if that happened, you could do a very mindful, large-scale, data-driven, and targeted implementation."[36] He advised against launching those efforts at the Dukes, Hopkins, and Mayo Clinics of the country that are the number one players in their respective markets.[37]

"You need to go to the third-ranked hospital in a market led by a 40-year-old CEO who wants to make a name for himself and wants to move up to number 1 or 2. Pick a handful of those hospitals and do it. Slowly get these wins and proceed from there to a large-scale commercialization. I think Eugene must take a page out of the startup world," Smith suggested. "Those are disruptive changes that people like. He can promise better things. In this world, you have to do a data-driven, strategic, and targeted rollout and commercialization of the model and build traction and acceptance. I think that's what's been missing. There haven't been enough of the right people to come together to convince private finance guys of its worth."[38]

Ellis "Mac" Knight, MD, the former chief medical officer for the Palmetto Health system in Columbia, South Carolina, does not foresee a "eureka" moment that converts the nation's hospitals to adopting surgical smoothing.[39] "Unfortunately, it will be similar to all the changes for better that have occurred in healthcare: they occur slowly and incrementally. That's the way things are done. It will take time and may require regulatory changes to be put into place to force hospitals to alter their ways," Knight said.[40] But if the Joint Commission – America's largest hospital accreditation organization – set operations management standards to accredit hospitals across the industry and enforced them, that could escalate the pace of change.[41]

Knight believes that commercial health insurers eventually will get involved. "I'd love to see the Leapfrog Group [a healthcare quality standards organization] or the Centers for Medicare and Medicaid Services (CMS) or Aetna [health plan] or the Blues plans [Blue Cross/Blue Shield health plans] and other big payers coming up with quality measures that they say hospitals must achieve to get reimbursed. If they did, that would make a huge difference."[42]

Mark Smith, MD, an internist, university professor, and former president of the California Health Care Foundation, said overcoming the hospital industry's institutional malaise and other barriers is complicated. "There are cultural and economic factors. One thing I've learned is the maddening variability of adoption of things that have been widely proven, along with the rapid adoption of things not widely proven. On the one hand people rush to implant drug-eluding stents, only to find years later they that don't work. It's taken 150 years of struggling to get people to wash their hands," Smith said. "So it's not surprising to see Litvak's ideas have ironclad proof of their effectiveness, but have not been universally adopted. I'm pessimistic in the short run, but optimistic in the long run that these will be adopted. When he goes on book tours people in the signing audience will turn to their neighbors and ask: why aren't we doing this?"[43]

Smith said 10 years ago, hospital CEOs could dismiss quality concerns by claiming their hospitals treat sicker patients and are doing a better job than neighboring hospitals. But, he said, those quality performance scores are more widely disseminated now, and hospitals are facing greater economic pressures and challenges to maintain their profit margins and give up old habits to remain financially viable.[44]

"They've done the easy things first: buy the competing hospital down the street and jack up their rates 10%. But all those things wear out eventually. Eventually, they will have to adopt greater efficiency and quality," Smith said. "To him [Litvak], it is about the mission to improve the quality and function of our healthcare system. He has the persistence of a scientist who understands the importance of his work. That's what it takes. Few scientific advancers become heroes. It often takes 20 years. But Eugene is a great example of someone pushing and pushing until everyone else comes to understand the importance of his ideas."[45]

Epilogue

In the past two years Litvak's methods for improving hospital patient flow and quality of care have found even greater support among leading medical specialties and healthcare leaders. Reports and editorials in emergency medicine publications, top medical journals, and even the National Academies of Sciences, Engineering, and Medicine (NASEM), have endorsed his tested and validated programs. Those pieces show his IHO techniques for reducing variability can help not only to ease overcrowding in hospitals and emergency rooms, but even improve the quality and quantity of human organ transplants.

A NASEM report, "Realizing the Promise of Equity in the Organ Transplantation System," revealed that more than 20% of all US donated organs – 23% of donated kidneys in 2021 – are unused and wasted. That rate is significantly higher than other developed nations and twice the rate of France. At the same time, an average of 17 people in America die daily from the lack of available transplant organs.[1]

That February 2022 report determined that the primary cause of wasted and unused donated human organs was a lack of available surgeons to perform surgery at the appropriate times to harvest and transplant those donated organs. The report also concluded that the US transplant system is "demonstrably inequitable," noting that, "Black Americans are three times more likely to suffer from kidney failure than white Americans, but they are substantially less likely to be placed on transplant waitlists or ultimately get an organ transplant."[2]

That report chiefly explores ways of making the transplant system more transparent and equitable for all within the next five years. But it also offers recommendations for reducing waste and inefficiency that Litvak has developed and championed.

The authors concluded that the nonuse and waste of donated organs is higher on weekends, though donations occur seven days per week. The report recommended, among other things, adopting operations management methods for smoothing surgical schedules and spreading out surgeries and transplant procedures throughout the week, including weekends; separating operating rooms for scheduled (planned) and unscheduled (emergency) surgeries; classifying the time and resource needs of surgical patients and other strategies to improve hospital efficiency and quality of care. These recommended courses of action are at the core of Litvak's IHO program, and he and his research are identified in the report.[3] Another prestigious endorsement of his work came from the Association of Academic Chairs of Emergency Medicine in a piece published in the *New England Journal of Medicine Catalyst*.[4]

That September 2021 opinion piece by eight prominent chairs of hospital emergency departments titled, "Emergency Department Crowding: The Canary in the Health Care System," identified causes of overcrowding and the many harms inflicted on patients.

Prior to the COVID pandemic, emergency room visits had grown by more than 60% since 1997 to 146 million in 2016. The pandemic intensified overcrowding, including waiting times and lengths of stay in the ER.[5]

"The normalization of ED crowding by hospitals as a tolerable dysfunction had resulted in patient endangerment during 'normal' times and has contributed to capacity failure and affected the ability to meet the challenges of public health emergencies," the authors observed.[6] "The impact of ED crowding on morbidity, mortality, medical error, staff burnout, and excessive cost is well documented, but remains largely underappreciated."[7]

The authors wrote that smoothing the surgical schedule throughout the entire week has been shown to exert "a major impact" on crowding and overall hospital operations. "Hospitals often start each week with a heavy surgical schedule, straining if not outright overloading capacity. Surgical volumes typically trail off as the end of the traditional workweek approaches, resulting in hospitals being above capacity during the week and below capacity on weekends."[8]

The report said ED overcrowding must be acknowledged as a serious threat to patient safety, not just as an inconvenience. The ED directors likened ED status to the sentinel canary in the coal mine – reflective of health system dysfunction. "The canary's condition is critical. Without action, patients will continue to be at a heightened risk of harm," they wrote.[9]

More opinion pieces and editorials, by Litvak and top healthcare leaders, cast light on flaws in the US healthcare system and the potential solutions Litvak's methods offer. In an October 2022 opinion piece published in the publication covering Congress, *The Hill*, Litvak and his physician co-authors Harvey Fineberg and Mark Smith identify improving patient flow through surgical smoothing as a way to increase access to organ transplants and reduce patient deaths. "It can alleviate emergency department and hospital overcrowding, as well as stress on frontline workers, improve nurse retention, increase clinicians' satisfaction, and yield multi-million-dollar improvements in hospital margins," the authors wrote in the piece, "A Key Step in the Road to Health Equity: Improving Patient Flow."[10]

"The COVID pandemic has revealed and exacerbated inequities in health care and produced disproportionate deaths among people of color. It has stretched hospital staffing to the breaking point. In such times of stress, improving health care equity requires more than noble intentions or even money. It requires something more difficult – commitment and practical steps to increase efficiency by overcoming impediments of habit and traditional ways of doing things."[11]

They concluded that if "hospitals open their eyes to the advantages of smoothing patient flow, and CMS applies financial incentives to end organ waste and improve access to care across the United States via this intervention, the benefits for patients and society will reverberate long after the COVID pandemic has subsided. Our commitment to fairness in health care deserves no less."[12]

Canada's largest hospital surgery program, the University Health Networks in Toronto, adopted Litvak's IHO program even before the pandemic struck in 2020, which was discussed earlier in the book. Dr. Shaf Keshavjee, UHN's chief surgeon, told a *Canadian Press* reporter in a December 2021 story that the program served the system well in a time of chaos and uncertainty.

"It is the silver bullet in that we're doing more than we've ever done with less, more efficiently," explained Keshavjee, then-president of the medical specialty society, the American Association for Thoracic Surgery. "We've created the capacity to do more. So we are working at 105% [to] 110%."[13]

Another opinion piece focused on how to reduce ambulance diversions. In a July 2022 story, also published in *The Hill*, Litvak and co-authors Susan Dentzer, president and chief executive officer of America's Physician Groups and a former PBS health correspondent, and Renee Hsia, MD, professor of Health Services Research in the Department of Emergency Medicine at the University of California San Francisco, and an ER physician, pointed out the high levels of diversions experienced by San Francisco hospitals during and before the COVID pandemic.

In the fourth weekend of July 2022, for example, Zuckerberg San Francisco General Hospital was on ambulance diversion for

61% to 87% of the time. Diversions occur when hospital ERs are no longer able to accept ambulance traffic and treat new patients due to overcrowding.[14]

Ambulance diversions are not unique to San Francisco or even Los Angeles, but are occurring throughout California and the United States. "For the most part, hospital crowding isn't due to a lack of physical beds, but inefficient use of nursing resource," the authors wrote, noting that diversion is more common in hospitals serving poorer patient populations. But the delays in the entire 911 system affect all patients, not just the poor."[15]

The authors wrote that California is the only state in the nation to have passed legislation mandating nurse-patient staffing ratios, a proposed solution to nursing stress and shortages Litvak and the authors generally oppose because it pushes the problem down the road without addressing the root causes. Their solution – identified in detail throughout this book – involves "managing the peaks and valleys of patient flow created by elective surgery schedules."[16]

They suggested that "Addressing systemic issues in the healthcare system with techniques like surgical smoothing will improve safety for our patients and nurses and ensure a more sustainable system for the long term. If not now, when?"[17]

What You Can Do Now

Litvak will continue to advocate for patients through IHO and his work with hospitals, championing the cause of improving patient flow and safety to media outlets, healthcare organizations, and anyone who will listen to him.

But the hard work ahead is up to patients and their families and friends. Contact your local hospitals' boards of directors and executives to ask whether they have adopted proven solutions to patient flow problems and are employing operations management tools. And if not, why not?

Call or email the Joint Commission, the nation's leading hospital accreditation organization, to ask why it does not require patient flow and other operations management tools to become standards of care when Joint Commission teams accredit hospitals. That simple step would require hospitals to pay attention to patient flow and change local culture and practices to truly put patients first.

Phone, mail, email, or text your state and federal elected officials to demand that they hold hospitals accountable for patient safety and require hospitals to adopt patient flow strategies to avoid overcrowding in hospitals and their emergency departments, methods that would improve quality of care, save taxpayer dollars, reduce medical errors, and save patient lives. And don't just settle for a "yes" or "yeah, but" explanation; demand specifics.

Join with patient advocacy and protection organizations in demanding changes that put patients before local traditions and practices that are harming them.

The following are lists of hospital organizations and their leadership and contact information.

Hospital Membership, Trade, and Lobbying Associations

The American Hospital Association is the umbrella lobbying and trade organization representing US hospitals. The AHA lists its state hospital associations on its website at:

https://www.aha.org/directory/2020-06-09-state-hospital-associations

The Federation of American Hospitals is the trade and lobbying organization for more than 1,000 US for-profit hospitals. It can be reached at:

750 9th St. NW, Suite 600, Washington, DC, 20001-4524

(202) 624-1500

Their corporate leaders can be found at:

https://www.fah.org/about-fah/fah-staff/

Many of the Federation's members are for-profit hospital companies, which own and operate chains of local hospitals around the country, perhaps including your hometown hospital.

Many of those chains can be reached at this website:

https://www.fah.org/membership/member-companies/

National Rural Health Association (NRHA)

http://www.nrharural.org

American College of Healthcare Executives is an educational and professional organization of hospital and healthcare leaders.

http://www.ache.org

Listing of American Healthcare Organizations

An extensive listing of healthcare organizations and associations and their websites:

https://www.aha.org/websites/2006-01-11-other-health-care-associations-b

Patient Safety and Quality Organizations

Here is a list of patient advocacy organizations and their leadership and contact information.

American Patient Rights Association is an independent, nonpartisan nonprofit consumer organization advocating for patient rights.

P.O. Box 2073, Mount Dora, FL 32756

Phone: (407) 212-7685, https://www.americanpatient.org/

AARP Public Policy Institute is an arm of the consumer protection and lobbying organization for people 50 and over, AARP, the PPI analyzes and formulates policy solutions to issues that include Medicare, health care, and aging.

Email: ppi@aarp.org, Phone: (202) 434-3840

Leapfrog Group is an influential private, not-for-profit organization that gathers, analyzes, and publishes data about healthcare quality and patient safety for the purpose of driving improvement.

1775 K St. NW, Suite 400, Washington, DC 20006

Phone: (202) 292-6713, https://www.leapfroggroup.org/

Families USA is a nonpartisan healthcare consumer rights organization that advocates for improved quality, access, healthcare equity, and patient safety.

1225 New York Avenue NW, Suite 800, Washington, DC 20005

Phone: (202) 628-3030, www.familiesusa.org

Institute for Healthcare Improvement is one of the pre-eminent organizations advocating for improved healthcare outcomes, quality, and patient safety. IHI had supported Litvak's methods for improving patient flow.

53 State Street, 18th Floor, Boston, MA 02109 USA

Phone: (617) 301-4800, Toll-Free: (866) 787-0831, www.ihi.org

National Quality Forum (NQF) is a national, nonpartisan, not-for-profit organization that seeks to improve healthcare quality and safety through its tested measures and standards.

1099 14th St NW, Suite 500, Washington, DC 20005

Phone: (202) 783-3434, www.qualityforum.org

National Patient Safety Board Advocacy Coalition is an organization seeking to pass a US House bill, the National Patient Safety Board Act, which would establish a board to address safety in healthcare modeled after the National Transportation Safety Board. Its members include large hospitals and health systems, quality and patient safety organizations, and unions representing healthcare workers.

EQT Plaza, 625 Liberty Ave., Ste. 2500, Pittsburgh, PA 15222 https://npsb.org/

Patients for Patient Safety is a network of people and organizations aligned with the World Health Organization (WHO) working to improve patient safety in the United States.

Phone: (678) 309-9605, http://www.p4ps.org/

Patient Safety Movement Foundation is a global organization aiming to improve patient safety and quality of care.

15642 Sand Canyon Ave. #51268, Irvine, CA 92619

Phone: (877) 236-0279, www.Patientsafetymovement.org

State Government Officials

The National Governors Association lists governors of American states and their websites. Inquire to find the governors' healthcare advisors:

https://www.nga.org/governors/

National Conference of State Legislatures (NCSL) Here is how to contact state legislature members:

https://www.ncsl.org/legislative-leaders/2023-state-legislative-leaders

Association of State and Territorial Health Officials is a directory of top individual state health department directors, commissioners, secretaries, and chief medical officers. While their powers vary from state to state, many oversee boards and commissions, some of which have oversight or regulatory authority over hospitals.

https://www.astho.org/members/member-directory/

Us Elected Officials: Senate and House of Representatives

A free directory of US Congress representatives:

https://www.house.gov/representatives

There are several congressional committees that have oversight on healthcare issues. They include:

Committee on Ways and Means/Subcommittee on Health
Chairman Vern Buchanan (R-FL)
(202) 225-5015, 111 S. Orange Ave. #202W, Sarasota, FL 34236
(941) 951-6643

Committee on Energy and Commerce/Subcommittee on Health

Chairman Brett Guthrie (R-KY)

2434 Rayburn H.O.B., Washington, DC 20515

(202) 225-3501

Committee on Appropriations/Subcommittee on Labor, Health, and Human Services, Education and Related Agencies

Chairman Robert Aderholt (R-AL)

Committee on the Budget/Senate Subcommittees on Health/ Subcommittee on Primary Health and Retirement Security

Chairman is Senator Bernie Sanders (I-VT), and the ranking member is Senator Susan Collins (R-ME). The Subcommittee has jurisdiction over a wide range of issues.

US Senate Committee on Health, Education, Labor, and Pensions (HELP)

As of the printing of this book in 2024, Senator Bernie Sanders was the chairperson.

The contact information for that committee is:

https://www.help.senate.gov/about

428 Senate Dirksen Office Building, Washington, DC 20510

(202) 224-5375

Subcommittee on Primary Health and Retirement Security

Chairman Senator Bernie Sanders

Dirksen Building

(202) 224-5141

Ranking Member Senator Susan Collins

Dirksen Building

(202) 224-2523

Federal Agencies and Departments That Finance and Support Healthcare

Agency for Healthcare Quality and Research https://www.ahrq.gov/

Centers for Medicare and Medicaid Services [MI1] https://www.cms.gov/

Department of Health and Human Services https://www.hhs.gov/

Centers for Disease Control and Prevention (CDC) https://www.cdc.gov/index.htm

Food and Drug Administration (FDA) https://www.fda.gov

Notes

Preface

1. Linda T. Kohn, Janet M. Corrigan, and Molla S. Donaldson, eds., *To Err Is Human: Building a Safer Health System* (Washington, DC: Institute of Medicine, National Academy Press, 1999).
2. Centers for Disease Control and Prevention (CDC), "The Leading Causes of Death in US, 2019," CDC Vital Statistics Report, September 22, 2020.
3. Centers for Medicare and Medicaid Services, "National Health Expenditure Data Fact Sheet, Historical NHE 2020," https://www.cms.gov/Research-Statistics-Data-and-ystems/Statistics-Trends-and-Reports/nationalHealthExpendData/NHE-Fact-Sheet.
4. Ibid.
5. Eugene Litvak, interview, October 30, 2017.
6. Ibid.
7. Ibid.
8. Ibid.
9. Ibid.
10. Eugene Litvak, interview, August 12, 2019.
11. Arnold Milstein and Stephen Shortell, "Innovations in Care Delivery to Slow Growth of US Health Spending," *Journal of the American Medical Association* 308 (October 10, 2012): 1439.
12. National Academies of Sciences, Engineering and Medicine, "Realizing the Promise of Equity in the Organ Transplantation System," February 2022.
13. Ibid.

14. Eugene Litvak, Harvey Fineberg, and Mark Smith, "A Key Step in the Road to Health Equity: Improving Patient Flow," *The Hill*, October 7, 2022.

15. Ibid.

16. Ibid.

17. Eugene Litvak, interview, December 12, 2022.

18. Ibid.

19. Eugene Litvak, interview, October 10, 2017.

20. Ibid.

21. Ibid.

22. Ibid.

23. Ibid.

24. Ibid.

Chapter 1

1. Jim Anderson, interview, April 13, 2016.

2. Cincinnati Children's Hospital website, https://www.cincinnatichildrens.org/.

3. Anderson, interview.

4. Fred Ryckman, interview, December 12, 2017.

5. Eugene Litvak, interview, December 11, 2017.

6. Organization for Economic Cooperation and Development (OECD) (2022), Hospital beds (indicator). doi: 10.1787/0191328e-en (accessed on September 2, 2022).

7. Litvak, interview.

8. Ibid.

9. Ibid.

10. Anderson, interview.

11. Ryckman, interview.

12. Litvak, interview.

13. Ibid.

14. "About the Affordable Care Act," US Department of Health and Human Services website, https://www.hhs.gov/healthcare/about-the-aca/index.html#:~:text=Make%20affordable%20health%20insurance%20available, below%20 138%25%20of%20the%20FPL.

15. Litvak, interview.
16. Ryckman, interview.
17. Ibid.
18. Anderson, interview.
19. Ibid.
20. Scott Hamlin, interview, December 11, 2017.
21. IHI podcast, "All Hospitals in Favor of Saving Money: Say "Patient Flow!" https://www.ihi.org/resources/Pages/AudioandVideo,   December 2, 2009.
22. Hamlin, interview.
23. Mark Taylor, "Meet the Man Who Says He Can Reduce the ER Overcrowding Problem," *Chicago Tribune*, May 2, 2016.
24. Ryckman, interview.
25. Ibid.
26. Ibid.
27. Ibid.
28. Ibid.
29. Ibid.
30. Ibid.
31. Ibid.
32. Ibid.
33. Daniel Von Allmen, interview, February 13, 2020.
34. Ibid.
35. Ibid.
36. Ibid.
37. Ibid.
38. Brooke Mullett, interview, February 13, 2020.
39. Ibid.
40. Taylor, "Meet the Man."
41. Litvak, interview.
42. Ibid.

Chapter 2

1. Johns Hopkins Medicine website, https://www.hopkinsmedicine .org/news/articles/is-sunken-chest-more-than-a-cosmetic-problem, November 11, 2011.
2. Hopkins website, Fizan Abdullah, MD.
3. Helen Haskell, interview, July 20, 2023.
4. Ibid.
5. Ibid.
6. Peter McKenna et al., "Emergency Department and Hospital Crowding: Causes, Consequences, and Cures," *Clinical and Experimental Emergency Medicine* 6, no. 3 (September 2019): 189.
7. Haskell, interview.
8. Ibid.
9. Ibid.
10. Ibid.
11. Ibid.
12. Ibid.
13. Ibid.
14. Ibid.
15. Ibid.
16. Ibid.
17. Litvak, interview, October 10, 2017.
18. Eugene Litvak, "Don't Get Your Operation on a Thursday," *Wall Street Journal*, December 2, 2013.
19. Haskell, interview.
20. Litvak, interview.
21. Ibid.
22. Ibid.
23. Ibid.
24. Litvak, "Don't Get Your Operation on a Thursday."
25. Litvak, interview.
26. Ibid.
27. Ibid.

28. Ibid.

29. Jack Kitts, interview, October 30, 2017.

30. Ibid.

31. Ibid.

32. Ibid.

33. Ibid.

34. Ibid.

35. Ibid.

36. Ibid.

37. Ibid.

Chapter 3

1. Katherine Keisler Starkey and Lisa N. Bunch, *Health Insurance Coverage in the United States: 2021*, September 2022, https://www.census.gov/content/dam/Census/library/publications/2022/demo/p60-278.pdf.

2. Ibid.

3. Ibid.

4. Aiden Lee et al., "National Uninsured Rate Reaches All-Time Low in Early 2022," US Department of Health and Human Services' Assistant Secretary for Planning and Evaluation, https://aspe.hhs.gov/reports/2022-uninsurance-at-all-time-low.

5. Lloyd D. Hughes and Miles D. Witham, "Causes and Correlates of 30-Day and 180-Day Readmission Following Discharge from a Medicine for the Elderly Rehabilitation Unit," *BMC Geriatrics*, August 28, 2018.

6. U.S. Department of Health and Human Services' Office of the Secretary for Planning and Evaluation (ASPE), *Health Coverage Changes Under the Affordable Care Act: End of 2021 Update*, April 29, 2022.

7. Centers for Medicare and Medicaid Services (CMS) National Health Expenditure Data Fact Sheet, Historical NHE 2020, https://www.cms.gov/Research-Statistics-Data-and-Systems/Statistics-Trends-and-Reports/NationalHealthExpendData/ NHE-Fact-Sheet.

8. "To Err Is Human: Building a Safer Health System," *Institute of Medicine*, 1999.

9. Daniel R. Levinson, "Adverse Events in Hospitals: National Incidence Among Medicare Beneficiaries," Office of HHS Inspector General, November 2010, 19.
10. John T. James, "A New, Evidence-Based Estimate of Patient Harms Associated with Hospital Care," *Journal of Patient Safety* 9, no. 3 (September 2013): 122–28.
11. Ellis Knight, interview, October 10, 2017.
12. Ibid.
13. Ibid.
14. Ibid.
15. Eugene Litvak and Harvey Fineberg, "Smoothing the Way to High Quality, Safety, and Economy," *New England Journal of Medicine* 369 (October 23, 2013): 1583.
16. Arnold Milstein and Stephen Shortell, "Innovations in Care Delivery to Slow Growth of US Health Spending," *Journal of the American Medical Association* 308 (October 10, 2012): 1439.
17. Ibid.
18. Arnold Milstein, interview, November 14, 2017.
19. Ibid.
20. Ibid.
21. Ibid.
22. Ibid.
23. Ibid.
24. Ibid.
25. Eugene Litvak, interview, November 12, 2017.
26. Ibid.
27. Mark Taylor, "Meet the Man Who Says He Can Reduce the ER Overcrowding Problem," *Chicago Tribune*, May 2, 2016.
28. Donald Berwick, interview, October 29, 2017.
29. Ibid.
30. Ibid.
31. Ibid.
32. Ibid.
33. Harvey Fineberg, interview, October 6, 2017.

34. Ibid.

35. Ibid.

Chapter 4

1. Eugene Litvak, interview, October 27, 2017.
2. Peter Kenez, *Civil War in South Russia, 1919–1920: The Defeat of the Whites* (Berkeley: University of California Press, 1977), 166.
3. Ibid.
4. Litvak, interview.
5. Ibid.
6. Ibid.
7. Ibid.
8. Ibid.
9. Ibid.
10. Ibid.
11. Ibid.
12. Ibid.
13. Ibid.
14. Ibid.
15. Ibid.
16. Ibid.
17. Ibid.
18. Ibid.
19. https://encyclopedia.ushmm.org/content/en/article/kiev-and-babi-yar.
20. Litvak, interview.
21. Ibid.
22. Ibid.
23. Ibid.
24. Ibid.
25. Ibid.
26. Ibid.
27. Eugene Litvak, interview, October 30, 2017.

28. Soviet Public Holidays: https://www.wikiwand.com/en/Public_holidays_in_the_Soviet_Union.

29. Litvak, interview, October 30, 2017.

30. Ibid.

31. Ibid.

32. Catriona Kelly, *Children's World: Growing Up in Russia, 1890–1991* (New Haven: Yale University Press, 2007).

33. Litvak, interview, October 30, 2017.

34. Ibid.

35. Ibid.

36. Ibid.

37. Ibid.

38. Ibid.

39. Mykhailo Vasiliovych Koval, "Kiev Defense Operation 1941," *Encyclopedia of the History of Ukraine*, vol. 4 (2007), 528.

40. Litvak, interview, October 30, 2017.

41. Ibid.

42. Ibid.

43. Ibid.

44. Ibid.

45. Ibid.

46. Ibid.

47. Ibid.

48. Ibid.

49. Ibid.

50. Ibid.

51. Ibid.

52. Ibid.

53. Ibid.

54. Ibid.

55. Ibid.

56. Ibid.

57. Eugene Litvak, interview, May 11, 2018.

58. Ibid.

Notes

59. Ibid.

60. Ibid.

61. Ibid

62. A. Mark Clarfield, "One Foot in the Past: The Soviet "Doctors' Plot"—50 Years On," *BMJ*, December 21, 2002.

63. Ibid.

64. Litvak, interview, May 11, 2018.

65. Ibid.

66. Ibid.

67. Ibid.

68. Ibid.

69. Eugene Litvak, interview, September 27, 2019.

70. Ibid.

71. Ibid.

72. Ibid.

73. Ibid.

74. Ibid.

75. Ibid.

76. Ibid.

77. Ibid.

78. Ibid.

79. Ibid.

80. Ibid.

81. Eugene Litvak, Interview, September 26, 2019.

82. Ibid.

83. Ibid.

84. Ibid.

85. Ibid.

86. Ibid.

87. Ibid.

88. Ibid.

89. Ibid.

90. Ibid.

91. Ibid.

225

Notes

92. Berta Vtorov, interview, September 29, 2019.

93. Ibid.

94. Litvak, interview, September 26, 2019.

95. Ibid.

96. Vtorov, interview.

97. Mikhail Shifman, *You Have Failed Your Math Exam, Comrade Einstein: Adventures and Misadventures of Young Mathematicians, or Test Your Skills in Almost Recreational Mathematics* (Singapore: World Scientific Publishing, 2005).

98. Shifman, interview, January 23, 2020.

99. Ibid.

100. Ibid.

101. Ibid.

102. Eugene Litvak, interview, December 27, 2019.

103. Ibid.

104. Mikhail Yastrebenetsky and Alexander Bochkov, "In Memory of Professor Igor Ushakov," presented at the 2016 Second International Symposium on Stochastic Models in Reliability Engineering, Life Science, and Operations Management (Beer Sheva, Israel, February 15–18, 2016).

105. Litvak, interview, December 27, 2019.

106. Ibid.

107. Ibid.

108. Ibid.

109. Ibid.

110. Ibid.

111. Ibid.

112. Vtorov, interview.

113. Iryna Stoianova, interview September 29, 2019.

114. Ibid.

115. Vtorov, interview.

116. Ibid.

117. Litvak, interview, December 27, 2019.

118. Ibid.

119. Shifman, *You Have Failed Your Math Exam, Comrade Einstein.*

Notes

120. Ibid.
121. Stanislav Lipovetsky, letter to Mikhail Shifman, 2005.
122. George Szpiro, "Bella Abramovna Subbotovskaya and the 'Jewish People's University,'" *Notices of the American Mathematical Society* 54, no. 10 (November 2007): 1327.
123. Ibid.
124. Shifman, *You Have Failed Your Math Exam, Comrade Einstein.*
125. Litvak, interview, December 27, 2019.
126. "First Department," *Encyclopedia of Soviet Life,* 125, https://books .google.com/books?id=XFje-RiHeisC&pg=PA125&lpg=PA125&dq= %22Encyclopedia+of+Soviet+Life%22+%22First+Department%22& source=bl&ots=qSbgs9D4CI&sig=ACfU3U2m8RfjqWzP71iH3Ubsrg PFcIYpGg&hl=en&sa=X&ved=2ahUKEwjmj77q-sf8AhWykokEHfr HAUsQ6AF6BAgIEAM#v=onepage&q=%22Encyclopedia%20of %20Soviet%20Life%22%20%22First%20Department%22&f=false
127. Litvak, interview, December 27, 2019.
128. "First Department."
129. Ibid.
130. Eugene Litvak, interview, October 30, 2017.
131. Ibid.
132. Ibid.
133. Ibid.
134. Ibid.
135. Ibid.
136. Ibid.
137. Ibid.
138. Ibid.
139. Ibid.
140. Ibid.
141. Ibid.
142. Ibid.
143. Ibid.
144. Ibid.
145. Ibid.

146. Stoianova, interview.

147. Vtorov, interview.

148. Litvak, interview, October 30, 2017.

149. Ella Litvak, interview, November 19, 2020.

150. Ibid.

151. Ibid.

152. Litvak, interview, October 30, 2017.

153. Ibid.

154. Ibid.

155. Vtorov, interview.

156. Litvak, interview, October 30, 2017.

157. Ibid.

158. Ibid.

159. Shifman, interview.

160. Ibid.

Chapter 5

1. Massachusetts General Hospital website: https://www.massgeneral .org/about.

2. "Economic Impact Report 2023", Mass General Brigham.

3. Eugene Litvak, interview, August 12, 2019.

4. Ibid.

5. Ibid.

6. Ibid.

7. Ibid.

8. Peter Slavin, interview, August 13, 2019.

9. Ibid.

10. Ibid.

11. Ibid.

12. Ibid.

13. Ibid.

14. Ibid.

15. Mike Long, interview, August 29, 2019.

16. Ibid.
17. Litvak, interview.
18. Ibid.
19. Long, interview.
20. Ibid.
21. Ibid.
22. Ibid.
23. Ibid.
24. Ibid.
25. Ibid.
26. Ibid.
27. Ibid.
28. Ibid.
29. Ibid.
30. Ibid.
31. Ibid.
32. Ibid.
33. Ibid.
34. Ibid.
35. Ibid.
36. Ibid.
37. Ibid.
38. Ibid.
39. Long, interview.
40. Ibid.
41. Ibid.
42. Ibid.
43. Ibid.
44. Ibid.
45. Ibid.
46. Ibid.
47. Litvak, interview.
48. Ibid.
49. Ibid.

50. Eugene Litvak, and Michael C. Long, "Cost and Quality Under Managed Care: Irreconcilable Differences?" *American Journal of Managed Care* 6, no. 3 (2000): 311.

51. Ibid.

52. Ibid.

53. Litvak, interview.

54. Ibid.

55. Other Litvak and Long Papers: Eugene Litvak, Mike Long, A. B. Cooper, and Michael McManus, "Emergency Room Diversion: Causes and Solutions," *Academic Emergency Medicine* 8, no. 11 (November 2001): 1108–10; Eugene Litvak, Mike Long, and J. S. Schwartz, "Cost Effectiveness Analysis Under Managed Care: Not Yet Ready for Prime Time?" *American Journal of Managed Care* 6, no. 2 (February 2000): 254–56.

56. Slavin, interview.

57. Ibid.

58. Ibid.

59. Litvak, interview.

60. Ibid.

61. Ibid.

62. Eugene Litvak and Harvey Fineberg, "Smoothing the Way to High Quality, Safety, and Economy," *New England Journal of Medicine* 369 (October 23, 2013): 1583.

63. Harvey Fineberg, interview, October 6, 2017.

64. Litvak, interview.

65. Ibid.

66. William Pierskalla, interview, November 3, 2017.

67. Ibid.

68. Ibid.

69. Ibid.

70. Ibid.

71. Don Berwick, interview, October 29, 2017.

72. Litvak, interview.

73. Berwick, interview.

74. Ibid.

75. Ibid.
76. Litvak, interview.
77. Ibid.
78. Ibid.
79. Ibid.

Chapter 6

1. Eugene Litvak, interview, December 11, 2019.
2. P. A. Rutherford et al., *Achieving Hospital-Wide Patient Flow: Second Edition*, Institute for Healthcare Improvement White Paper (2020), 5.
3. Litvak, interview.
4. Ibid.
5. Ibid.
6. Ibid.
7. Ibid.
8. Ibid.
9. Ibid.
10. Ibid.
11. Ibid.
12. Ibid.
13. Ibid.
14. Allison Connolly "Hospitals Eye BU Plan to Boost Care, Add Revenue," *Boston Business Journal*, May 20, 2002.
15. Kathleen O'Dell, "St. John's Cuts Errors, Increases Efficiency," Springfield (Missouri) *News-Leader*, July 5, 2006.
16. Ibid.
17. Ibid.
18. Ibid.
19. Institute for Healthcare Improvement, "Improvement Stories," https://www.ihi.org/resources/Pages/ImprovementStories/ImprovingSurgical FlowatStJohnsRegionalHealthCenterSpringfieldMOALeapofFaith.aspx.
20. Christina Dempsey, interview, November 13, 2019.
21. Ibid.

22. Ibid.

23. Eugene Litvak, "Optimizing Patient Flow by Managing its Variability," in *Front Office to Front Line: Essential Issues for Health Care Leaders*, ed. S. Berman, 91–111 (Oakbrook Terrace, IL: Joint Commission Resources, 2005).

24. O'Dell, "St. John's Cuts Errors,"

25. "The Future of Emergency Care in the United States Health System," Institute of Medicine (now the Academy of Medicine), 2006.

26. Ibid.

27. Eugene Litvak, interview, October 14, 2019.

28. Ibid.

29. Scott Allen, "Getting in the Flow Helps Hospital Time Deliveries," *Boston Globe*, January 25, 2005.

30. Ibid.

31. Ibid.

32. Ibid.

33. Boston Medical Center website, https://www.bmc.org/sites/default/files/For_Medical_Professionals/BMC-Facts.pdf.

34. Litvak, interview.

35. Ibid.

36. Laura Landro, "Unsnarling Traffic James in the O.R.," *Wall Street Journal*, September 10, 2005.

37. Niels Rathlev, Interview, October 17, 2019.

38. Litvak, "Optimizing Patient Flow."

39. Rathlev, interview.

40. Niels Rathlev, John Chessare, and Eugene Litvak, "Redesigning the Surgical Schedule to Enhance Productivity in the Operating Room," *HSOA Journal of Emergency Medicine Trauma and Surgical Care* 5, no. 1 (2018).

41. John Monk, "How a Hospital Failed a Boy Who Didn't Have to Die," *The State* (Columbia, South Carolina), June 16, 2002.

42. Litvak, interview, October 14, 2019.

43. William Cameon, interview, January 14, 2019.

44. Ibid.

45. Ibid.
46. Ibid.
47. Ibid.
48. "Strategies Related to Emergency Department Output," Government Accountability Office (GAO), 2009.
49. Ibid.
50. Ibid.
51. Marcia J. Wilson, Bruce Siegel, Mike Williams, "Perfecting Patient Flow: America's Safety Net Hospitals and Emergency Department Crowding," Robert Woods Johnson Foundation "Urgent Matters Program," National Association of Public Hospitals and Health Systems, January 1, 2005, p. 11.
52. "Institute of Medicine Report: The Future of Emergency Care in the United States Health System," National Academies of Sciences, 2006, p. 1084.
53. Charlotte Yeh, interview, November 11, 2019.
54. Boston University Program for the Management of Variability in Health Care Delivery for the Massachusetts Department of Public Health, "Root Cause Analysis of Emergency Department Crowding and Ambulance Diversion in Massachusetts," October 2002.
55. Ibid.
56. Michael McManus et al., "Variability in Surgical Caseload and Access to Intensive Care Services," *Anesthesiology* 98, no. 6 (June 2003).
57. "Smoothing OR Schedule Can Ease Capacity Crunches, Researchers Say," *OR Manager: The Monthly Publication for OR Decision Makers* 19, no. 11 (November 2003): 9.
58. Litvak, interview, October 14, 2019.
59. "Massachusetts to End Emergency Department Ambulance Diversions," *Kaiser Health News*, June 11, 2009.
60. Litvak, interview, October 14, 2019.
61. Ibid.
62. Ibid.
63. Ibid.
64. Ibid.

Notes

65. Ibid.
66. Yeh, interview.
67. Ibid.
68. Ibid.
69. Ibid.
70. Ibid.
71. Ibid.
72. Jesse Pines, interview, November 12, 2019.
73. Ibid.
74. Richard Wolfe, interview October 4, 2019.
75. Ibid.
76. James Augustine, interview, December 19, 2019.
77. Ibid.
78. Ibid.
79. Seth Trueger, interview, November 21, 2019.
80. Ibid.
81. Ibid.
82. Ibid.
83. Litvak, interview, October 14, 2019.
84. Eric Goralnick, interview, December 19, 2019.
85. Ibid.
86. Ibid.
87. Peter Viccellio, interview, November 19, 2019.
88. Ibid.
89. Ibid.
90. Ibid.
91. Ibid.
92. Ibid.
93. Ibid.
94. Peter Viccellio, Eric Morley, Samita Heslin, "Smoothing of Operative Admissions and Effective Weekend Discharge Planning Opportunities for Decreasing Hospital Crowding" (manuscript), 2020.
95. Ibid.
96. Ibid.

97. Ibid.

98. Ibid.

99. Mary Lou Buyse, interview, November 29, 2019.

100. Mark Smith, interview, September 10, 2019.

101. Ibid.

102. John Diedrich, "We Found 21 Deaths Nationwide After Hospitals Turned Ambulances Away, But No One Is Tracking Them," *Milwaukee Journal-Sentinel*, October 28, 2019.

103. Ibid.

104. San Francisco Emergency Medical Response Ambulance Diversions: http://sfemergencymedicalresponse.weebly.com/ambulance-diversion.html.

105. Litvak, interview, October 14, 2019.

106. Ibid.

107. Ibid.

108. Susan Dentzer, interview, August 13, 2019.

109. Ibid.

110. Ibid.

111. Ibid.

112. Ibid.

113. Eugene Litvak, interview, August 10, 2019.

114. Ibid.

115. Ibid.

116. Ibid.

117. Ibid.

118. Ibid.

119. Ibid.

120. Ibid.

Chapter 7

1. Eugene Litvak, interview, September 22, 2019.

2. Ibid.

3. Scott Allen, "Getting in the Flow Helps Hospital Time Deliveries," *Boston Globe*, January 25, 2005, https://www.ihoptimize.org/wp-content/uploads/2005/01/Boston-Globe-on-Elliot-Hospital.pdf.

4. Michelle Hillman, "Research Delves into Medical Errors," *Milford Daily News*, October 14, 2003, https://www.milforddailynews.com/story/lifestyle/health-fitness/2003/10/14/research-delves-into-medical-errors/41164281007/.

5. Dawn Gould, "Promoting Patient Safety: The Rapid Medical Response Team," *Permanente Journal* 11, no. 3 (Summer 2007).

6. Deonni Stolldorf and C. B. Jones, "Deployment of Rapid Response Teams by 31 Hospitals in a Statewide Collaborative," *Joint Commission Journal on Quality and Patient Safety*, April 1, 2015.

7. "Rapid Response Teams," Institute for Healthcare Improvement website: https:// www.ihi.org/Topics/RapidResponseTeams/Pages/default.aspx#:~:text=The%20 Rapid%20Response%20Team%20%E2%80%94%20known, (or%20wherever%20 it's%20needed).

8. Eugene Litvak and Peter Pronovost, "Rethinking Rapid Response Teams," *Journal of the American Medical Association Commentary* 304, no. 12 (2010): 1375–76.

9. Litvak, interview.

10. Ibid.

11. Ibid.

12. Peter Pronovost, interview, February 7, 2020.

13. Peter Pronovost and Eric Vohr, *Safe Patients, Smart Hospitals: How One Doctor's Checklist Can Help Us Change Health Care from the Inside Out* (New York: Hudson Street Press, 2010).

14. Pronovost, interview.

15. Ibid.

16. Ibid.

17. Congress.gov website, S.1567: Nurse Staffing Standards for Hospital Patient Safety and Quality Care Act of 2021, https://www.congress.gov/bill/117th-congress/senate-bill/1567/text H.R.3165: Nurse Staffing Standards for Hospital Patient Safety and Quality Care Act of 2021, https://www.congress.gov/bill/117th-congress/house-bill/3165.

Notes

18. Linda Aiken et al., "Implications of the California Nurse Staffing Mandate for Other States," *Health Services Research* (August 2010).

19. Ibid.

20. Ibid.

21. Pronovost, interview.

22. Litvak, interview.

23. Ibid.

24. Ibid.

25. Ibid.

26. Ibid.

27. Ibid.

28. Ibid.

29. Ibid.

30. Ibid.

31. Ibid.

32. Ibid.

33. "The Nurse Shortage: Perspectives from Current Direct Care Nurses and Former Direct Care Nurse – An Opinion Research Study Conducted By Peter D. Hart Research Associates for the Federation of Nurses and Health Professionals," April 2001.

34. "Strategies for Addressing the Evolving Nursing Shortages," *Joint Commission Journal on Quality and Patient Safety* 29, no. 1 (January 2003).

35. Ibid.

36. Ibid.

37. Linda Aiken, Sean Clarke, and Douglas Sloane, "Hospital Nurse Staffing and Patient Mortality, Nurse Burnout, and Job Dissatisfaction," *Journal of the American Medical Association*, October 30, 2002.

38. Ibid.

39. Ibid.

40. American Hospital Association and The Lewin Group, "The Hospital Workforce Shortage: Immediate and Future," *Trend Watch* 3, no. 1 (2001).

41. Jack Needleman et al., "Nurse-Staffing Levels and Quality of Care in Hospitals," *New England Journal of Medicine* (May 30, 2002).

42. Marilyn Rudolph, interview, August 27, 2019.

43. Ibid.

44. Ibid.

45. Eugene Litvak et al., "Managing Unnecessary Variability in Patient Demand to Reduce Nursing Stress and Improve Patient Safety," *Joint Commission Journal on Quality and Patient Safety* 31, no. 6 (June 2005).

46. Ibid.

47. Ibid.

48. Ibid.

49. Mayo Clinic website: https://www.mayoclinic.org/about-mayo-clinic.

50. Arizona State University website: https://search.asu.edu/profile/1538616.

51. Denis Cortese, interview, September 18, 2019.

52. Ibid.

53. Ibid.

54. Ibid.

55. Ibid.

56. Ibid.

57. Ibid.

58. Ibid.

59. Allison Connolly, "Hospitals Eye BU Plan to Boost Care, Revenue," *Boston Business Journal*, May 20, 2002.

60. C. Dan Smith, interview, September 23, 2019.

61. Ibid.

62. Ibid.

63. Ibid.

64. Ibid.

65. Ibid.

66. Ibid.

67. Litvak, interview.

68. Ibid.

69. Julie Freischlag, interview, November 4, 2019.

70. Ibid.

71. Ibid.

72. Ibid.

73. Ibid.

Chapter 8

1. Eugene Litvak, interview, August 22, 2019.
2. Mark Smith, Robert Saunders, Leigh Stuckhardt, and J. Michael McGuinness, eds., *Best Care at Lower Cost: The Path to Continuously Learning Health Care* (Washington, DC: Institute of Medicine, National Academies Press, 2010), 264.
3. Henry J. Michtalik, Hsin-Chieh Yeh, Peter Pronovost, and Daniel Brotman, "Impact of Attending Physician Workload on Patient Care: A Survey of Hospitalists," *JAMA Internal Medicine* 173, no. 5 (2013): 375–77.
4. Eugene Litvak, interview, November 12, 2019.
5. Ibid.
6. Ibid.
7. Ibid.
8. Ibid.
9. Robert Lahita, interview, August 26, 2019.
10. Ibid.
11. Ibid.
12. Ibid.
13. Ibid.
14. Patrick McGinley, "N.J. Hospitals Improve Quality, Reduce Costs, Shorten Wait Times in Patient Flow Partnership," *Patient Safety and Quality Healthcare*, Oct. 29, 2013.
15. John Halamka, interview, November 13, 2019.
16. Ibid.
17. Ibid.
18. Ibid.
19. Ibid.
20. Ibid.
21. Ibid.
22. Ibid.
23. Ibid.
24. Ibid.
25. Ibid.
26. Helen Darling, interview, September 6, 2019.

27. Glen Steele, Jr., interview, September 20, 2019.
28. Ibid.
29. Ibid.
30. Ibid.
31. Ibid.
32. Ibid.
33. Ibid.
34. Richard Umbdenstock, interview, September 23, 2019.
35. Ibid.
36. Ibid.
37. Ibid.
38. Ibid.
39. Ibid.
40. Avalere Health for Physicians Advocacy Institute, "COVID-19's Impact on Acquisitions of Physician Practices and Physician Employment 2019–2021," Jan. 1, 2022.
41. Umbdenstock, interview.
42. Ibid.
43. Ibid.
44. Litvak, interview, November 12, 2019.
45. Umbdenstock, interview.
46. Mark Smith, interview, June 4, 2021.
47. Ibid.
48. Ibid.
49. Ibid.
50. Richard K. Leuchter et al., "Racial Disparities in Potentially Avoidable Hospitalizations During the COVID-19 Pandemic," *American Journal of Preventive Medicine* (March 2021).
51. Ibid.
52. Ibid.
53. Amina Khan, "Another Racial Disparity that May Be Heightened by the Pandemic: Access to Outpatient Care," *Los Angeles Times*, March 26, 2021.
54. Ronald Wyatt, interview, May 17, 2021.
55. Ibid.

56. Ibid.
57. Ibid.
58. Eugene Litvak, interview, May 18, 2021.

Chapter 9

1. Don Erwin, interview, May 20, 2021.
2. Ibid.
3. Ibid.
4. Ibid.
5. Ibid.
6. Ibid.
7. Ibid.
8. Ibid.
9. Ibid.
10. Ibid.
11. Eugene Litvak, interview, November 18, 2019.
12. Erwin, interview.
13. Ibid.
14. Ibid.
15. Ibid.
16. Ibid.
17. Ibid.
18. Ibid.
19. Ibid.
20. Ibid.
21. Ibid.
22. Ibid.
23. Ibid.
24. Ibid.
25. Definitive Healthcare website: https://www.definitivehc.com/blog/how-many-fqhcs-are-there.
26. https://bphc.hrsa.gov/about-health-centers/health-center-program-impact-growth#:~:text=In%202021%2C%20health%20centers%20achieved,one%20in%20five%20rural%20residents.

27. Erwin, interview.

28. Ibid.

29. Ibid.

30. Donald Erwin, interview, February 21, 2024.

31. Donald Erwin, interview, May 20, 2021.

32. Ibid.

33. Ibid.

34. Ibid.

35. Ibid.

36. Hakmeng Kang, interview, November 20, 2019.

37. Ibid.

38. Ibid.

39. Ibid.

40. Ibid.

41. Ibid.

42. Ibid.

43. Ibid.

44. Ibid.

45. Ibid.

46. Litvak, interview, November 18, 2019.

Chapter 10

1. Eugene Litvak, interview, January 12, 2020.

2. Peter Lachman, interview, January 16, 2020.

3. Litvak, interview.

4. Martin Elliott, interview, January 13, 2020.

5. Ibid.

6. Ibid.

7. Ibid.

8. Lachman, interview.

9. Ibid.

10. Ibid.

11. Ibid.

12. Ibid.
13. Ibid.
14. Ibid.
15. Ibid.
16. Ibid.
17. Ibid.
18. Ibid.
19. Ibid.
20. Jason Leitch, interview, November 19, 2019.
21. Ibid.
22. Ibid.
23. Ibid.
24. Ibid.
25. Ibid.
26. Ibid.
27. Ibid.
28. Ibid.
29. Ibid.
30. Ibid.
31. Ibid.
32. Ibid.
33. Eugene Litvak, interview, November 19, 2019.
34. Ibid.
35. Ibid.
36. Jack Kitts, interview, October 30, 2017.
37. Ibid.
38. Ibid.
39. Ibid.
40. Ibid.
41. Litvak, interview, November 19, 2019.
42. Shaf Keshavjee, interview, May 6, 2020.
43. Ibid.
44. Ibid.
45. Ibid.

46. Ibid.

47. Ibid.

48. Susan Brooke, interview, February 18, 2020.

49. Ibid.

50. Ibid.

51. Ibid.

52. Ibid.

53. Ibid.

54. Ibid.

55. Ibid.

Chapter 11

1. Julie Freischlag, interview, November 4, 2019.

2. Ibid.

3. Mike Long, interview, August 29, 2019.

4. Ibid.

5. William Pierskalla, interview, November 3, 2017.

6. Ibid.

7. Ibid.

8. Harvey Fineberg, interview, October 6, 2017.

9. Ibid.

10. Ibid.

11. Richard Umbdenstock, interview, September 23, 2019.

12. Ibid.

13. Ibid.

14. Ibid.

15. Glenn Steele, Jr., interview, September 20, 2019.

16. Ibid.

17. John Halamka, interview, November 13, 2019.

18. Helen Darling, interview, September 6, 2019.

19. Ibid.

20. Ibid.

21. Fred Ryckman, interview, December 12, 2017.
22. Ibid.
23. Ibid.
24. Denis Cortese, interview, September 18, 2019.
25. Peter Lachman, interview, January 16, 2020.
26. Peter Pronovost, interview, February 7, 2020.
27. Ibid.
28. Ibid.
29. Donald Berwick, interview, October 29, 2017.
30. Ibid.
31. Ibid.
32. Ibid.
33. Ibid.
34. Ibid.
35. C. Dan Smith, interview, September 23, 2019.
36. Ibid.
37. Ibid.
38. Ibid.
39. Ellis Knight, interview, October 10, 2017.
40. Ibid.
41. Ibid.
42. Ibid.
43. Mark Smith, interview, September 10, 2019.
44. Ibid.
45. Ibid.

Epilogue

1. Kenneth Kizer, Rebecca English, and Meredith Hackman, eds., *Realizing the Promise of Equity in the Organ Transplantation System*, National Academies of Sciences, Engineering, and Medicine, February 2022.
2. Ibid.
3. Ibid.

4. Gabor Kelen et al., "Emergency Department Crowding: The Canary in the Health Care System," Association of Academic Chairs of Emergency Medicine, *New England Journal of Medicine Catalyst*, September 28, 2021.

5. Ibid.

6. Ibid.

7. Ibid.

8. Ibid.

9. Ibid.

10. Eugene Litvak, Harvey Fineberg, and Mark Smith, "A Key Step in the Road to Health Equity: Improving Patient Flow," *The Hill*, October 7, 2022.

11. Ibid.

12. Ibid.

13. Laura Osman, "COVID-19 Surgery Delays Can Be Done Without Overburdening Workers, Say Experts," *Canadian Press*, December 12, 2021.

14. Susan Dentzer, Renee Hsia, Eugene Litvak, "One Key Step Toward Solving the Nation's Deadly Nursing Shortage," *The Hill*, July 29, 2022.

15. Ibid.

16. Ibid.

17. Ibid.

Acknowledgments

This book could never have been written without the cooperation, collaboration, and invaluable assistance of the man it was written about: Eugene Litvak. Dr. Litvak has shared contacts, photos, experiences, client information, and many other valuable details that informed and expanded this book. I am grateful to him and his wife, Ella, for their time and assistance. I also wanted to thank David Stern, publisher of Eckhartz Press in Chicago, for his help. Of course, I would also like to thank my former editor at the Gary (Indiana) *Post-Tribune*, Jim Proctor, for his keen eye, and Marilyn Rudolph, a nurse and quality improvement expert, who lent her editing skills to make this a cleaner and more accurate book than it would have been if left to my sadly lacking devices. Finally, my wife, partner, best friend, editor, and advisor, Marcia Taylor, who read this book more than anyone should ever have to: thank you. It's too late to thank my parents, Robert and Kathryn Taylor, personally, but I hope wherever they are in this universe, they can feel my gratitude and love. I'm also beholden to my children, Rysiu Velazquez, Katherine Taylor Kazakovtsev, and Benjamin Taylor. I'm so proud to be your father and grateful for your help and advice. I'm a lucky man.

About the Author

Mark Taylor is a veteran healthcare journalist who has covered health and medicine for newspapers and business publications for decades. He is a recipient of Kaiser and Knight fellowships and is a co-founder of the Association of Health Care Journalists. Taylor is a former steelworker, taxicab driver, waiter, and lifeguard who lives in a Northwest Indiana suburb of Chicago.

Index

Blackman, LaBarre "Bar," 14
Blackman, Lewis, 13–16, 111
Block times, 9–10, 83–84, 147
Blue Cross/Blue Shield health plans, 196, 200
Boarding, 3, 110, 115, 119, 121–123
Bolshevik Revolution, 32, 34
Boston Business Journal, 104
Boston Children's Hospital, 114
Boston Globe, 97, 108, 125, 130
Boston Medical Center (BMC), xxi, 8, 96, 108, 110
Boston University (BU), 95–96, 101, 103, 114, 125, 130, 135
Brezhnev, Leonid, 50, 136
Brigham and Women's Hospital, 79, 121
Brigham Health, 121
Buchanan, Vern, 213
Bulgakov, Mikhail, 71
Burnout, xxiv, 3, 25–26, 83, 90, 101, 138, 188, 205. *See also* Nurse stress; Physician burnout
Buyse, Mary Lou, 123

California Health Care Foundation, xxii, 160, 200
California Nurses Association, 134
Cameon, Bill, 112
Canadian Ministry of Health, 19, 185
Canadian Press, 106
CDC (United States Centers for Disease Control and Prevention), xv, xx, 215
Centers for Medicare and Medicaid Services (CMS), xx, 23, 27, 94, 116, 122, 150, 170. *See also* Medicaid; Medicare

Cheka, 67
Chessare, John, 108–110
Chicago Tribune, 7, 11
Children's Health Insurance Program (CHIP), 21
Churchill, Winston, 11
Cincinnati Children's Hospital, xxi, 1–11, 127, 148, 177
Cleveland Clinic, 93, 193
CNN Digital, xxi
The Coker Group, 11
Collins, Susan, 214
Community Hospital of Munster, 112
Conn, Joseph, 154
Cooper, Abbot, 96, 114
Cooper, James Fenimore, 44
Cortese, Denis, 142–144, 196
COVID-19 pandemic, xv, xix, xxii, 64, 129–130, 159, 161–162, 204–206

Darling, Helen, 156, 195–196
Definitive Healthcare, 170
Dempsey, Christina, 104–106
Dentzer, Susan, 125–127, 206
Department of Visas (OVIR), 73
Dickens, Charles, 40
Diversion:
block time as solution to, 10
California's high rates of, 135
due to overcrowding, xix, 3, 26–27, 104, 110
from ICUs, 114–115, 188
ineffectiveness of, 111–113
and nursing shortages, 139
and patient deaths, 126
problems caused by, 118
prohibition of, 115–116
public reaction to, 122

257

Operating rooms (ORs):
  block times for, 83
  competition for, 92
  elective surgeries at, 80, 95
  for emergency cases, 104–105,
    108–109
  improving access to, 8–11
  inefficiency of, 81
  nursing problems at, 26
  overcrowding at, xviii, 80
  patient flow at, 19–20
  scheduled surgeries at, 14, 86
  shared problems of, 96
  specialty surgery at, 102
  variability in, 89–90
  work schedules at, 106–107
Operations management
    techniques:
  application of, 90, 174, 209
  investment in, 93–94
  at Mass General, 76, 78, 90–91
  NASEM report on, 204
  need for, 24
  and patient flow, 189, 191
  setting standards for, 200
  teaching, 192
  in Ukraine, xvi
  understanding of, 87
  and variability, 124
Operations Research Society of
    America, 192
Organization for Economic
    Cooperation and
    Development (OECD), 3
OR Manager magazine, 115
Ottawa Hospital, 18–20, 185–187
Overcrowding:
  bad health outcomes of,
    xix–xx, 132

at beginning of week, 122–123
causes of, 14
costs of, 19
during COVID-19 pandemic, 130,
  204
and ED expansion, 126–127
in EDs, 89–90, 99–138,
  204–205
in ERs, xviii–xix, xxi, xxiii, 25–26
growth of, 119
inefficient care during, 1
nursing shortage as cause of, 139
at ORs, xviii, 80
ORs as cause of, 114
and patient diversion, 116, 124,
  207
and patient flow, 2, 18, 113, 149,
  209
planned surgeries as cause of, 83
prevalence of, xxv
as public issue, 91
regulatory agencies as cause
  of, 121
studies on, 23–24, 115
surgical flow as cause of, 136
OVIR (Department of Visas), 73

Pacific Business Group on Health,
  xx, 24
Palmetto Health system, 23, 27, 199
Pampuro, Vladimir Ilych, 58–59
Partners HealthCare, 75, 79, 89
Partnership for Patients program,
  150
Patient censuses. *See also* Bed
  occupancy
  and elective surgeries, 186
  late in the week, xxv, 18
  overloaded, xxiv

Index